PIERRE LAROQUE AND THE WELFARE STATE IN POSTWAR FRANCE

OXFORD HISTORICAL MONOGRAPHS

Editors

P. CLAVIN   R. J. W. EVANS

L. GOLDMAN   J. ROBERTSON   R. SERVICE

P. A. SLACK   B. WARD-PERKINS

J. L. WATTS

Pierre Laroque and the Welfare State in Postwar France

ERIC JABBARI

OXFORD
UNIVERSITY PRESS

OXFORD

UNIVERSITY PRESS

Great Clarendon Street, Oxford, OX2 6DP,
United Kingdom

Oxford University Press is a department of the University of Oxford.
It furthers the University's objective of excellence in research, scholarship,
and education by publishing worldwide. Oxford is a registered trade mark of
Oxford University Press in the UK and in certain other countries

British Library Cataloguing in Publication Data
Data available

Library of Congress Cataloguing in Publication Data
Library of Congress Control Number: 2011942649

ISBN 978–0–19–928963–9

Printed in Great Britain
on acid-free paper by
MPG Books Group, Bodmin and King's Lynn

Contents

Abbreviations

AMGOT	Allied Military Government of Occupied Territories
AN	Archives Nationales
ANC	Assemblée Nationale Constituante
Ass. Nat.	Assemblée Nationale
BP	Belin papers
CAC	Centre des Archives Contemporaines
CET	Conseil Économique du Travail
CFLN	Comité Français de Libération Nationale
CFTC	Confédération Française des Travailleurs Chrétiens
CGC	Confédération Générale des Cadres
CGE	Comité Général d'Entente
CGE	Comité Général d'Études
CGPF	Confédération Générale de la Production Française
CGPME	Confédération Générale des Petites et Moyennes Entreprises
CGT	Confédération Générale du Travail
CHSS	Comité d'Histoire de la Sécurité Sociale
CIDC	Comité de Défense des Intérêts du Personnel et des Cadres
CNE	Conseil National Économique
CNPF	Conseil National du Patronat Français
CNR	Conseil National de la Résistance
FFI	Forces Françaises de l'Intérieur
FNMF	Fédération Nationale de la Mutualité Française
FNSP	Fondation Nationale des Sciences Politiques
IHS	Institut d'Histoire Sociale
LP	Laroque papers
MAS	Ministère des Affaires Sociales
MRP	Mouvement Républicain Populaire
OURS	Office Universitaire de Recherche Socialiste
PBP	Peter Baldwin papers
PCF	Parti Communiste Français
POB	Parti Ouvrier Belge
PP	Parodi papers
SFIO	Section Française de l'Internationale Ouvrière
SHAEF	Supreme Headquarters of the Allied Expeditionary Force

Introduction

In the autumn of 1944, Pierre Laroque, a senior civil servant assigned to the Ministry of Labour, launched a policy review which culminated in the establishment of a French social security system the following year. Laroque was well versed in the area of social policy, and he had advocated the reform of social insurance for over a decade. Before the outbreak of the Second World War, however, he had focused on other issues, namely the prospective reform of the collective bargaining system. For much of the thirties, in fact, he had advocated the creation of new corporatist structures which aimed to defuse social tensions by uniting the representatives of business and labour in the management of industrial relations. These proposals reflected his concern with the persistence of industrial strife in contemporary France, but they also reflected his preoccupation with the necessity of promoting social solidarity, an objective which he believed was to be met through an interventionist state which encouraged public participation through the medium of decentralized services. Laroque's corporatist views owed much to his exposure to administrative law as a student, and its underlying themes would remain central to his conception of social policy long after he had lost his illusions about corporatism. Most importantly, these concerns would eventually influence the development of the social security system of post-Liberation France.

By October 1945, Pierre Laroque had already enjoyed a long, varied and successful career. From the early thirties onwards, his work had been concerned with various questions of public law and social policy. After joining the *Conseil d'État* in 1930, he dealt with important cases in administrative law, served in various administrative posts, taught a course at the *École Libre des Sciences Politiques*, and wrote a host of articles and books which highlighted the wide scope of his interests.[1] During the war, his career had taken an unexpected turn; he was dismissed from the civil service because of his Jewish origins, and then became involved in the

---

[1] See the exhaustive bibliography which is included in his memoirs. P. Laroque, *Au service de l'homme et du droit: souvenirs et réflexions*, 363–76.

Resistance and Free French movements. By the autumn of 1944, he had returned to the *Conseil d'État* and the Ministry of Labour, and he initiated a review that culminated in the introduction of the social security ordinances of October 1945. Laroque was thus a man of thought and action, and his contribution to the rise of the French welfare state was shaped by a set of ideological preoccupations which can be traced back to this extensive record of published writings.

While Laroque's thought evoked a diverse set of influences and evolved during the span of a few decades, it remained defined by a solidaristic conception of the state and society throughout his career. Echoing the thought of Émile Durkheim, he believed in the functional interdependence of the individual members of society, and stressed that the task of social policy was to promote social solidarity. These views were an outgrowth of his study of administrative law, and they explained his advocacy of corporatism and social security during the thirties and forties. Solidarist rhetoric permeated his writings, and his memoirs, published in 1993, reveal that he remained committed to these principles nearly five decades after the Liberation:

> Men and women are interdependent. Existence, the well-being of each individual, is to a large extent a function of that of others. It is incumbent, therefore, for each to become aware of this interdependence, of this solidarity, and to take stock of its consequences with regard to his behaviour towards others. It is also the duty of the community to organize, when it is required, this solidarity. Mutual assistance is a natural duty of each individual towards one's peers. Liberty therefore does not mean selfishness. On the contrary it implies an active obligation to bring one's assistance to those who are in need, to those who perceive a direct or indirect threat to their own liberty. Solidarity must mean fraternity.[2]

In Laroque's mind, social solidarity was both an objective fact and a normative ideal, and these preoccupations lay at the root of the development of the Laroque Plan, his proposals concerning social security relief, from the autumn of 1944 onwards.

As Laroque saw it, social security promoted a radical agenda since it aimed to cultivate a new climate of solidarity uniting all Frenchmen, resulting in a new social order defined by an active citizenry and a new social consciousness. These objectives were first outlined in a speech which he had delivered in March 1945:

> The effort required to accomplish this will transform our political democracy into a real social democracy, insuring both the security of tomorrow and the

---

[2] *Au service*, 19.

development of the responsible participation of each and everyone in the . . . management of this undertaking. This can only be achieved through the profound transformation of our society. The problem which must be resolved is not only or principally a technical problem. It consists specifically of creating and developing new forms of behaviour, of profoundly transforming the very spirit of our society.[3]

The ultimate task of social security was not of a material nature, since it served a cultural and psychological purpose. These objectives reflected his longstanding views concerning the psychological dimension of social conflict, reflecting a line of analysis which he had espoused since the thirties while evoking the utopian rhetoric of the Resistance and the Free French movement.

The reformist environment of the post-Liberation period might have made it possible to introduce social security, but its underlying themes and stated objectives proved consistent with the principles which had driven Laroque's career for over a decade. As a result of his study of Léon Duguit and Maurice Hauriou, prominent legal scholars associated with the public service and institutionalist schools of French public law, he had adopted a solidarist view of society which explained his support for an interventionist state. The latter had been mitigated by his belief in a form of administrative decentralization that encouraged public participation in the management of public services. While serving on the staff of the Minister of Labour in 1931–1932, Laroque became interested in the development of social policy, and the research that he had conducted for the *Conseil National Économique* turned him into an advocate of corporatism by 1934. Impressed by the purported achievements of Fascist corporatism, he argued that the corporation would provide the disciplinary constraints required to make collective bargaining agreements binding and effective. The corporatist management of industrial relations was meant to foster a new climate of social solidarity between labour and management by uniting them in a new forum for the regulation of working conditions.

Laroque's support for corporatism was by no means unique, since interest in corporatist politics had been a recurring theme in the public discourse during the preceding decades. Intellectuals like Durkheim and Duguit had supported corporatism, while the creation of the *Conseil National Économique* in 1925 had been inspired by the corporatist policies outlined in the minimum programme of the *Confédération Générale du Travail*.[4] During

---

[3] Ibid. 199. While this excerpt is taken from his memoirs, it was originally part of a lecture he had delivered in March 1945.

[4] T. V. Kaufman-Osborn, 'Émile Durkheim and the Science of Corporatism', *Political Theory*, xiv, 4, (1986) 638–59; C. Laborde, *Pluralist Thought and the State in Britain and*

the thirties, moreover, there had been a renewal of interest in corporatism as a response to the perceived crisis of the Third Republic. It was in this context that Laroque was able to find a receptive audience for his proposals, and he participated in the intellectual debates of these years, publishing articles in reviews such as *L'Homme Nouveau* and *Les Nouveaux Cahiers*, and participating in discussion groups like the *Groupe du 9 Juillet* and *X-crise*.[5] By the end of the decade, however, he had quietly forsaken his support for a democratic variant of corporatism. The tacit admission that his views had been somewhat naive was a product of his realization that the ultimate success of any given policy depended upon a change in public attitudes, a lesson he learned from observing the impact of the Blum government's reform of the collective bargaining system. At the same time, Laroque had become increasingly aware that Fascist corporatism had not lived up to his expectations. In Italy, corporatism had merely represented a means of extending state control over the population, an objective which ran counter to his own conception of corporatist policy.

Laroque's pre-war activism dovetailed with the rise of the technocratic and neo-socialist movements. Laroque was representative of the rise of so-called 'technocrats' who sought to modernize the French state in light of the social, political, and economic problems of the interwar period. The technocratic movement was defined by a desire to implement new approaches towards governance that were influenced by recent developments in science, technology, and management.[6] On a political level, this translated into support for state interventionism, namely in the form of economic planning, in light of the perceived failure of laissez-faire capitalism. The *planiste* movement, as it came to be known, was not limited to technocratic circles, since others also came to believe in the necessity of introducing some form of planning in the midst of the economic crisis of the thirties. Most notably, the neo-socialists favoured the implementation of such a policy, but they had come to support planning in light of their efforts to renew the socialist discourse.[7] Laroque's association with the neo-socialists exposed him to alternative explanations of class conflict, as

France, 1900–1925; A. Chatriot, *La Démocratie sociale à la française: l'expérience du Conseil national économique 1924–1940*, 101–24 and 150–2.

[5] Laroque, *Au service*, 113; *Témoignage* Laroque. For a discussion of these reviews and groups, see: J.-L. Loubet del Bayle, *Les Non-conformistes des années trente*; O. Dard, *Le Rendez-vous manqué des relèves des années 30*; P. Andreu, *Le Rouge et le blanc, 1928–1944* and *Les Révoltes de l'esprit. Les revues des années trente*.

[6] G. Brun, *Technocrates et technocratie en France 1918–1945*; R. F. Kuisel, *Capitalism and the State in Modern France*.

[7] P. Dodge, *Beyond Marxism: the faith and works of Hendrik de Man*; P. Burrin, *La Dérive fasciste: Doriot, Déat et Bergery 1933–1945*.

illustrated by Hendrik de Man's contention that cultural and psychological factors were at the root of these social tensions. From the thirties onwards, Laroque would argue that social policy had to address the non-economic dimensions of working class alienation, an objective which he first sought to achieve through the corporatist management of industrial relations and later through the introduction of the post-war social security system.

The development of the Laroque Plan in 1944–1945, the name attributed to Laroque's proposals in the field of social security, also benefited from his expertise concerning the social insurance system which had been established during the interwar period. As a member of the *Conseil d'État* and chief of the staff of Adolphe Landry, the Minister of Labour of the Laval government of 1931–1932, Laroque had studied the relevant legislation and had been involved in the setting up of its administrative infrastructure. These experiences had convinced him of the necessity of reforming social insurance. In his view, the legislation of 1928–1930 had sought to reconcile a compulsory system of insurance with a voluntarist network of mutual aid societies, resulting in an exceedingly complex administrative structure. Furthermore, he was later involved in the first major attempt to rationalize its services and benefits during the months that followed the establishment of the Vichy regime. The Ministry of Labour would prove unable to pursue its objectives, and a succeeding attempt would meet with the same fate in the spring of 1942. By this time, however, Laroque was no longer involved in the development of social policy, having been excluded from the civil service in October 1940.

Laroque was dismissed because of his Jewish origins, a result of the anti-Semitic legislation of the Vichy regime, and he soon joined the French Resistance. While he participated in the deliberations of the *Comité Général d'Études*, the think tank set up to ponder the challenges of a liberated France, his work did not focus on the issues of social insurance or social security. By the time he reached London in the spring of 1943, he had been assigned new responsibilities which bore no relation to the problems of social policy. Returning to France in the days that followed the Allied landings in Normandy, Laroque would only revisit these questions in the autumn of 1944, after he had been readmitted to the *Conseil d'État* and named director general of social insurance in the Ministry of Labour. At this point, the problems encountered by the social insurance system confirmed his belief in the necessity of its overhaul. After commissioning an actuarial review of its benefit programmes, he began developing a plan which promoted the rationalization of the administrative structure of social insurance while integrating other social policies, such as family allowances and industrial accident insurance in a new social security system. From the outset, Laroque had made it clear that he believed that the ultimate objective of social security had to be the creation of a universal system of benefits that would cover the entire population of post-war France.

By the summer of 1945 concerned interest groups, such as the mutual aid societies and the Catholic trade unions, had risen in opposition to the Laroque Plan. Their criticism focused largely on the *caisse unique*, the lynchpin of the administrative structure of the proposed system. These critics were defending the status quo, objecting to the rationalization of services that would dispossess them of the pre-eminent role which had been granted to the mutual aid societies as a result of the social insurance legislation of 1928–1930. While similar objections had proved successful in frustrating past attempts at reforming social insurance, Laroque would succeed where others had failed, save for the provisional government's decision to abandon plans to integrate family allowances into a unified administrative structure. The ordinances of October 1945 officially created social security, and the stage was set for the subsequent expansion of coverage to the rest of the population. Within a few months, however, the situation changed dramatically when a growing anti-reformist coalition emerged in opposition to the creation of a universal system of old age insurance. Groups such as the *cadres*, artisans, small- and medium-sized business owners refused to participate in a system which they believed would impose new financial burdens without providing them with a corresponding level of benefits. By 1947, the decision to pursue the universalization of old age insurance would result in a widespread social revolt which compelled the government to retreat from implementing this objective. The following year, the National Assembly created an old age insurance system that was defined along vocational lines, an approach which negated the solidaristic objectives of the Laroque Plan. Instead of transforming social relations, as Laroque had originally intended, the implementation of social security had provoked the revival of deep-seated social tensions in post-war France.

The welfare state has been the subject of much historical scholarship in German and Anglo-American circles, and the existing work focuses largely on the British, German, and Scandinavian experiences.[8] Until recently, historians of contemporary France have shown little interest in studying the French welfare state, and the relative absence of research in the field

---

[8] J. F. Harris, *Sir William Beveridge: a biography*; P. Baldwin, *The Politics of Social Solidarity*; G. Ritter, *Der Sozialstaat: Entstehung und Entwicklung im Internationalen Vergleich*.

explains the persistence of various misconceptions concerning its origins and development in contemporary France.[9] Much of the existing literature has been written from the perspectives of law, sociology, and political science, resulting in studies which have generally neglected the consultation of various primary sources. These limitations are all the more apparent in light of the commonly accepted narratives concerning the development of social security in post-Liberation France. The latter is generally attributed to the reformist spirit of the Resistance and Free France, but this does little to explain how the Laroque Plan was developed or what influences inspired its architect. Furthermore, there is no evidence that the ideas developed by the Resistance or Free France played any role in defining the plan's substance, but this has not discouraged scholars from advancing unsubstantiated claims concerning the origins of post-war social security. Some historians continue to assert that social security was devised by the services of the exiled Free French community, but Laroque rejected these claims when he was asked about the origins of the Laroque Plan.[10] While both Free France and the Resistance had come to promote the cause of social and economic reform in post-Liberation France, their commitment to change did not translate into a specific blueprint for social security policy, and it was Laroque who bore the ultimate responsibility for the substance of the plan which was to be elaborated after his return to the civil service.

The existing literature has been handicapped by other problems, namely the fact that it all too often ignores the importance of non-institutional factors in determining the actual substance of social security. Many of those who have attempted to examine the conceptual origins of social security have been reduced to advancing other questionable assertions. As Nicole Kerschen has noted, many still believe that the Laroque Plan was modelled upon the Beveridge Report, despite the fact that there is no evidence that the latter had served as a model for the former.[11] While Laroque might have been familiar with the content of the Report, his plan was designed in response to the problems which were specific to French social insurance. Nevertheless, it is true that both Laroque and Beveridge shared a belief in the virtue of an interventionist state, and stressed that social benefits had to be conceived as part of a comprehensive set of social

---

[9] H. C. Galant, *Histoire politique de la sécurité sociale*; J. Ambler, ed. *The French Welfare State*; P. V. Dutton, *Origins of the French Welfare State*; B. Palier, *Gouverner la sécurité sociale*; and B. Valat, *Histoire de le sécurité sociale 1945–1967*.

[10] Dutton, *Origins*, 202–8. *Témoignage* Laroque (*archives orales de la sécurité sociale*); P.-J. Hesse interview, 9 December 1998.

[11] N. Kerschen, 'L'influence du rapport Beveridge sur le plan français de sécurité sociale de 1945', in B. Palier (ed.), *Comparer les systèmes de protection sociale en Europe*, i, 128.

and economic policies aimed at promoting both the security of income and full employment.[12] Sir William Beveridge might have made social policy fashionable, but his Report was based upon a study of benefit programmes which had been established in the United Kingdom during the preceding decades; similarly, the Laroque Plan was based upon an analysis of initiatives which had been introduced in France during the thirties and forties.

The failure to examine the intellectual history of the French welfare state has made it difficult to determine how given ideologies influenced the development of social policy in twentieth-century France. Some scholars have pointed to the influence of Keynesian or Christian democratic ideas on French policymakers,[13] but there is no evidence that either doctrine played a role in the development of social security. The welfare state, however, was influenced by deep-seated demographic concerns, and these fears led to the creation of a family allowance system that aimed to reverse the threat of demographic decline.[14] While Laroque shared many of the same assumptions concerning the national birth rate and the importance of the family, these considerations played no role in influencing his work from the autumn of 1944 onwards.

Laroque's memoirs provide the reader with some indication of the ideological preoccupations that influenced his work, but, while they answer certain questions, they are of limited use. While Laroque outlined the solidarist principles that influenced his career, he does not explain how he came to espouse these views in the first place.[15] Oddly enough, Laroque did not discuss how his legal background had contributed to his conception of the state and society, an omission which is all the more peculiar since this background helps explain his support for corporatism and social security.[16] The cursory treatment of his background in administrative law is all the more surprising given the fact that its substance was directly related to the changing role of the state in twentieth-century

---

[12] Harris, *Beveridge* See also Sir William Beveridge, *Social Insurance and Allied Services* and *Full Employment in a Free Society*; Laroque, *Au service*.

[13] P. Rosanvallon, *L'État en France*, 184–95; D. Wilsford, 'The Continuity of Crisis: Patterns of Health Care Policymaking in France, 1978–1988', in J. Ambler (ed.), *The French Welfare State: surviving social and ideological change*, 97; B. Jobert, 'Democracy and Social Policies: the example of France', in Ambler (ed.), *The French Welfare State*, 240.

[14] S. Pedersen, *Family, Dependence and the Origins of the Welfare State in Britain and France 1914–1945*; MAS, LP, box 139. Laroque was a member of the *Alliance nationale pour l'accroissement de la population française*, the leading natalist lobby group of the first half of the twentieth century. Furthermore, he devoted a number of radio broadcasts, between 1936 and 1938, to the demographic question.

[15] Laroque, *Au service*, 197–8.

[16] Ibid. 107–8.

France. As his early writings demonstrate, his reading of the works of scholars such as Hauriou and Duguit explained his solidaristic views and turned him into a proponent of a state interventionism which simultaneously decentralized the relevant public services. Laroque's memoirs are tainted by other frustrating omissions. For example, he barely mentions his participation in the so-called nonconformist movement of the thirties, and does not discuss his advocacy of the corporatist management of industrial relations during this same period.[17] The corporatist phase of his career, however, was of critical importance since it represented the first practical application of the interventionist bias that had characterized his legal writings, and its underlying principles continued to influence his work in the following decades. In the end, these memoirs probably reflect the problems raised by the advanced age of an author who had probably lost sight of the complex interplay of the diverse set of factors that had shaped his thought during the twenties, thirties, and forties.

The ideological influences that underpinned Laroque's work has not entirely eluded the scrutiny of the academic community. François-Xavier Merrien, a political sociologist, was the first scholar to study Laroque's corporatist proposals and his involvement in the nonconformist movement.[18] While his work broke new ground in the study of the French welfare state, he referred to a limited number of primary sources and drew some rather hasty conclusions concerning the nature of Laroque's pre-war views and activities. Indeed, Merrien portrayed Laroque as a slavish admirer of Fascist corporatism who was ambivalent if not hostile towards democracy and republicanism, a conclusion which is not necessarily supported by the published record of his writings or the materials found in his private papers.[19] While Laroque was initially impressed by Fascist corporatism, this did not necessarily entail support for an authoritarian or a totalitarian politics. The corporatist views which he advocated during this period did not betray any ambivalence towards democratic and republican principles, a point which he had bothered to make clear at the time.

The following study is based upon an extensive array of archival sources, including the private papers of Pierre Laroque, and it focuses upon the highlights of his career as a legal scholar, social policy expert, and

---

[17] Ibid. 97.

[18] F.-X. Merrien, *Étude comparative de l'édification et de l'évolution de l'état protecteur en France et en Grande-Bretagne*, 231–49. Based on his *doctorat d'état*, this study was produced for the *Mission interministérielle de recherche et d'expérimentation* (MIRE).

[19] Ibid. 242–4.

architect of post-war social security. It examines the evolution of his thought over the course of two decades, explaining how it informed his work in the field of social security. Laroque's contribution to the rise of the French welfare state shall be examined within the political, intellectual, and institutional context of early twentieth-century France. While it will be necessary to consider some of the technical and administrative questions which pertain to the implementation of social insurance and social security during these years, the book will not examine the development of the family allowance and industrial accident systems of the period, since they largely escaped the purview of Laroque's specific contribution to French social policy. The book is divided into six chapters, excluding the introduction and the conclusion. Chapter 1 examines the origins of solidarism and the creation of social insurance. Chapter 2 discusses Laroque's legal background and his advocacy of corporatism. Chapter 3 details his pre-war activism and the evolution of his views, while Chapter 4 focuses upon his service with Vichy, the Resistance, and Free France during the Second World War. Chapter 5 looks at the development of the Laroque Plan from the autumn of 1944 to the introduction of the ordinances of October 1945, while Chapter 6 discusses the failure to implement a universal system of old age insurance during the early months of 1947.

1

Solidarism and Social Insurance

INTRODUCTION

Pierre Laroque's contribution to the development of the French welfare state must be understood in relation to the intellectual and institutional legacy of the French social policy tradition. The development of a social security plan in post-Liberation France owed much to past experience, since its design represented a practical response to the perceived short-comings of the social insurance system that had been introduced during the interwar period. At the same time, both social insurance and social security shared a common ideological lineage since they were both conceived in a political environment that was defined by the ideological legacy of a solidarist movement which had wielded a significant influence on the public discourse of the early twentieth century. While Laroque would respond to the structural problems of social insurance, a product of its uneasy juxtaposition between the statist and non-statist aspects of the legislation of 1928–1930, the solutions which he came to advocate were influenced by the solidarist values which he had come to espouse during his formative years as a student of administrative law and a rising expert in the field of social policy in interwar France.

SOLIDARISM: ORIGINS, IDEOLOGY, AND POLITICS

The solidarist movement emerged in response to the rising social and political tensions of late nineteenth-century France. Social relations had been transformed by the rise of an industrial workforce, and a pressing focus upon the social consequences of the capitalist system led to the creation of trade unions (*syndicats*), not to mention socialist parties.[1] The

---

[1] T. Zeldin, *France 1848–1945*, Vol. 1: *Ambition, Love and Politics*, 199–264 and 723–87.

emergence of these groups represented a direct challenge to existing social, political and economic order, and this contributed to the elaboration of doctrines that sought to address the root causes of this phenomenon. By the end of the century, various thinkers attempted to develop a new ideological synthesis that could bridge the gap between liberalism and collectivism while promoting a reformist politics which could diffuse social conflict without subverting the foundations of the social and economic system. For its advocates, solidarism represented a third way of sorts: an attempt at devising a new form of politics which would make it possible to transcend the ideological polarization of the public discourse. The ideology of solidarism evoked many of the themes which had been developed by a previous generation of thinkers, and the very notion of social solidarity had been a leitmotif of Proudhonian anarchism

Pierre-Joseph Proudhon, the famed anarchist thinker and erstwhile rival of Karl Marx, developed many of the themes which were later to be associated with the solidarist movement.[2] A fierce critic of the capitalist system, Proudhon sought to establish a new social, political, and economic order which would be founded on the principles of liberty and equality. In order to achieve this objective, he advocated the decentralization of political and economic power through the creation of a mutualist economic system and a federalist political structure.[3] The principle of mutualism referred to the establishment of an egalitarian system of cooperation and exchange. According to Proudhon, his proposed economic system would be defined by the free association of workers who would assume control of their workshops and factories.[4] The principle of workers' control of industry was central to Proudhonian anarchism and it entailed the reorganization of the economy along corporatist lines, a notion which would become a recurring theme of French politics during the course of the following decades.

While the free association of workers would permit the creation of a cooperative system of exchange in the economic sphere, the introduction of federalism would promote the same libertarian and egalitarian objectives when it came to the political organization of society. In Proudhon's view, federalism provided the best means of achieving this goal since it diffused state power between the constituent elements of the federal

---

[2] C. Bouglé (ed.), *Proudhon*; Bouglé, a Durkheimian sociologist who was a committed solidarist, even claimed that Proudhon was a 'pre-sociologist', in the Durkheimian sense of course.

[3] G. Guy-Grand, *Pour connaître la pensée de Proudhon*, 164–85, J. Lajugie (ed.), *Pierre-Joseph Proudhon: textes choisis et présentés par J. Lajugie*, 130–70.

[4] P.-J. Proudhon, *Idée générale de la révolution*, in C. Bouglé (ed.), *Oeuvres complètes de Pierre-Joseph Proudhon*, 302.

system.[5] The pursuit of increased individual liberty and the creation of a more egalitarian society were essential to the anarchist project, and the attainment of these objectives would transform the moral foundations of French society. The introduction of mutualism and federalism served to foster the development of a new civic virtue, a new sense of public morality which would define social relations.[6] The transformed social climate would be defined by egalitarian values, thus strengthening the bonds which united the members of society.[7] The relations between the latter would be defined by a new sense of social solidarity. For Proudhon, the pursuit of individual liberty did not represent a negation of the collective dimension of social life since it promised to renew the bonds of society by placing its members on a free and equal footing. In the end, the introduction of mutualism and federalism would lead to the development of social solidarity, the collective realization of the interdependence of the all individuals.

The thoughts of Pierre-Joseph Proudhon exercised a widespread influence upon the social, political, and intellectual life of early twentieth-century France. Long after his death in 1865, his thoughts continued to elicit the interest of a wide array of intellectuals, politicians, and syndicalists,[8] including prominent figures such as Maurice Hauriou, Léon Duguit, Léon Bourgeois, and Célestin Bouglé.[9] Whatever their respective differences, these figures shared a common belief in the importance of cultivating a new civic virtue through the medium of decentralized socio-political structures, a concern that characterized both Proudhonian and solidarist thought. In fact, Bourgeois, Bouglé, and Duguit were closely associated, with the solidarist movement, and their shared interest in Proudhon was by no means accidental, since Proudhon's writings dealt with the very issues which were central to the solidarist movement of the late nineteenth and early twentieth centuries.

The rise of solidarism was intimately related to the development of the social sciences, namely the emergence of sociology as a new academic discipline within the academy. In the first quarter of the twentieth century, Émile Durkheim and his followers would play a key role in the development of both sociology and solidarism, their academic research

---

[5] P.-J. Proudhon, *Du principe fédératif* in C. Bouglé (ed.), *Oeuvres complètes*, 324–5.
[6] Ibid. 329.
[7] Lajugie, *Pierre-Joseph Proudhon*, 126.
[8] A. Kriegel, *Le pain et les roses*, 84–7; J. Hayward, *After the French Revolution*, 217–21.
[9] J. Bancal, *Proudhon: pluralisme et autogestion*, ii, 215–20.

providing both theoretical and factual arguments in support of solidarist doctrine. From the publication of *La division du travail social* onwards, Durkheim had focused upon a limited set of themes including the establishment of sociology upon an empirical basis, the issue of individualism in modern society and the sources of moral authority.[10] In his view, empirical data demonstrated the importance of moral norms in determining individual and collective behaviour, a view which would define the solidarist discourse of the following decades. At the same time, Durkheim provided a new argument in favour of state interventionism, the latter being justified by the state's obligation to pursue solidaristic objectives.

Émile Durkheim believed that society was shaped by the increased specialization of tasks, a result of the division of labour required by the advent of the industrial system. This phenomenon had resulted in the diffusion of solidaristic sentiments throughout society, since the functional interdependence of human beings led to a collective consciousness of the importance of this network of human relationships.[11] Durkheim explained this phenomenon through a historical analysis of social change. The shift from mechanical to organic solidarity, which extended and intensified the bonds of the individual to society, inspired this process of moral transformation; he believed that this was illustrated by the evolution of legal concepts, namely the replacement of punitive sanctions by compensatory mechanisms.[12] Whatever its scientific value, this analysis offered a compelling interpretation of contemporary social change, since it argued that the increasing complexity of modern life tended to reinforce the collective moral imagination which bound the members of society.

Durkheimian sociology provided a social scientific rationale for the pursuit of solidaristic objectives. The concept of social solidarity was defined as a collective moral phenomenon that was central to the evolution of human societies, but it was not necessarily an inevitable outcome of the interplay of social and economic forces. The transition from mechanical to organic solidarity was an imperfect and ongoing process, and Durkheim's belief in social and political reform reflected the voluntaristic dimension of his thought. In fact, his observation of current social trends led him to believe that European societies were being undermined by the divorce of economic forces from any binding moral framework.[13] This moral critique of social and economic development helped explain

<hr>

[10] A. Giddens, *Durkheim*, 9–10.
[11] É. Durkheim, *La division du travail social*, 57–66.
[12] Ibid. 137.
[13] É. Durkheim, *Leçons de sociologie*, 16–17.

his support for a reformist politics, since the positive action of the state could compensate for the adverse effects of economic development.

The solution to this problem lay with the creation of new sociopolitical structures that would promote the moralization of economic relations. Durkheim advocated the establishment of professional corporations which would serve to cultivate social solidarity. This corporatist agenda was based upon his sociological analysis; he noted that vocational groups were a vital source of moral discipline since they fostered a sense of community around shared occupations, ideas, and sentiments.[14] According to Durkheim, it was this occupational solidarity that made social solidarity possible, and the corporation would simply consolidate this existing trend. By regulating economic activity, linking those who contributed to the productive process, the corporation was meant to provide the socio-economic system with a moral framework that had been hitherto lacking in modern capitalist society.[15] The corporation would build upon the functional specialization of labour and enforce the moral discipline that was a necessary precondition of organic solidarity. Durkheimian reformism thus complemented the supposedly empirical analyses of its underlying sociology.

The emergence of the Durkheimian school of sociology proved critical to the development of the political discourse in turn of the century France. As William Logue has argued, the rise and triumph of the Durkheimian school marked the emergence of a new kind of liberalism based upon sociological principles.[16] The redefinition of liberal ideology along sociological lines attempted to reconcile individualist with communitarian concerns, and the case that was made by its advocates was supposedly objective and normative. According to this view, modern society was characterized by the growth of organic solidarity, a phenomenon that was both moral and functional in nature. Moreover, the strength of these social bonds also a function of the individual's capacity to contribute to the development of this solidarity. The state had the obligation to provide the means through which this could be achieved, namely though interventionist policies and the establishment of corporatist economic structures. While these concepts were developed within the confines of French academia, they also came to permeate the political discourse of the

---

[14] Ibid. 23–32.

[15] Ibid. 37–9.

[16] W. Logue, *From Philosophy to Sociology*, 16; V. Karady, 'Stratégies de réussite et mode de faire valoir de la sociologie chez les Durkheimiens', *Revue Française de Sociologie*, 20 (1979), 49–53; G. Weisz, 'L'Idéologie républicaine et les sciences sociales', *Revue Française de Sociologie*, 20 (1979), 111–12.

belle époque, as would be demonstrated by the rise of a solidarist faction within the Radical Party.

Léon Bourgeois, a prominent deputy and future prime minister, became one of the leaders of this tendency, and he authored his own theoretical exposé of solidarist doctrine. With the publication of *Solidarité* in 1896, Bourgeois presented a case for a pragmatic reformism which would take account of social concerns and economic realities,[17] an objective which implied the pursuit of reformist policies within the framework of a capitalist society. Bourgeois defined solidarism as the *via media* between socialist collectivism and liberal individualism. Much like its Durkheimian variant, this form of solidarism was inspired by similar ethical and sociological concerns. The concept of *solidarité*, according to Bourgeois, was symptomatic of the objective of social interdependence of individuals as well as representing a normative ideal for the individual, society, and the state.[18] The social organism was defined by its functional and moral characteristics, and Bourgeois called for the implementation of interventionist public policies that aimed to facilitate the pursuit of this individual and collective objective.

The solidarist argument for state intervention reconciled liberal and communitarian concerns within a contractarian framework. Bourgeois stressed that the individual benefited from the historical legacy bequeathed by society; as a result, the former had the duty to protect this legacy for the benefit of future generations. From birth onwards, he argued, man was a debtor of human association, a consequence of the quasi-contract which bound all men and distributed their respective rights and responsibilities.[19] Bourgeois referred to the contractual principle in order to redefine the relationship of the individual with society. While solidarism called for an interventionist state, it simultaneously called for the limitation of the scope of its policies. Bourgeois argued that public intervention only served to recognize the natural allocation of rights and responsibilities determined by the quasi-contract.[20] Of course, this was excessively vague and provided little guidance to those who sought to determine the precise boundaries of state interventionism, but it illustrated the tensions of a doctrine that remained ambivalent towards the expansion of the state.

The solidarist doctrines elaborated by Durkheim and Bourgeois were remarkably similar, and it is therefore unsurprising that Durkheimians were to be found in the ranks of the Radical Party. Most notably, Célestin

---

[17] L. Bourgeois, *Solidarité*, 2nd edn, 37.
[18] Ibid. 16–17.
[19] Ibid. 116–17, 138.
[20] Ibid. 153.

Bouglé, a prominent sociologist and representative of the Durkheimian school, became a leading intellectual spokesman for the Radical Party and its solidarist agenda, and he repeatedly sought election to office as a Radical candidate.[21] While Bouglé might have failed to obtain elective office, his political activism highlighted the ideological proximity and the personal links which united the political and academic variants of solidarism. Furthermore, his career as a political militant illustrated the ambivalence of the solidarist attitude towards the issue of state intervention. While Bouglé and his fellow solidarists accepted the necessity of state interventionism in social and economic affairs, its support was conditioned by a simultaneous desire to limit the extent of these statist policies.

According to Bouglé, the solution to this dilemma was to be found in the various associations which made up civil society. Groups such as the mutual aid societies and the trade unions served to promote a common solidaristic objective,[22] and this function made it possible to limit the recourse to state intervention. By defining solidarity outside the scope of the state, highlighting the importance of intermediary groups in cultivating positive liberty, the solidarists sought to preserve a balance between their individualist and communitarian concerns. For Bouglé, the social and moral objectives of solidarism were to be attained through the mutually supportive pressure of the state and society, and this would limit the need for state intervention.[23] The cultivation of social solidarity was to be assured within a decentralized social and political framework, and this conception of solidarist reform would prove essential to the development of social policy during the coming decades.

The principles of solidarism also found an echo in French legal circles, as demonstrated by the writings of Léon Duguit and the public service school of administrative law. Duguit gained notoriety as the prime exponent of a sociological approach to the study of law. Most importantly, his doctrine was premised upon the notion that the law could only be understood within a sociological framework; the law was a product of social trends, but it also served to promote a specific objective: the cultivation of social solidarity.[24] The law had to be based upon the empirical observation of social phenomena, the most important of which was the question of the moral and functional interdependence of

---

[21] P. Vogt, 'Un durkheimien ambivalent: Célestin Bouglé, 1870–1940', *Revue Française de Sociologie*, 20 (1979), 123–4; W. Logue, 'Sociologie et politique: le libéralisme de Célestin Bouglé', *Revue Française de Sociologie*, 20 (1979), 150–1.

[22] C. Bouglé, *Le Solidarisme*, 192–3.

[23] Ibid. 170.

[24] Ibid. 162–4.

all individuals, and it was the result of this analysis which defined the ultimate purpose of the law and the state.

According to Duguit, the state had the obligation to provide services that would cultivate social solidarity.[25] As had been the case with Durkheim, he viewed social solidarity as an objective reality and a normative ideal, arguing that the growth of public services was both a response to, and a mechanism for, the development of social interdependence.[26] From this perspective, French administrative law served a solidaristic purpose, since it provided the legal framework for the expansion of public services in early twentieth-century France. Moreover, Duguit advocated specific reforms in order to achieve this solidarist objective. Like Durkheim, he was in favour of the creation of professional corporations which would assemble the representatives of various social and economic interests.[27] This promotion of corporatist reform, in fact, not only reiterated Durkheim's views on the matter but also anticipated the diffusion of similar proposals during the twenties and thirties.

Pierre Laroque owed much to the thought of Léon Duguit and the public service school, as he adopted its solidarist bias and believed in the necessity of new forms of state interventionism to promote social solidarity. In a doctoral thesis which he published in 1933, Laroque argued that the modern state had become defined by the notion of public service, and this had been demonstrated by the increasing scope of its obligations and functions.[28] In contrast to Duguit, he provided a more precise definition of the notion of public service and explicitly related it to the perceived failure of non-state actors to provide for given social needs. Laroque defined a public service as an activity continuously exercised by a public administration in response to the incapacity of the private sector to ensure this service.[29] In his mind, state interventionism was determined by practical necessity, but it also served to fulfil the moral obligation of the state. The latter's increased role, Laroque concluded, was the practical manifestation of its responsibility to ensure the satisfaction of public needs.[30] As his career would later demonstrate, these views concerning the nature of the state and society were destined to influence his conception of social policy during the thirties and forties.

The principles associated with solidarism would prove influential throughout the course of the Third Republic, and the issue of social

<hr>

[25] L. Duguit, *Souveraineté et liberté*, 165.
[26] L. Duguit, *Traité de droit constitutionnel*, 2nd edn, ii, 55–7.
[27] Duguit, *Souveraineté et liberté*, 186.
[28] Laroque, *Les Usagers des services publics industriels*, 2.
[29] Ibid. 5.
[30] Ibid. 5–7.

solidarity would become a recurring leitmotif of the debates surrounding social insurance, though its impact would prove ambiguous. While solidarist arguments could serve to justify state interventionism, they could also be invoked by those who sought to limit the scope of state power. The debates surrounding the question of social insurance reflected this ambivalence, as would the result achieved by the legislative process. While the social insurance legislation of 1928–1930 did mark an extension of state power, its administrative infrastructure also confirmed the enduring influence of the non-statist dimension of solidarism, as demonstrated by the pre-eminent role that it would confer upon the mutual aid societies with regard to the administration of the social insurance system.

THE SOCIAL INSURANCE LEGISLATION
OF 1928–1930

From the *belle époque* to the Depression, succeeding French governments initiated various forms of industrial accident, pension, and family allowance legislation. While these measures were undoubtedly limited in scope, as was illustrated by the legislation which introduced the *Retraites ouvrières et paysannes* in 1910,[31] they did confirm the gradual extension of state intervention in the social and economic spheres. The end of the First World War ushered in a new phase in French social policy, a shift that was the direct result of the recovery of Alsace-Lorraine from a defeated Germany. French policymakers had to contend with the fact that the population of these territories had enjoyed a wide gamut of social benefits as a result of the introduction of Bismarck's social reforms in the late nineteenth century,[32] and this situation inspired an effort to extend similar programmes to the rest of the French population. By 1921, a social insurance project would be submitted to the Chamber of Deputies, but the content of this proposal elicited the opposition of various groups, and this gave rise to discussions and negotiations which would last until the beginning of the thirties.

The first version of the social insurance project was devised by Georges Cahen-Salvador, a civil servant who was a member of the *Conseil d'État* and would later serve as secretary general of the *Conseil National Économique*, the consultative body which was to be established in 1925.[33]

---

[31] See B. Dumons and G. Pollet, *L'État et les retraites*.

[32] M. Dreyfus et al., *Se protéger, être protégé: une histoire des assurances sociales en France*, 57–9.

[33] A. Chatriot, *La Démocrative sociale à la française: expérience du Conseil national économique, 1924–1940*, 51.

Georges Cahen-Salvador, the architect of the first social insurance project of interwar France, had much in common with Pierre Laroque, the bureaucrat who would devise the social security system of the post-war era. The paths of Cahen-Salvador and Laroque would cross at the *Conseil d'État* and the *Conseil National Économique*, and their contributions in the field of social policy was marked by a shared commitment to social reform which did not shy away from recourse to greater state intervention. Their work in the fields of social insurance and social security was defined by a common statist bias that was mitigated by their shared belief in the necessity of encouraging public participation in the management of social services, an objective which was to be met through a form of administrative decentralization.

At the outset, the social insurance proposal owed much to the Bismarckian model, a testimony to the advanced nature of its various benefit programmes. In fact, Cahen-Salvador had undertaken an extensive study of the latter in the immediate aftermath of the First World War.[34] The foreign imprint of the project might have been clear, but its public rationale was characterized by a reference to the principles promoted by the solidarist movement that had emerged at the turn of the century. According to Cahen-Salvador, the implementation of a nationwide social insurance programme would serve to promote a social solidarity throughout a reunited France:

> By granting these advantages to those who ignore them still, taking our inspiration from the experience of Alsace-Lorraine to create new legislation which is more complete, better adapted to our needs and applicable on all of French territory, we are tightening by a new bond the solidarity which unites the children of the same homeland. Through renewed structures, we are giving to all French workers guarantees against insecurity, and a pledge of social peace to the country as a whole.[35]

The solidaristic rationale for social insurance was explicitly stated, but Cahen-Salvador was not simply reiterating the solidarist discourse of the belle époque, since his attitude towards state intervention proved less amenable to recurring liberal anxieties concerning the growth of state power.

The social insurance project of 1921 was aimed at the most vulnerable elements of French society, and it provided coverage to all wage earners under 60 who earned less than 10,000 francs a year, offering them

---

[34] É. Antonelli, *Comment furent votées les assurances sociales*, 5; AN, CAC 760145, *Rapport sur la situation financière de l'Institut d'Assurance Sociale d'Alsace-Lorraine*, 10 March 1919.

[35] *Les Motifs et le projet de loi sur les assurances sociales*, 3.

protection against a variety of insurable risks, including sickness, old age, death, and maternity.[36] This wide array of benefits would not be financed through the national budget, but would be self-financed through the contributions of those who were registered with the social insurance system. The contributions of the insured, moreover, were to be matched by the contributions of their employers.[37] Finally, a network of regional *caisses* would cover metropolitan France, thus ensuring the distribution of benefits throughout the country.[38] The structure of social insurance was to be defined by a form of administrative decentralization, and it was this proposed structure that became the source of controversy during the following years.

The mutual aid societies and their legislative allies were adamantly hostile to the initial form of the social insurance project, arguing that it represented an exercise in state expansion and administrative centralization which was anathema to the French tradition of social reform. According to the views expressed by Étienne Antonelli, a Socialist deputy and proponent of Proudhonian ideas who served as a *rapporteur* of a parliamentary commission which examined the proposed social insurance legislation, Cahen-Salvador had been unduly influenced by the Bismarckian model, and his project was oblivious to the fact that the mutual aid societies had long played a critical role in the delivery of social benefits to the population.[39] These concerns could be easily understood: the movement towards a national and obligatory pension scheme had resulted in a hybrid social policy model that combined state intervention with recourse to the mutual aid societies, as had been demonstrated by the design of *Retraites ouvrières et paysannes* which had been adopted in 1910.[40] Throughout the following years, this approach towards social policy remained influential, as was to be confirmed by the lobbying and legislative activity that would engulf the social insurance question throughout the decade.

Cahen-Salvador, however, did not share the concerns of the mutual aid societies. While he did not shy away from state interventionism, he also stressed that the social insurance system would encourage the participation of the insured through the management structure of the various regional *caisses*, a point which nonetheless ignored the fact that the latter would no

---

[36] G. Cahen-Salvador, *Les Assurances sociales*, 9.

[37] Ibid. 11–12.

[38] Ibid. 23–8.

[39] Antonelli, *Comment*, 6–7; Antonelli, *La Démocratie sociale*, 25; J. Milhau, 'L'Action politique d'Étienne Antonelli', *Revue d'Histoire Économique et Sociale*, 31, 4 (1953), 364–5.

[40] Dumons et Pollet, *L'État et les retraites*, 357.

longer be administered by the mutual aid societies.[41] The threat of excessive bureaucratization and centralization was to be averted by the encouragement of public participation, but the fact remained that Cahen-Salvador had designed an administrative structure which excluded groups who had played a fundamental role in defining the French social policy model and who exerted much influence among the members of the legislature. The mutual aid societies could only reject a project which reduced their role in the delivery of social benefits, but this opposition owed as much to narrow self-interest as to the anti-statist dimension of the solidarist discourse of the early twentieth century.

From the spring of 1921 onwards, the insurance commission of the Chamber of Deputies began its study of the government's social insurance project. For the next couple of years, the commission consulted various groups representing different social and economic interests. While these organizations tended to support the principle of social insurance, many were uneasy with its financial and administrative implications, and this controversy delayed the legislative process. By 1924, this consultation had resulted in a variety of amendments aimed at placating the medical profession, the mutual aid societies, and the agricultural lobby.[42] By the time that the social insurance bill was passed by the Chamber of Deputies, the clash of extra-parliamentary interests would be exacerbated by the obstructionism of key members of the Senate.

The reform's most enthusiastic supporters were to be found in the trade union movement. Both the *Confédération Générale du Travail* and the *Confédération Française des Travailleurs Chrétiens* voiced their support for the social insurance initiative. While the CGT called for a universal system that would insure the entire population and cover the risk of unemployment, its Catholic counterpart advocated a system which was to be designed along corporatist lines.[43] The support of the labour movement was indeed important, but it was by no means sufficient to ensure the success of social insurance. In a marked contrast to the views of the labour movement, the business community proved sceptical, if not hostile, to social insurance. The *Confédération Générale de la Production Française* believed that the scheme would place a new and excessive burden on the economy while threatening the existence of its own policy initiatives; as a result, it proposed that a more limited form of social insurance be

---

[41] Cahen-Salvador, *Les Assurances sociales*, 33.

[42] Antonelli, *Comment furent votées*, 8–9.

[43] AN, C 14646, *p-v de la commission d'assurance*, Laurent and Perrot, 19 November 1921. AN, C 14646, *p-v*, CFTC note, 25 November 1921.

introduced in successive stages over a number of years.[44] Concerned by the economic implications of the proposed reform, the CGPF eschewed any direct assault upon the principle of social insurance, a position which mirrored the criticism raised by other concerned social and economic interests.

The mutual aid societies and the medical profession represented the two groups most concerned by the proposed legislation. As previously mentioned, the *Retraites ouvrières et paysannes* had given the mutual aid societies a central role in the management of pension benefits.[45] It was not surprising that the representatives of the mutual aid societies clamoured for the extensive modification of the government's social insurance proposal. Fearing to be displaced by an expanded state bureaucracy, they wished to play a central role in the management of the future social insurance programme.[46] These ambitions were threatened by the statist implications of the reform and found a receptive ear in the legislature, a predictable development given the size and scope of the mutual aid societies. The claims of the mutual aid societies could not be discounted easily: they had a membership of two and a half million and had created between 30 and 40 *caisses* responsible for the management of existing benefit schemes.[47] These statistics explained the political influence of the mutual aid societies, and one can surmise that many legislators were well aware of the difficulties they might encounter if they chose to ignore their concerns.

The medical lobby voiced its hostility towards a key element of the health insurance scheme. The social insurance bill proposed that a flat fee be introduced for the payment of medical services, but this measure contradicted one of the cardinal tenets of liberal medicine, namely the right of doctors to establish their own rates of honoraria.[48] The hostility to any potential limitation of income explained the intransigent position of the medical profession. Finally, the agricultural lobby also voiced its concern with the social insurance project. Its leading organizations called for the creation of a separate insurance regime for the agricultural sector, which was to be organized along mutualist lines.[49] They defined solidarity in exclusively vocational terms, a position which ran counter to

---

[44] AN, C 14646, *p-v*, 3 February 1922, CGPF note.

[45] Dumons and Pollet, *L'État et les rotraites*, 357.

[46] AN, C 14646, *p-v de la commission d'assurance*, 7 July 1921, Lariolle and Miroël; AN, C 14646, *p-v*, 9 December 1921, *Voeux du Conseil Supérieur de la Mutualité*.

[47] AN, C 14646, *p-v*, 3 March 1922, Cahen-Salvador.

[48] AN, C 14646, *p-v*, 12 October 1921, Dr Legras, Dr Grivey.

[49] AN, C 14646, *p-v*, 25 November 1921, Toussaint. AN, C 14646, *p-v*, 2 December 1921, memorandum of the *Confédération Nationale des Associations Agricoles*.

Cahen-Salvador's conception of social solidarity. In a general sense, the principle of national solidarity was confronted by various sectional demands that complicated the development of policy and jeopardized the future of the social insurance project.

The willingness to acquiesce to the demands of these various lobbies delayed the legislative process, and the final vote of the Chamber of Deputies would only take place in April 1924, three years after the submission of the first social insurance proposal. Though the insurance commission had preserved many of the features of the original project, the final bill was characterized by a series of measures that aimed to placate the concerns of diverse interests. The most notable success was achieved by the medical lobby and the mutual aid societies, as demonstrated by the bill's treatment of the proposed health insurance system as well as the administrative structure of social insurance as a whole.[50] Most notably, the mutual aid societies would be entrusted with the administration of various regional *caisses*, while medical fees were to be determined by the *caisses* and the representatives of the medical profession.[51] While it was altogether apparent that the mutual aid societies and the medical lobby had managed to influence the final shape of the social insurance bill, their successes did not put an end to the controversy which surrounded the social insurance question. The Chamber of Deputies might have passed the bill, but the Senate was now determined to review its very substance, and this prolonged the deliberations of the legislature.

Dr Chauveau, the president of the Senate's hygiene commission, was determined to rework this piece of legislation, since he believed that the authors of the project had grossly underestimated its economic impact while creating a complicated scheme for the distribution of benefits.[52] In his mind, the bill would impose a heavy burden on the economy while creating an unwieldy bureaucratic structure. According to his estimates, between 800 and 5,300 new bureaucrats would be employed by the system; as a consequence, this would make it difficult for the Ministry of Labour to supervise its social insurance system.[53] Whatever the value of this analysis, it should be noted that his counterproposals would have made it impossible to create a viable system. For example, Dr Chaveau suggested that the *caisses* should be permitted to determine their own contributory rates and specific levels of benefits.[54] Such recommendations

[50] Dreyfus et al., *Se protéger*, 81.
[51] AN, CE 65, *projet de loi 1632*, articles 23, 83, 84, 88, 92, 94.
[52] *Sénat, p-v de la commission d'hygiène*, 25 June 1924, Dr Chauveau.
[53] *Sénat, p-v de la commission d'hygiène*, 9 July 1924, Dr Chauveau.
[54] *La Nouvelle Revue*, 15 November 1924.

could only spell the end for a single and uniform system of coverage and this was not lost on those bureaucrats who were intimately associated with the issue of social insurance.

Jean-Louis Dreyfus, one of the leading actuaries of the Ministry of Labour, submitted a confidential note to the Minister of Hygiene in response to these latest developments. Dreyfus believed that if these suggestions were acted upon, they would provoke the hostility of the labour movement while jeopardizing the financial basis of social insurance.[55] Furthermore, he argued that the redistributive objectives of social insurance would be imperilled by the hygiene commission's proposals. Moreover, a move towards a uniform level of benefits would undermine the redistributive purposes of a scheme which sought to aid those who earned the lowest wages.[56] This defence of redistribution was matched by a fierce critique of Dr Chauveau's views concerning the management of the system. As Dreyfus noted, it would be difficult for the state to exercise any control over the system if the various *caisses* were allowed to establish their own rates of contributions and benefits.[57] In brief, the proposals circulated by the head of the hygiene commission suggested that the issue of social insurance was at an impasse and that a new series of negotiations would be required to break the deadlock.

In the summer of 1925, the Ministry of Labour sought to conciliate the positions of the Senate, the Chamber of Deputies, and the concerned interest groups. Assisted by parliamentarians such as Dr Édouard Grinda and Étienne Antonelli, the minister was able to conclude an agreement through the deliberations of a special extra-parliamentary commission.[58] This negotiating process resulted in the practical repudiation of most of Dr Chauveau's proposals. By 1928, both legislative chambers would pass social insurance legislation that reiterated many of the principles which had defined the bill first passed by the Chamber of Deputies a few years before.[59] By the beginning of the next decade, a new social insurance system would finally be established, and both its benefits and structure would reflect the multiple influences which had marked its inception during the first decade of the interwar period.

Throughout the twenties, the unremitting pressure of ambivalent and hostile special interests defined the social insurance question. First inspired by practical necessity, namely the repatriation of Alsace-Lorraine, social

---

[55] AN, CE 65, *Note confidentielle pour M. Justin Godart*, 19 November 1924, 1.
[56] Ibid. 6–7.
[57] Ibid. 14.
[58] AN, C 14768, *p-v de la commission d'assurance*, 5 February 1928, Durafour.
[59] AN, C 14768, *p-v*, 25 November 1927, Dr Grinda.

insurance was soon defined by the complex interplay of ideological and political considerations. The concern for public consultations, which was largely confined to the activism of the aforementioned lobbies, further inhibited a policy process that was held hostage to a myriad of separate and conflicting sectional demands. The legislation expanded upon the limited purview of the state in social and economic affairs, but its content illustrated the non-statist dimension of the solidarist legacy, not to mention the political influence of different interest groups. By the end of the next decade, the Ministry of Labour would address the administrative limitations of the social insurance regime, revisiting an issue which had prolonged the legislative process in the first place. These subsequent adjustments were inevitable since the legislation of the interwar period had largely been shaped by conflicting interest group pressures which defied any rational conception of public policy but which had sought to placate their respective political objectives.

PIERRE LAROQUE AND SOCIAL INSURANCE

In the autumn of 1944, Pierre Laroque, the newly appointed director of social insurance, would launch a policy review which culminated in the development of French social security. The work undertaken in the aftermath of the Liberation benefited from Laroque's long-standing exposure to the problems of social insurance, and his knowledge of the matter owed much to his professional background as a civil servant who had dealt with the implementation of the social insurance legislation of 1928–1930. These experiences had made him familiar with social insurance law as well as the administrative structures of the system, and he had long been convinced of the necessity of reforming French social insurance.

Laroque's first encounter with the question of social insurance came within a few months of his admission to the *Conseil d'État*. In the summer of 1930, he was assigned as a *rapporteur* on a commission which examined the legislation that had been passed by the legislature,[60] though little is known about the actual substance of his experience. During the following years, he would repeatedly revisit the issue as a member of the staff of Adolphe Landry, the Minister of Labour who served in the Laval government of the early thirties. While serving as legal adviser and chief of staff to the minister,[61] he became involved with the implementation of the social

---

[60] *Témoignage* Laroque (oral history interview conducted by the *Comité d'histoire de la sécurité sociale*); P. Laroque, *Au service de l'homme et du droit*, 95.

[61] Laroque, *Au service*, 98–101.

insurance system, and this experience provided him with an intimate knowledge of its inner workings. During this period, in fact, he came into contact with the groups which played a central role in the functioning of the social insurance system, and he was personally acquainted with the leaders of the medical lobby and the mutual aid societies.[62] More importantly, Laroque developed his expertise in the more technical aspects of social insurance law. For example, he was involved in the development of the separate system of benefits which was to serve the needs of the agricultural sector.[63] These combined experiences provided him both with a technical expertise and a practical experience that would serve him well as the architect of the post-war social security plan.

In the meantime, Laroque wrote about the issue of social insurance, and he stated his belief that the system would have to be reformed during the coming years. In 1932, he authored a study of the existing legislation[64] which proved to be an incisive treatment of a dry and complicated subject. Laroque was well aware that the social insurance system was the product of a political compromise between different interest groups, but he also believed that it was necessary to reform it at some later date.[65] In fact, he would reiterate this view in his subsequent writings. In 1935, he contributed an article on the topic of *prévoyance* for the *Encyclopédie Française*, and the resulting piece dealt with the fundamental problems which would later be addressed by the social security plan of 1945. According to Laroque, the social insurance legislation of 1928–1930 had resulted in bureaucratic chaos, a result which was compounded by the financial limitations of its system of benefits:

> The allocated benefits only cover partially and incompletely the insured risks, the administrative mechanism is heavy, complex, the obligatory principle is not even strictly enforced. The compromise achieved by French legislation between the necessity of state intervention and the mutual aid societies has not always produced happy results. Perhaps it would have been better to give more autonomy to organizations where there truly exists a spirit of mutual aid and increase the role of the state wherever this spirit does not exist.[66]

---

[62] MAS, LP, box 4, letter from Dr Cibrie (*Confédération des Syndicats Médicaux*), 23 February 1932; MAS, LP, box 4, letter from the *Comité Central des Assurances Sociales*, 26 February 1932; *Témoignage* Laroque.

[63] *Témoignage* Laroque.

[64] P. Tissier, P. O. Sardan, and P. Closset, *Traité des assurances sociales. Supplément de mise courant an 31 october 1932, par Pierre Laroque.*

[65] Ibid. 21.

[66] MAS, LP, box 50, article on *prévoyance* submitted to the *Encyclopédie Française*, 13.

The haphazard nature of the decentralization of services might have reflected the political realities of the time, but it did not facilitate the delivery of benefits, and the latter did not adequately provide for the needs of the insured. As a consequence, it was necessary to consider recourse to a greater degree of state intervention, but this did not preclude his support for the maintenance of some form of administrative decentralization wherever possible.

CONCLUSION

Early twentieth-century France was marked by the rise of the solidarist movement, a wide-ranging ideological and political phenomenon which came to define the reformist discourse of the Third Republic. While Pierre-Joseph Proudhon had anticipated many of the themes later associated with solidarism, the latter emerged as a force in its own right by the turn of the century, as demonstrated by the careers of its most prominent advocates, which included Émile Durkheim, Léon Bourgeois, Célestin Bouglé, and Léon Duguit. These thinkers were united by a shared concern with social solidarity, a concept which referred to both the moral and functional interdependence of all members of society. While they believed that this interdependence was an objective reality of social development, they also promoted various initiatives aimed at fostering this sense of social solidarity, whether defined through state intervention or the organized activity of given civic groups. The solidarists accepted the necessity of a greater degree of state intervention, but they remained uneasy about its scope, a reflection of the liberal anxieties which permeated their attempt at reconciling individualist and collectivist principles.

The ambivalence of the solidarist movement was also reflected in the development of social insurance. In the aftermath of the First World War, Georges Cahen-Salvador argued that his proposal was defined by the desire to pursue solidaristic objectives, but his reliance on an expanded state infrastructure elicited the opposition of the mutual aid societies, a group which had played a critical role in the administration of the *Retraites ouvrières et paysannes* which had been established a decade before. These societies were able to influence the legislative process, and this resulted in the revision of a social insurance project which came to reflect their desire to play a central role in the administration of social insurance. The opposition of the mutual aid societies might have been based on self-interest, but it also confirmed the non-statist dimension of the solidarist conception of social reform, namely its belief that intermediary bodies and structures could also serve to promote social solidarity. The ensuing legislation combined both statist and non-statist elements, as illustrated by the central role that was attributed to the mutual aid societies in the management of a publicly mandated social insurance system.

Pierre Laroque was first exposed to the question of social insurance soon after he began his career as a civil servant. As a student of administrative law, he had come to espouse a solidarist conception of the law and the state which owed much to the thought of Léon Duguit and the public service school. For Duguit, the state had the obligation to provide new services attuned to public needs, and this role was intimately linked to the pursuit of solidarist objectives. These principles would inform Laroque's conception of social policy, as became apparent once he embarked upon the study of various social problems. At the same time, he became aware of the practical realities of the social insurance system as a result of his work during the early thirties. As a consequence, Laroque came to believe that the system was hampered by its juxtaposition of obligatory and voluntary principles, since it had resulted in a haphazard form of decentralization which was exceedingly complex and inefficient. These observations would explain his support for the reform of social insurance, though his recommendations in this matter would only be officially formulated in the following decade.

2

The Law and Corporatism

INTRODUCTION

Pierre Laroque's reputation as the architect of French social security has overshadowed the wide scope of his interests, and it was this intellectual curiosity which inspired his work in the fields of administrative law and industrial relations. As a student of the leading theoreticians of French public law, Laroque came to believe in the virtues of administrative decentralization, the means through which the state could adapt to social diversity without jeopardizing its role as the custodian of the general interest. At the same time, he adopted a solidarist conception of society and the state, and this explained his advocacy of a greater degree of state interventionism in order to promote social solidarity. These views would later influence his conception of social policy, and they help explain why he came to support the corporatist management of industrial relations. In 1934, the *Conseil National Économique* entrusted him with the task of studying existing collective bargaining procedures, and his research turned him into an admirer of Fascist corporatism. In his view, the creation of corporatist structures would provide labour with a strengthened role in the negotiation of working conditions and the mediation of industrial conflict. The corporation would implement the disciplinary constraints which had been lacking in the collective bargaining process, thus making this legal mechanism more effective while fostering a new sense of social solidarity in a pacified social climate.

BACKGROUND AND EDUCATION

Pierre Laroque was born in November 1907, the son of a Jewish father and an Anglo-Catholic mother.[1] While we know little of how these origins might have influenced his early development, they would eventually

---

[1] P. Laroque, *Au service de l'homme et du droit*, 65–6.

account for his expulsion from the civil service in the fall of 1940, when he became a victim of the anti-Semitic legislation of the Vichy regime.[2] During the years of his childhood and adolescence, however, it is altogether clear that Laroque benefited from the various social and educational advantages which one readily associates with a background of privilege. The father of his best friend, for example, was a prominent lawyer and local politician who often entertained many of the prominent figures of early twentieth-century France.[3] From a young age, he was exposed to a world where social prominence mingled with professional success. Later on, as a student of the Faculty of Law of the University of Paris, he befriended various individuals who were destined to achieve great success and fame in the course of the following decades. It was during this period that he met Edgar Faure, a future prime minister, and Raymond Aron, the famed sociologist, acquaintances who would eventually become members of the *Académie Française*.[4] Throughout these years, he socialized with influential elders and brilliant young contemporaries who represented the nation's present and future social, political, and intellectual elite.

Laroque's memoirs and personal archive provide interesting glimpses into his life and character. The Laroque papers provide additional detail concerning issues and events barely mentioned in his memoirs, and thus represent a useful record of his life during the twenties and thirties. On a more intimate level, his papers provide us with a sense of his personality, giving one the impression of a highly developed sense of organization and a propensity for hard work, traits which were mirrored in his abundant production of published works dealing with a wide array of subjects.[5] Moreover, his contemporaries seemed to share this perception of his character, and this was demonstrated by a prank played by a couple of friends who had his handwriting submitted for analysis. During the thirties, a couple of his friends had his writing studied by graphologists (though one may question the seriousness of the enterprise); according to the results obtained by one analysis, Laroque possessed highly developed intellectual faculties which were abetted by a capacity for hard work, a reasonable temperament, and a meticulous sense of organization.[6] The following year, another friend would confirm these findings. The person noted that Laroque's writing denoted clarity, order, and honesty; furthermore, the subject also demonstrated a remarkable capacity for intellectual

---

[2] Ibid. 126–7.
[3] Ibid. 69.
[4] Ibid. 71–5.
[5] Laroque, *Au service*, 363–75. Chronological list of publications (1926–1992).
[6] MAS, LP, box 140, see analysis and accompanying letter from Ms Yvonne Guillet, 1 November 1937.

synthesis.[7] While these comments might have been made in jest, they do provide us with an amusing but altogether accurate portrait of the man's character and intellect, illustrating personal traits which contributed to his professional success.

Like his father before him, Laroque decided to pursue a career in the law, and he enrolled at both the Faculty of Law of the University of Paris and the *École Libre des Sciences Politiques* in the autumn of 1924.[8] While he chose to focus upon administrative law, he was also interested in the study of history, as reflected in his attendance of Élie Halévy's lectures on the history of European socialism.[9] The course focused upon the changing nature of state responsibility, a phenomenon that had sparked much interest in French academic circles. The course of Laroque's studies, in fact, was very much affected by the gradual erosion of state minimalism and the rise of state interventionism, and it was during these years that he became interested in the practical implications of this shift in the responsibilities of the modern state.

Élie Halévy's lectures on the history of European socialism were delivered during the academic year of 1925–1926. While it is difficult to ascertain the actual influence of these lectures upon Laroque's thought, it is clear that they exposed him to the changing nature of politics and governance during the first quarter of the twentieth century. At the time, Halévy argued that the existing economic system was a hybrid of sorts, since it combined elements of both liberal capitalism and statist collectivism.[10] The historian had noted the fundamental shift in public responsibilities that had rendered the minimalist state obsolete. Decried by the advocates of classical forms of liberalism, the new role of the state was embraced by others, namely those who favoured various forms of social, political, and economic reform. Laroque was introduced to the study of law during this momentous period, and its legacy was to be felt throughout the following decades.

In the spring of 1926, he wrote a paper on the influence of socialist doctrines on the legislation and institutions of the Third Republic. Laroque argued that the redefinition of the responsibilities of the state had resulted in new forms of interventionism, thus reducing the scope of private law and calling into question the legal system's capacity to protect individual rights.[11] Since the end of the nineteenth century, he noted,

---

[7] MAS, LP, box 140, letter from Mrs Colette Lagrange, 21 November 1938.

[8] Laroque, *Au service*, 71.

[9] Ibid. 75.

[10] MAS, LP, box 8, *Le socialisme en Europe au XIX siècle (1925–1926)*, second notebook, 285–6.

[11] MAS, LP, box 140, paper, 17 May 1926, 2–7.

both the public discourse and the practice of government had undergone a profound transformation:

> ... it seems that the influence of socialist doctrines upon our institutions is increasing, it seems, according to one contemporary economist, that our epoch is a time of socialistic capitalism which some want to replace with a capitalistic socialism. Revolutionary doctrines are in disfavour. And the socialism being promoted is characterized by its statism: it represents a coordinated and systematic grouping of all national forces.[12]

In a sense, the evolution of the modern state represented a process of modernization and rationalization of a public administration which was confronted with new social and economic challenges. These practices, in turn, raised serious legal questions regarding the nature and limits of state power, and these concerns came under the purview of administrative law.

As Stuart Jones has noted, the drive to expand the scope of the responsibilities of the state had inspired a revolution in the field of French legal thought, thus allowing for the renewal of the French state tradition in the light of rising popular democracy and incipient collectivism.[13] French public law sought to engage with the problems presented by the rise of an industrial society, namely a growing preoccupation with the social consequences of industrialization. As a result, administrative law attempted to reconcile traditional individualist concerns with a communitarian perspective, seeking to balance individual rights with these new interventionist practices.[14] French administrative law was not ideologically neutral, and both its scholars and practitioners contributed to the shift in the responsibilities of the French state during the early twentieth century.

By the mid twenties, the field of administrative law had been deeply influenced by the works of Léon Duguit and Maurice Hauriou, legal scholars who were associated with the public service and institutionalist schools of French administrative law. Whatever their differences, both Hauriou and Duguit shared a common interest in the redefinition of public law in the light of wide ranging sociological and philosophical influences, and their research was characterized by their sustained interest in the relationship between the law and social theory.[15] As we have seen, Léon Duguit was the exponent of a sociological approach to the law, and this explained his belief that the law and the modern state had to serve a

---

[12] Ibid. 12.
[13] H. S. Jones, *The French State in Question*, 28.
[14] Ibid. 51.
[15] Ibid. 150.

solidarist objective.[16] The public service doctrine thus provided a solidarist rationale for the rise of state interventionism. As discussed in the previous chapter, Laroque was influenced by Duguit and the public service school, a bias which was to be confirmed in the doctoral thesis he published in 1933. Like Duguit, he argued that the state had to promote social solidarity through expanded public services, but it should be noted that his thought also bore the imprint of contending schools of administrative law.

Maurice Hauriou, the leading theoretician of the institutionalist school, was concerned with the same social and administrative phenomena as Duguit and his followers, but his thought was based on different ideological premises. Like Duguit, Hauriou was concerned with the relationship of the individual with society, but his analysis of this problem combined a sociological approach with an idealistic perspective, the latter of which owed much to the Catholic and Bergsonian aspects of his thought.[17] From the institutionalist perspective, the evolution of society was defined by the constant interaction of the individual and the social context. The individual expressed ideas and values, and these subjective elements would find a practical manifestation in the creation of social groups that constituted the objective reality of social existence.[18] These groups represented the practical manifestation of ideas and principles, and it was this notion which was at the core of the doctrine put forward by Hauriou and his followers. The theory of the institution, as it was called, made it possible to understand social development, and the same doctrine also explained the emergence of the state and the multiplication of its services. According to institutionalist theory, the state enjoyed a pre-eminent status over other institutions since it represented the will of the nation, a consequence of the rise of political democracy.[19] The theory of the institution thus provided an explanation for the development of the modern state, and its approach was both normative and descriptive in nature.

Hauriou believed that his theory made it possible to explain the function of the state and its constituent services. These institutions could not be understood if one chose to focus upon their material reality alone, since

[16] See Chapter 1, and Jones, *The French State*, 149–79; É. Pisier-Kouchner, *Le Service public dans la théorie de l'État de Léon Duguit*.

[17] L. Sfez, *Essai sur la contribution du doyen Hauriou au droit administratif français*, 7–8; F. Fournié, *Recherches sur la décentralisation dans l'œuvre de Maurice Hauriou*, 38–40; Jones, *The French State*, 180–204.

[18] M. Hauriou, 'La Théorie de l'institution et de la fondation (Essai de vitalisme social)' (1925), in P. Archambault (ed.), *Aux sources du droit. Le Pouvoir, l'ordre, la liberté*, 96.

[19] M. Hauriou, 'L'ordre social, la justice et le droit' (1927), in Archambault, *Aux sources du droit*, 60.

they were also defined by their underlying moral purpose. The notion of institution was the cornerstone of his thought, and he argued that its importance lay with the fact that the institution promoted social cohesion through the development of a spirit of communion, a collective awareness which bound individuals to a given institution.[20] The latter were active participants in social reality, and they both embodied and diffused the values of civil society at large. Hauriou was an advocate of administrative decentralization, and his support for this form of bureaucratic organization was an outgrowth of his pluralistic conception of individual and collective existence. The state had to adapt its services in light of the inherent complexity of society,[21] but this was no simple task because the state remained the custodian of the general interest. The principle of administrative decentralization resolved this dilemma by adapting services according to local or functional needs without calling into question the pre-eminent status of the central authority of the state.[22] In other words, decentralization reconciled contradictory requirements by adapting the state to a pluralistic social reality while safeguarding its central and pre-eminent role.

While Laroque came to espouse the solidarist views associated with the public service school, he also was influenced by the institutionalist conception of the state, as would be demonstrated in his early legal writings. In 1930, Laroque co-authored with Roland Maspétiol a prize-winning study of the *tutelle administrative*, the legal mechanism which regulated the relationship between the state and its decentralized services.[23] The *tutelle administrative* outlined a particular conception of the state, since its authors believed that the latter had to provide expanded public services without abandoning its responsibilities as the custodian of the general interest. The increase in state interventionism had eroded the unitary character of the state, since the latter had decentralized its services on both technical and geographical grounds. The *tutelle administrative* referred to the supervisory control exercised by the state over its constituent services. For the authors, this coordinating mechanism preserved the unity of the former while providing for the relative autonomy of the latter. If anything, the *tutelle* was an instrument of liberty:

> The *tutelle administrative* is thus, and one cannot insist too strongly on this point, an institution of liberty. It finds its origin and its end in decentralization. Undoubtedly it might seem paradoxical to bring together two notions

<hr>

[20] Hauriou, 'La Théorie de l'institution et de la fondation', 105–6.
[21] M. Hauriou, *Précis de droit constitutionnel*, 2nd edn, 74–5.
[22] Fournié, *Recherches sur la décentralisation*, 501–54.
[23] R. Maspétiol and P. Laroque, *La Tutelle administrative*.

> which are apparently contradictory; but if, in fact and in the realm of ideas,
> the *tutelle administrative* is opposed to decentralization in order to mark its
> limits, it is nonetheless true that these ideas are intimately linked and in a
> unitary state decentralization cannot proceed without the *tutelle* and the
> *tutelle* without decentralization.[24]

In the light of a constitutional system which remained influenced by a centralizing tradition, the *tutelle* was a legal instrument that made decentralization possible without calling into question the fundamental unity of the state.

Maspétiol and Laroque believed that the state was the custodian of the general interest. They argued that the *tutelle administrative* simultaneously protected the population, the relevant services, and the state itself, thereby promoting the cohesion of the nation as a whole.[25] This explicit reference to the nation was altogether significant. Unlike the advocates of the public service school, Laroque and Maspétiol believed in the pre-eminence of the state, since the latter represented the legal and political manifestation of the nation:

> The state cannot be reduced to a series of independent and autonomous
> public services; a cohesive power is necessary for any social grouping; this is
> what is meant when one speaks of state sovereignty, and if this expression
> has been criticised in terms of legal theory, it does nevertheless correspond
> to an imperious political necessity, and social institutions must make it
> prevail.[26]

The authors' concern with social cohesion was explicitly related to an underlying belief in state sovereignty, since it was the state that was entrusted with the task of promoting the general interest.

Laroque and Maspétiol believed that decentralization represented an essential mechanism for popular participation in the management of public affairs. They argued that this increased faculty for public involvement was the single most important social, political, and administrative development of the contemporary era.[27] The expansion of public authority, they believed, resulted in the development of the reciprocal ties between the state and society. It provided for the association of private groups with the state, and decentralization thus laid the basis of a corporatist structure which cultivated a true spirit of citizenship amongst the population at large.[28] The reference to corporatism was all the more

----

[24] Maspétiol and Laroque, *La Tutelle administrative*, 9.
[25] Ibid. 14–15.
[26] Ibid. 376.
[27] Ibid. 373.
[28] Ibid. 373–5.

interesting, given the evolution of Laroque's interests during the course of the following decade.

In their conclusion, the authors employed language that evoked the concerns of the solidarist ideology of the past as well as the technocratic doctrines which were in vogue among their contemporaries. They believed that state interventionism was inspired by the need to rationalize economic activity, while administrative decentralization was motivated by the increased functional specificity of the state's new responsibilities.[29] By invoking the notion of rationalization and technical expertise, the authors confirmed the influence of technocratic ideas upon legal thought and administrative practice. Furthermore, they believed that decentralization promoted greater social, political, and administrative cohesion. The *tutelle administrative*, they concluded, was an instrument of collaboration and solidarity since it was intimately related to increased public involvement in the management of public services.[30] While managing the relationship between the state and its constituent organs, the *tutelle* also represented an instrument of solidarity, since it made it possible to associate different social and economic groups with the French state.

As a student, Laroque had devoted little attention to social problems, but his work revealed a budding awareness of these questions. Élie Halévy's course on European socialism had exposed him to the rise of reformist ideologies that had emerged in response to the social consequences of industrialization, while his study of public law had forced him to reflect upon the changing nature of state power. While the public service school was defined by its solidaristic conception of the role of the state, the institutionalist argued that the modern state was the embodiment of liberal and democratic values, and that administrative decentralization was a practical response to the pluralistic nature of society. Laroque was influenced by both doctrines, since his legal writings evoked the concerns of both the public service and the institutionalist schools of public law. The eclectic nature of his thinking would be confirmed throughout the course of the thirties, as new personal and professional experiences contributed to the development of his ideas concerning the nature of society and the role of the state.

---

[29] Ibid. 378.
[30] Ibid. 382.

CONSEIL D'ÉTAT, MINISTRY OF LABOUR, AND CONSEIL NATIONAL ÉCONOMIQUE

Upon the completion of his studies, Laroque aimed for a position with the *Conseil d'État*, the administrative court entrusted with the task of adjudicating cases pertaining to administrative law and which provided legal counsel to the government and the bureaucracy.[31] The members of the council were involved in virtually every aspect of French governance, tasks which contributed to their reputation as being part of an elite corps of the civil service. Entry to the *Conseil d'État* was determined by a rigorous examination process, which came at the end of at least one year of preparation. By the end of 1929, Laroque had passed the *concours* which gained him entry into this select group of administrative lawyers, and he was named an *auditeur de deuxième classe* of the council with his employment beginning on 1 January 1930.[32] Like many of the council's junior members, he was assigned to whatever government agency or commission that required the services of a specialist in administrative law. It was in this context that he was appointed to serve as the *rapporteur* of a commission that dealt with the implementation of social insurance in the summer of 1930. By the following year, he had joined the staff of the Minister of Labour. Family connections had provided him with this new professional opportunity: he was recommended by an acquaintance of his father, who also happened to be the minister's son-in-law.[33] As a result of these fortuitous circumstances, he began working for a man who would become a mentor of sorts, and the experience would contribute to the burgeoning of his interest in social policy in the widest sense.

The Minister of Labour, Adolphe Landry, was a scholar and a statesman who had published a wide array of studies in philosophy, history, economics, and demography; he was also a deputy from Corsica who had long been committed to social reform and was particularly concerned by the issue of demographic decline.[34] As Alfred Sauvy later recalled, these reformist and natalist views were central to his political outlook:

> But these reforms, he knew, would take time before they came into being: the advent of communism in the world and the existence of a purely revolutionary party, could only, in his view, slow down this process. And,

---

[31] See M.-C. Kessler, *Le Conseil d'État*; Y. Robineau and D. Truchet, *Le Conseil d'État*; B. Latour, *La Fabrique du droit: une ethnographie du Conseil d'État*.

[32] Laroque, *Au service*, 89

[33] *Témoignage* Laroque; Laroque, *Au service*, 98.

[34] Alfred Sauvy, 'Adolphe Landry', *Population*, 11 (1956), 609–11.

in the meantime, France had to live. What could a triumphant socialism achieve in a country deprived of youth? What many socialists did not understand, A. Landry saw with his lucid mind, and he was rarely proven wrong. The essential goal, the first objective, was to stop the fatal decline and this could only take place within the context of the existing political regime.[35]

Most importantly, his concern with demographic decline led him to campaign for the introduction of family allowances,[36] an objective which came to be shared by a wide array of French policymakers, and would contribute to the shaping of French social policy during the following decades.

Who was Adolphe Landry? The scion of a prominent Corsican family, he was born in 1874 and had attended the prestigious *École Normale Supérieure* before embarking on an academic career.[37] Publishing a myriad of books and articles from an early age, he rapidly ascended the academic hierarchy and was appointed to the chair of economic history at the *École Pratique des Hautes Études* in 1907.[38] This academic success did not deter him from engaging in other pursuits, and he would soon depart the staid life of academia for the tumult of electoral politics. In 1910, Landry was elected to the Chamber of Deputies as a Radical-Socialist.[39] Landry quickly established the main priorities of his legislative work: most notably, he promoted laws aimed at increasing the national birth rate. Within a couple of years, in fact, he would become a member of the board of the *Alliance Nationale contre la Dépopulation*, a leading natalist pressure group.[40] This interest in demographic issues not only drove his political career, but was also expressed in his scholarly publications.

In 1934, Landry published *La Révolution démographique*, a study that argued that the decline in the birth rate threatened the future of the French nation while affecting the relationship between different members of the international community. According to the author, the international balance of power would be permanently altered as a result of a worldwide demographic shift.[41] Laroque was well aware of the nature of Landry's preoccupations, and he would write a sympathetic review of his

---

[35] Ibid. 616–17.

[36] S. Pedersen, *Family, Dependence, and the Origins of the Welfare State: Britain and France 1914–1945*, 289, 373, 381, and 386. As Pedersen notes, Landry was one of the leaders of natalist opinion in the legislature.

[37] Sauvy, 'Adolphe Landry', 609.

[38] Ibid. 611.

[39] Ibid.

[40] Ibid.

[41] See A. Landry, *La Révolution démographique*.

work for the *Revue Française de Science Politique*.[42] Interestingly enough, he even sent a draft of his review to the one-time minister, a move which the latter did not consider appropriate:

> My dear Laroque,
> I am very pleased that my book interested you. But when you send me a copy of your review so that I may correct it, aren't you being led astray by affection? Could you see a judge requesting the approval of the person on trial?
> At the end, however, I wrote a comment in pencil. It is to restate my view: that the demographic revolution, after taking place among the peoples of the European races, is destined to spread throughout humanity as a whole.[43]

This correspondence suggests that the two enjoyed a close relationship, an impression which is confirmed by Landry's repeated entreaties to his former subordinate to come by his home for a visit or to consult the resources of his personal library.[44] Both men exhibited a common devotion to public service and a wide-ranging intellectual curiosity, and most importantly, they shared a commitment to a reformist agenda which was influenced by a fear of demographic decline.[45] Laroque never lost sight of the lessons he had learned while working for Adolphe Landry, and this was made clear in an article he penned for the centenary of Landry's birth. With the benefit of four decades of hindsight, he noted that events had confirmed the prescience of the minister's views, noting that an anaemic birth rate helped explain the decline of the Third Republic while a baby boom had contributed to the recovery of post-war France.[46] In brief, Laroque shared the natalist concerns which shaped French social policy during the early twentieth century, even if his own work in the field of social security was the product of a different set of priorities.

Though it is often difficult to determine which particular set of experiences contribute to the evolution of an individual's world view, it does appear that Laroque was deeply influenced by his sojourn at the Ministry of Labour. Before he had reached the age of 30, he had been confronted with the problems of ministerial politics and was able to contribute to the development of public policy from a privileged vantage point. Furthermore, he developed a lasting interest in the diverse aspects of social policy,

---

[42] MAS, LP, box 66, *Revue Française de Science Politique* (Avril–Juin, 1934), 305–7.

[43] MAS, LP, box 4, letter from Landry, 28 February 1934.

[44] MAS, LP, box 4, note from Landry, 17 October 1936; Laroque, *Au service*, 100–1.

[45] Laroque, *Au service*, 100–1; MAS, LP, box 139, Laroque was a member of the *Alliance nationale pour l'accroissement de la population française*, a leading pro-natalist lobby, and he devoted a number of radio broadcasts to the issue of demography during 1936–1938.

[46] MAS, LP, box 42, typescript of article submitted to *Population et Avenir* (1974), 5.

viewing the latter as the outcome of the complex interplay of a wide array of social, economic, and historical factors. In 1934, one friend would write that he thought that Laroque's experience at the ministry had shaped his interests and outlook:

> I noticed that your sojourn at the Ministry of Labour had led you to reflect upon serious problems that were less administrative and more philosophical in nature and that you had conceptions which go singularly beyond the bureaucratic mentality in which I thought, perhaps by analogy, all civil servants were forced to confine themselves.[47]

In other words, his time under Landry's tutelage had contributed to the maturation of his ideas, and in the process he came to focus upon the problems of social policy.

The opening of these new horizons also coincided with his work for the *Conseil National Économique*, the consultative body which assembled the representatives of the various social and economic interests of interwar France.[48] In 1934, Laroque was entrusted with the task of producing a report on the existing forms of collective bargaining legislation, an assignment which provided him with a unique opportunity to deepen his knowledge of industrial relations. Most importantly, his study of collective bargaining procedures led him to advocate the adoption of a corporatist approach to the management of industrial relations, and these proposals would come to define his contribution to the field of social policy during the interwar period. While his views on corporatism would evolve during the following years, he remained committed to its fundamental objectives, and this would be amply demonstrated by his later work in the field of social security.

The first draft of the report on collective bargaining was submitted on 20 June 1934. Eighty-seven pages long, it examined the issue of collective bargaining from a comparative perspective, focusing upon the mechanisms currently in place in France, Italy, Germany, and Britain.[49] Though written in an even-handed manner, the ideological bias of the report was apparent to any reader. Its analysis of social relations was marked by a critical attitude towards the business community, sympathy for the working class, and a belief in the necessity of state intervention in order to mediate social conflict. The report noted that industrial relations in contemporary France had to be understood within a proper historical

---

[47] MAS, LP, box 4, undated letter from Claude (probably Zimmern), sometime in 1934.

[48] A. Chatriot, *La Démocratie sociale à la française: l'Expérience du Conseil National Économique 1924–1940.*

[49] MAS, LP, box 22, *Rapport sur les conventions collectives*, 20 June 1934.

framework, since the pattern of these relations was an outcome of the struggles which had pitted labour against management during the previous decades. Since the middle of the nineteenth century, Laroque argued, the labour movement had sought to empower a working class which remained at the mercy of an authoritarian and paternalistic management.[50] French social relations were governed by force, a pattern that had been partially mitigated by the development of the law and the expansion of the state. It was the persistence of industrial conflict, in Laroque's view, which had led to a gradual increase in state intervention in social and economic affairs.[51] The emergence of collective bargaining mechanisms was representative of this phenomenon. As Laroque noted, collective bargaining represented an attempt at achieving a binding legal accord between conflicting economic interests, thus providing for the peaceful resolution of their respective differences.[52] The mechanism of collective bargaining had been developed in order to diffuse social tensions, and it established a legal framework that compensated for the limitations of a legal system that remained influenced by the individualist biases of the civil code and the contractual principle.

According to the report, the promise offered by the advent of collective bargaining procedures had never been achieved in practice, and these limited results reflected the persistent influence of obsolete liberal principles. French labour legislation was still defined by the influence of an individualist outlook which compromised its capacity to achieve its social and economic objectives.[53] Collective bargaining agreements, according to the existing legislation, depended solely upon the accord of their respective parties, and this lack of legal constraints called into question their effectiveness. As a result, existing legislation could do little to promote the peaceful resolution of industrial conflict.[54] The deficiencies of this legislation were matched by the prevalence of individualist attitudes which further complicated attempts at promoting the peaceful resolution of industrial conflict:

> The basic individualism, of business owners as well as workers, has slowed this movement of organization down in France. But this backwardness cannot continue without compromising the stability of the social and economic order. The prospect of social troubles, which can only happen after the revival of economic activity and the sacrifices imposed upon the

---

[50] MAS, LP, box 22, *Rapport*, 1.
[51] Ibid.
[52] Ibid.
[53] Ibid. 40.
[54] Ibid. 79–80.

working class, makes it particularly urgent to establish an organization permitting the adaptation, through pacific means, of working conditions to economic circumstances and substituting legal solutions for solutions of force in industrial relations.[55]

It was the prospect of renewed industrial strife that made it imperative to reform existing collective bargaining procedures, and it was in this context that Laroque outlined his recommendations.

Since French collective bargaining legislation had proved incapable of achieving its objective, it was necessary to create a system which would provide the disciplinary constraints that would make it more effective. The introduction of corporatist structures was intended to serve this purpose, and his proposals owed much to his research on the corporatist policies of Italian Fascism, the achievements of which he deemed to be 'remarkable'.[56] The corporation, in his view, provided a solution to the problems associated with a laissez-faire approach to industrial relations, since it would provide a new forum for the negotiation and enforcement of collective bargaining agreements. More specifically, Laroque suggested that the arbitration of labour disputes and the negotiation of working conditions in each sector of industrial activity be placed under the authority of departmental or regional commissions uniting the representatives of labour and management.[57] These corporations would thus facilitate the task of social mediation which befell the modern state by involving the contending parties in a permanent structure which served to manage industrial relations.

LAROQUE, CORPORATISM, AND FASCISM

While Laroque might have found Fascist corporatism impressive, his proposals could also be seen as an outgrowth of his research in the field of administrative law. By virtue of his exposure to the works of the public service and institutionalist schools, he had come to believe that the state had to promote social solidarity, and that the decentralization of public services could be achieved without calling into question the pre-eminent role of the state as custodian of the general interest. This administrative decentralization would associate various social and economic groups in the

---

[55] Ibid. 83.

[56] Ibid. 14.

[57] Ibid. 86–7. Laroque's proposals were similar to the ideas promoted by Georges Scelle, an author he consulted for his report. See G. Scelle, *Le Droit ouvrier. Tableau de la législation française actuelle.*

management of these services, a development that was consistent both
with the development of democratic forms of governance as well as with
the need to cultivate social solidarity in a modern industrial state. Laroque's espousal of these ideas predated his discovery of Fascist corporatism, but it was his report on collective bargaining that set the stage for a
new application of these principles.

The corporatist proposals outlined in his report were influenced by his
study of the Fascist model of industrial relations, and this has led some
scholars to argue that Laroque had espoused pro-Fascist views during the
thirties.[58] While Laroque might have been impressed by Fascist corporatism, his proposals were developed within an explicitly democratic and
republican framework. Though he might have been seduced by the
promise of Fascist corporatism as a result of his research, his views were
not tainted by sympathy for an authoritarian or totalitarian politics, but
simply added to the rich and diverse corpus of a corporatist discourse
which had never been monopolized by any particular group or regime.

Notwithstanding these considerations, it is useful to consider the
origins and development of Fascist corporatism, for the simple reason
that Laroque came to espouse a corporatist politics as a result of his
exposure to the Fascist experience in this particular area of social policy.
This particular variant of corporatism can be viewed as the practical
manifestation of the ideological legacy of revolutionary syndicalism, a
movement which had influenced the emergence of Fascist thought in
the early part of the twentieth century.[59] Fascism was the product of the
synthesis of a diverse set of ideological influences, and this heritage was
openly acknowledged by the founder of the movement. Benito Mussolini
would later concede the influence of the ideas associated with Sorel,
Leone, and Olivetti, the leading representatives of the French and Italian
variants of revolutionary syndicalism.[60] These influences, however, coexisted with other tendencies, and ideological concerns had to contend with
the necessities of practical politics once Fascism came to power. This
ambiguity would be confirmed by Mussolini's conduct of public affairs,
and he repeatedly refrained from enacting policies which might upset his
attempt to balance contending political interests.[61] Nevertheless, the
rhetoric of Fascist corporatism reflected the imprint of the syndicalist

---

[58] F.-X. Merrien, *Étude comparative de l'édification et de l'évolution de l'état protecteur en
France et en Grande-Bretagne*, 231–49.

[59] Z. Sternhell, *The Birth of Fascist Ideology*, 32–3.

[60] B. Mussolini, 'The Doctrine of Fascism', in A. Lyttelton (ed.), *Italian Fascisms from
Pareto to Gentile*, 44–5. The article, however, was ghostwritten by Giovanni Gentile.

[61] R. Sarti, *Fascism and the Industrial Leadership in Italy 1919–40*, 2–3.

discourse, and this remained significant despite the limited achievements of Fascism and the corporate state.

Before the advent of the First World War, the syndicalists had promoted the ideal of the free producer, a concept which grouped both workers and employers, and thus made it possible to transcend traditional social cleavages.[62] The producer became an organizing principle which united a concern with the functional specialization of economic activity with an organic conception of Italian society. The syndicalists believed that employers and workers should collaborate in the management of industry through the medium of professional corporations.[63] The corporation became a mechanism for the democratization of industrial relations, an objective which recalled the objectives promoted by Proudhon and Durkheim during the course of the nineteenth century.

Once Mussolini came to power, syndicalist ideology would enjoy a limited and ambiguous impact on the course of Fascist social policy. The existence of conflicting interests made it difficult to introduce a comprehensive corporatist programme. In the years that followed the march on Rome, Edmondo Rossoni, the leading exponent of Fascist syndicalism, was repeatedly frustrated in his attempts to revolutionize industrial relations; indeed, the Fascist regime would abolish factory councils and refrain from creating mixed syndicates during the early years of its rule.[64] The rhetoric of corporatism was thus undermined by the regime's unwillingness to transform social and economic relations. The conservative reality of this corporatist model would be confirmed even as the government officially moved away from traditional liberal and capitalist conceptions of economic policy. For example, the Labour Charter of 1927, a document characterized by its corporatist language, represented little more than a general statement of principles devoid of practical impact.[65] Nevertheless, corporatist themes continued to permeate the Fascist discourse, and this was to be confirmed by the establishment of the corporate state in 1933–1934.

With the passing of the corporate law of 1934, the Fascist regime created an extensive network of professional corporations which were meant to regulate industrial relations, an initiative which represented a disavowal of the principles of economic laissez-faire. On 14 November 1933, Mussolini declared that the corporations implied public control of the economy without calling into question the private ownership of

[62] Sternhell, *Birth*, 144–6.
[63] Ibid.
[64] Sarti, *Fascism*, 58–77.
[65] Ibid. 95.

property; in this sense, corporatism represented a new ideological synthesis which transcended the divide between liberal individualism and socialist collectivism.[66] Notwithstanding the pretensions of the corporate state, its advent did little to alter the foundations of economic power, since the means of production remained in private hands, and the corporations did not exercise effective control over the management of industry.[67] The creation of new corporatist structures did not introduce democratic principles into the workplace, but the Fascists continued to proclaim that corporatism would revolutionize industrial relations and promote the social integration of the working class.

In a speech delivered before the workers of Milan, Mussolini stressed that the regime sought to achieve a greater degree of social justice:

> Fascism establishes the real equality of individuals before the nation. The difference is in the scale of responsibilities. In speaking to the thickly populated and venturesome city of Bari, I said that the object of the regime in the economic field is to ensure higher social justice for the whole Italian people . . . What does higher social justice mean? It means work guaranteed, fair wages, decent homes; it means the possibility of continuous evolution and improvement. Nor is this enough. It means that the workers must enter more and more intimately into the productive process and share its necessary discipline . . . As the past century was the century of capitalist power, the twentieth century is the century of the power and glory of labour.[68]

The ultimate objective of Fascist corporatism, if one was to take such rhetoric at face value, was to transform social and economic relations, thus creating a society which fully integrated those who had been exploited and marginalized by the capitalist system.

Fascist corporatism focused on the producer, a concept which denied the fundamental opposition between different socio-economic categories such as the proletariat and the bourgeoisie. The Fascist economy was to be based upon a form of industrial democracy, in so far as all producers were to be associated in the governance of a corporatist state. According to Edmondo Rossoni, corporatism sought to promote economic justice and social solidarity among these very producers.[69] By uniting all producers in a common representative structure, the corporate state served to promote a new form of social solidarity, an objective that had been promoted by the French solidarists. As we have seen, the solidarists had promoted a reformist politics which sought to foster a new sense of social solidarity,

66 B. Mussolini, *Four Speeches on the Corporate State*, 23.
67 Sarti, *Fascism*, 101–3.
68 Mussolini, *Four Speeches*, 39–40.
69 E. Rossoni, *Conférence de Edmondo Rossoni à Berlin, le 29 avril 1936*, 27.

and both Durkheim and Duguit had advocated a corporatist approach to the management of industrial relations. Unlike the Fascists, however, the solidarists had defined their project within a liberal and democratic framework.

Neither the Fascists nor the syndicalists had invented corporatism, and a recurring interest in corporatist ideas had long been a feature of French political and intellectual life. During the course of the nineteenth century, a wide array of thinkers had advocated corporatism, and this included figures such as Henri de St Simon and Pierre-Joseph Proudhon.[70] The appeal of corporatism could be explained by the disquiet felt by those who were unsettled by the social impact of the industrial revolution and the apparent incapacity of the state to address these problems. By the turn of the century, however, French corporatist ideology was generally associated with Catholic and Rightist thought. Most notably, René de La Tour du Pin emerged as the advocate of a form of corporatists politics.[71] Within the following decades, the advent of Rightist dictatorships in Italy, Spain and Portugal, each claiming to implement similar policies, seemingly confirmed this perception, but corporatism still attracted support among the French Left during the interwar period.[72] On the whole, the Left proved unreceptive to corporatist politics, and this owed much to its increased identification with the extreme Right.

The widespread currency of corporatist ideas in interwar France did not escape the notice of the Fascist regime, and it sought to capitalize on this trend by attempting a rapprochement with those elements of French political and intellectual life which seemed amenable to its brand of corporatist politics. As a result, the Fascist Institute of Culture organized a colloquium on corporatism in the spring of 1935 which assembled the representatives of various French political, intellectual, and labour organizations.[73] The meeting would demonstrate the fact that the corporatist movement was characterized by radically different conceptions as to what corporatism was supposed to mean, and this complicated the task of the organizers of the conference. Indeed, they failed to convince most of their guests of the virtues of their corporatist experiment, save for the enthusiastic response of the representatives of the neo-socialist movement.

---

[70] M. H. Elbow, *French Corporative Theory 1789–1948*, 23–51.

[71] Ibid. 53–80.

[72] F. Perroux, *Capitalisme et communauté de travail*, 160–2.

[73] G. Parlato, *Il convegno italo-francese di studi corporativi (1935) con il testo integrale degli Atti*; P. Andreu, *Révoltes de l'esprit: les revues des années 30*, 65. Andreu, in fact, helped organize and attended the conference; E. Mounier, *Mounier et sa génération: lettres, carnets et inédits*, 169–71. Emmanuel Mounier attended the meeting, as did Jean de Fabrègues, Maurice Noel, and Louis-Émile Galey.

The most incisive critiques of the corporatist state were voiced by an avowed exponent of syndicalist thought. Pierre Ganivet, the director of *L'Homme Réel*,[74] argued that Fascist corporatism contradicted the basic tenets of syndicalism. In his view, the totalitarian character of the Fascist regime could not be reconciled with the anti-statist bias of the syndicalist discourse:

> At the root of syndicalism we find the notion of class, at the root of Fascism, the notion of party. From this fundamental divergence ensues a number of consequences on the political plane and the economic plane... Instead of finding, like syndicalism, the legal, economic, and social norms which would facilitate the creation of a society without a state and without classes, a society of freely associated producers, of real men, Fascism, because it is based on the idea of a party, only renders more heavy the weight of the artificial machine of the state... The corporation, an abstract and dogmatic construction, only holds force because of the support provided to it by the state and the Fascist Party.[75]

Ganivet merely pointed out the obvious: the social and economic objectives of the Italian government were subordinated to its totaliarian politics. Instead of introducing industrial democracy into the management of social and economic relations, and thus radically decentralizing political and economic power, the corporation had consolidated the social control exercised by the state, thereby perverting the anti-authoritarian objectives of the syndicalist movement.

Georges Roditi and Paul Marion, individuals associated with the *Parti Socialiste de France* and *L'Homme Nouveau*, a political party and an intellectual review identified with neo-socialism, were impressed by the proclaimed achievements of corporatism. Roditi believed that the latter would set the stage for the radical transformation of social and economic relations, while Marion argued that its value lay with its introduction of democratic principles into the field of industrial relations.[76] Roditi and Marion were clearly swayed by the rhetoric of the Fascist regime, and their enthusiastic response could be explained by the fact that the neo-socialist movement was defined by a desire to develop a new form of reformist politics that would be liberated from the constraints of orthodox Marxism. The corporate state seemingly provided the means to achieve this end, but this perception depended upon one's willingness to accept the veracity of the claims put forward by the Italian government. Such an attitude might

---

[74] Andreu, *Revoltes de l'esprit*, 113–15, for a short description of the ideological orientation of *L'Homme Réel*.

[75] Parlato, Il convegno, 112–13.

[76] Ibid. 137, 139–40, 201–2.

have been the product of good faith, but it also demonstrated a remarkable degree of naivety on the part of men who sought to renew the political discourse of the Third Republic.

While Laroque might have been unduly impressed by the Fascist model of industrial relations, he made it clear that his brand of corporatism could not be mistaken for the policies pursued by the Fascists, as demonstrated by the lecture which he delivered at the *Conservatoire des Arts et Métiers* in April 1935. Like the Fascists, he believed that corporatism sought to combine the advantages of both liberal and statist approaches to industrial relations while discarding their corresponding disadvantages.[77] Corporatism thus signalled a break from both liberal individualism and socialist collectivism, but it did not necessarily imply the rejection of republican or democratic principles. The corporation, as Laroque understood it, would extend democratic principles into industrial relations by providing for the joint participation of business and labour in the management of industrial relations:

> The corporation would not be like in Fascist Italy an organisation under the strict control of the state, but an amalgam of all trade organisations, business and labour, involved in a given form of activity, an amalgam in which the profession would be organised by the interested parties themselves for the management of production and their working conditions. A formula that would avoid the inconveniences of liberalism, because it would submit both employers and employees to collective discipline; a formula that would avoid the inconveniences of statism, since decisions would be taken by the interested parties themselves represented by their own free organisations and not by state authorities who would only bring their support to the implementation of the decisions made by the corporation.[78]

Much like Durkheim, he believed that the corporation would promote the social integration of those who participated in French industrial life. Laroque sought to extend the democratic concept to the management of industrial relations while improving the efficiency of an interventionist state, and neither his writings nor his public declarations denote any hostility to the democratic system. According to the institutional typology elaborated by Mihail Manoilesco, a corporatist ideologue of the thirties, one might have concluded that he advocated a subordinated corporatist system in which the latter was subjected to the control of an elected parliament.[79] Divorced from any form of authoritarian or totalitarian politics, the corporation, as he understood it, was a decentralized administrative

---

[77] MAS, LP, box 22, notes of his lecture, 13 April 1935, 22.
[78] Ibid.
[79] M. Manoilesco, *Le siècle du corporatisme*, 156–60.

structure which would enforce the moral discipline necessary for the effective implementation of freely negotiated but ultimately binding collective bargaining agreements.

CORPORATISM IN FRANCE: THE CASE OF THE CNE

Pierre Laroque's corporatist proposals owed much to his background in administrative law and his study of collective bargaining procedures, but it should also be stressed that the elaboration of his ideas on the subject coincided with the rise of public interest in corporatism during the twenties and thirties. According to Maxime Leroy, a legal scholar and advocate of Proudhonian ideas, the creation of the *Conseil National Économique* in 1925 and the introduction of new collective bargaining legislation in 1936 reflected the emergence of a specifically French model of corporatist politics.[80] From this perspective, Laroque may be viewed as one representative of a wider movement which sought to introduce corporatist reforms during the interwar period.

The idea for a *Conseil National Économique* could be traced back to the minimum programme of the CGT, which, in the aftermath of the First World War, called for the creation of a *Conseil Économique du Travail* which would unite the representatives of production and consumption in the corporatist management of economic activity.[81] The programme called for the establishment of a new economic system. The CGT stressed that the ultimate objective of its proposal was to liberate all wage earners and promote the predominance of labour,[82] a purpose which recalled the ideas of Proudhon. In fact, the CET was conceived as the parliament of a future industrial republic. At the time, Maxime Leroy had declared that the minimum programme offered the promise of creating a community of free producers, and that this would usher in a new era defined by an expanded array of social and economic rights.[83] The reforms proposed by the CGT had been of a radical nature, and it was rather unsurprising that they were not adopted by the succeeding governments of the Third Republic.

Nevertheless, the minimum programme did inspire French policy-makers, though the ultimate result of this influence bore little relation

---

[80]   M. Leroy, *Les Tendances du pouvoir et de la liberté*, 123–43.

[81]   B. Georges and D. Tintant, *Léon Jouhaux*, i, annex VIII, *Le Programme minimum de la Confédération Générale du Travail*, 10 février 1921.

[82]   Ibid.

[83]   Leroy, *Les Techniques nouvelles du syndicalisme*, 184, 207–9; G. Guy-Grand, 'L'Ère Proudhon', in C. Bouglé (ed.), *Proudhon et notre temps*, 2–4.

to the radical intentions of the CGT. The *Conseil National Économique* represented but a pale imitation of the CET since it was intended to serve a consultative role and not a parliamentary function.[84] The creation of the CNE, however, did signal a shift in public attitudes towards the state and its responsibilities, and this change was noted in President Painlevé's address to the council at its inauguration:

> The serious problems that the end of 10 years of war and post-war impose on our activity cannot be resolved, in fact, without a deeper knowledge of technical and economic questions. In order to win the war, we had to employ all of the resources of science and modern industry. To achieve a real peace— because seven years after the armistice we are still working at it—we need a labour policy, raw materials, international trade. And we must coordinate these diverse efforts into coordinated action, directed towards a single goal.[85]

The CNE was conceived in light of the interventionist practices of the First World War, and the explicit reference to the experience of Total War suggested that the notion of a minimalist state was becoming increasingly irrelevant given the changing responsibilities of the modern industrial state.

The CNE was meant to advise the government on the diverse aspects of social and economic policy. According to the report submitted by the prime minister to the president of the Republic, the development of these policies would be facilitated by the consultation of the leading professional organizations, and this task could be performed by the council.[86] In other words, this new body institutionalized the consultative practices which formed an integral part of the political process. Accordingly, the CNE brought together the representatives of a wide array of social and economic groups, including the *Fédération Nationale de la Mutualité Française*, the *Confédération Générale de la Production Française*, the *Confédération Générale du Travail* and the *Confédération Française des Travailleurs Chrétiens*.[87] The scope of the council's membership reflected the desire to include the vast spectrum of interests which made up French socio-economic life, and this inclusiveness demonstrated the fact that the consultative role that had been attributed to the CNE was altogether important, even if the council was deprived of any decision-making authority.

[84] AN, CE 1, *discours de M. Painlevé*, 22 June 1925.
[85] Ibid.
[86] AN, CE 43, *rapport du Président du Conseil au Président de la République*.
[87] AN, CE 43, *arrêté du 9 avril 1925*.

While the CNE might have given short shrift to the objectives outlined in the minimum programme, it did represent a form of corporatist politics, and some viewed it as the nucleus of a future corporate state. By the mid thirties, George Cahen-Salvador, the secretary general of the CNE, would call for the consolidation of state interventionism in the social and economic spheres, and he argued that the council should be attributed a decision-making role in light of this new and expansive role which he attributed to the reformed state.[88] Cahen-Salvador believed that the council should be granted a political function, a view which harkened back to the original proposal of the CGT. These proposals were made in a political context which was defined by a revival in interest in constitutional reform, and the re-evaluation of the role of the council became a leitmotif of the discussions which took place during this period.

By the early thirties, the parliamentary regime came under increasing criticism, and this crisis of confidence contributed to the outbreak of political violence. The riot of 6 February 1934 illustrated this national malaise, and the Chamber of Deputies responded to this challenge by creating a parliamentary commission entrusted with the task of studying the question of constitutional reform.[89] The commission examined a proposal that might have granted political authority to the CNE, but its ensuing report proved sceptical of the feasibility of the corporatist agenda. Though it was not hostile to the principle of corporatist reform, it noted that it would be difficult to introduce such an ambitious reform in the current political climate.[90] According to its author, the rise of various corporatist ideologies, as well as the practical experience of the CNE, had not translated into a comprehensive political consensus which might have resulted in a new era of corporatist politics. In the end, the report rejected the proposal for two mutually supportive reasons. It argued that a divided labour movement would not be capable of exercising its new role, and the CNE would not be able to exert its authority in the absence of a consensus

[88] G. Cahen-Salvador, 'L'Économie disciplinée, ses méthodes et son programme', *Revue Politigue et Parliamentaire*, 15; Chatriot, *La Démocratie*, 73–108. Cahen-Salvador was by no means a lone voice in this regard. Deputies such as Joseph Paul-Boncour and Charles Spinasse had sought to transform the CNE into a corporatist structure.

[89] Chatriot, *La Démocratie*, 90–101; N. Roussellier, 'La Contestation du modèle républicains dans les années 30: la réforme de l'état', in S. Berstein and O. Rudelle (eds.), *Le Modèle républicain*, 319–35. Both Chatriot and Roussellier make the important point that other parliamentarians began considering the issue of state reform at the time.

[90] AN, CE 60, *Rapport fait au nom de la commission de la reforme de l'état chargée d'examiner le projet de loi relatif à un Conseil National Économique*, 14. It should be mentioned that Paul Ramadier, its author, was a Socialist deputy who returned to the SFIO after a short spell with the neo-socialists.

which would support its expanded responsibilities.[91] The rejection of corporatism was based upon a belief that the current divisions of French society would make it impossible for the council to exercise its political functions, a conclusion which turned the corporatist argument on its head, since its advocates argued that it was the corporation that would make it possible to address these very tensions.

The French corporatist phenomenon drew much of its inspiration from academic sociology and legal theory. Solidarist thinkers like Émile Durkheim and Léon Duguit had advocated corporatist policies, defining them as a mechanism to promote social solidarity, and similar views were expressed by other representatives of the legal profession. In 1937, Roger Bonnard, a legal scholar and a leading representative of the public service school, argued that corporatism was a form of interventionism which sought to conciliate individual economic interests with the collective general interest.[92] The corporatism of Bonnard, it should be stressed, was by no means an isolated occurrence within the legal community. In 1935, legal scholars established an Institute for Corporative and Social Studies which was devoted to development of corporatif policies.[93] In a sense, Laroque's espousal of corporatist policies was not only symptomatic of the currency of corporatist ideas in the social and political spheres, but also reflected the concerns of many of his colleagues within the legal profession.

CONCLUSION

Pierre Laroque's corporatist proposals were meant to provide a new decentralized administrative structure for the negotiation and enforcement of collective bargaining agreements, a system which served to make these agreements more effective. These views had been influenced by his background in administrative law, namely his exposure to the thought of Léon Duguit and Maurice Hauriou. Influenced by the thought of both the public service and institutionalist schools, he believed that the state was the custodian of the general interest and served to promote social solidarity, the latter of which could best be achieved through the administrative decentralization of public services. These ideological biases explained his response to the problem posed by existing collective bargaining legislation, namely his belief that corporatism could

---

[91] Ibid.

[92] R. Bonnard, *Syndicalisme, corporatisme et état corporatif*, 2–3.

[93] Elbow, *French Corporative Theory*, 133; Chatriot, *La Démocratie*, 81–5.

address its limitations while serving the solidaristic objectives which, he believed, were consubstantial to the law and social policy.

While Laroque might have supported a greater degree of state intervention in social and economic affairs, he also believed that it was necessary to foster public participation in the management of these expanded services. These principles would come to influence his corporatist views once he became interested in the study of industrial relations and the issue of collective bargaining. They would continue to shape his approach to social policy long after he had abandoned his support for the corporatist management of industrial relations. As his conception of the Laroque Plan would later demonstrate, he continued to believe in the virtue of an interventionist state that would conciliate contrasting social and economic interests. The promotion of solidarity, however, remained dependent on the participation of those who were destined to benefit from social policy, and this faith in a heightened form of public participation in the management of public services would come to define his conception of social security in post-Liberation France.

3

The Crises of the Thirties

INTRODUCTION

While Pierre Laroque was kept busy by his work for the *Conseil d'État*, the Ministry of Labour and the *Conseil National Économique*, he also found time to participate in the intellectual debates of the thirties. Throughout these years, he presented his corporatist views to a wide audience, publishing articles in reviews such as *L'Homme Nouveau* and *Les Nouveaux Cahiers*, and contributing to the activities of discussion groups such as the *Groupe du 9 Juillet* and *X-crise*. Laroque's involvement with these publications and organizations was by no means accidental since his critique of the collective bargaining system dovetailed with their wide-ranging critique of the social, political, and economic structures of inter-war France. Various advocates of planning, namely neo-socialists and technocrats, proved receptive to his corporatist proposals, but his ideas continued to evolve during the course of the decade. As he gained public recognition as an expert in the field of industrial relations, his enthusiasm for corporatism began to wane, but he remained committed to the principles which underlay his corporatist agenda. Like many young intellectuals of his generation, Laroque believed that the Third Republic was in the midst of a prolonged crisis, and his advocacy of corporatism became subsumed in a larger debate which focused upon the development of new solutions to the challenges of the time.

THE RIOT OF 6 FEBRUARY 1934 AND THE *GROUPE DU 9 JUILLET*

Pierre Laroque believed that France was undergoing a process of decadence and decline, and he voiced his concerns in his private correspondence, as revealed in the letters he exchanged with Henri Caillemer, a fellow law faculty graduate turned writer and journalist of extreme Right wing sympathies.[1] Both Laroque and Caillemer paid close attention to the unfolding of current events, and they were disturbed by what they witnessed, despite their respective ideological differences. While Laroque's missives have been lost, Caillemer's letters have been preserved in Laroque's private papers, and they provide us with a glimpse into the mindset of two young intellectuals who were concerned by the state of interwar France. As Caillemer wrote on 22 January 1933:

> Like you, the domestic situation does not appear to be good to me—indeed, I was informed by the papers, notably by the serious *Le Temps*, on the pitiful state of our finances. What appears to me to be of most concern is the moral and social aspect of this crisis, its political aspect as well, this insurrection against the state. We are far removed from the teaching we received at the rue Saint-Guillaume and the rue Soufflot![2]

The last remark was a reference to the curriculum of the prestigious faculties and schools of the Paris area, namely the *École Libre des Sciences Politiques* and the Faculty of Law, which had traditionally prepared students for careers in the civil service. Caillemer believed that there had been a decline in the value accorded to public service, and that the state itself was falling into disrepute. It would seem that Laroque shared this pessimistic outlook, but his response to these problems did not translate into the rejection of republican or democratic politics.

Both contemporary observers and later historians have referred to the pessimistic spirit of the thirties, a phenomenon defined by the diffusion of a sense of malaise which came to permeate the national consciousness.[3] At the time, this pessimism was most acutely felt by a rising generation of Frenchmen, many of whom contributed to the founding of a wide array of reviews and organizations that promoted different solutions to this sense of crisis. The intellectual ferment of the decade resulted in the elaboration of new ideas and new doctrines, contributing to what Jean-Louis Loubet del Bayle once called the 'nonconformist' movement of the thirties.[4] While these forums might have been nonconformist, in so far that they often sought to transcend traditional ideological divisions, their efforts were characterized by different areas of interest and emphasis. As

---

[1] J.-L. Loubet del Bayle, *Les Non-conformistes des années 30: une tentative de renouvellement de la pensée française*. See the biographical entry, 467–8. Henri Caillemer was a journalist and writer who also used the pseudonym Charles Mauban.

[2] MAS, LP, box 4, letter from Caillemer, 22 January 1934.

[3] O. Dard, *Le Rendez-vous manqué des relèves des années 30*, 1–12; J.-P. Maxence, *Histoire de dix ans: chronique des années 30*, 248–56; R. Aron, *Le Spectateur engagé*, 77.

[4] Loubet del Bayle, *Les Non-conformistes*, 11–21.

Olivier Dard has argued, these groups fell into two distinct categories: realists who focused on economic modernization and the reform of the state, and spiritualists who focused on moral and cultural issues.[5] These approaches were mutually supportive in the sense that they both addressed a perceived crisis which, in the minds of those who participated in the nonconformist movement, required an urgent and comprehensive solution. It was in this context that Laroque became involved with realist publications and groups,[6] an altogether unsurprising development, since his interest in corporatism touched upon industrial relations and the role of the state.

The national malaise which inspired this flurry of activity was not limited to intellectual circles, and it had the potential to become a source of social and political instability, a problem which became apparent during the events of the following year. At the end of 1933, the outbreak of the Stavisky affair, as relayed by the press of the extreme Right, fuelled a widely shared belief that the political elites of the Third Republic were hopelessly corrupt and willing to take any measure to prevent the unmasking of their involvement in shady political and financial dealings.[7] Most importantly, the scandal reinvigorated the *ligues* of the extreme Right, a loose collection of extra-parliamentary groups which were united by their unremitting hostility to the parliamentary regime.[8] On 6 February 1934, these groups convened in the vicinity of the Place de la Concorde and threatened to march on the Palais Bourbon, the seat of the Chamber of Deputies; this initiative culminated in a massive riot that left hundreds injured, an outcome that testified to the intense rage felt by these opponents of the political system.[9] The government might have averted catastrophe, but the failure of the *ligues* did not quell the anxieties of those who believed that the Republic was in jeopardy, and that it was necessary to promote a reformist agenda that might address its underlying problems.

In the aftermath of the riot, Jules Romains, a prominent writer, called for a renewal of the public debate. During the following weeks, Romains assembled a coterie of young activists and intellectuals of various persuasions who proceeded to discuss the state of current affairs; they then elaborated a political programme which aimed to appeal to a wide cross

---

[5] Dard, *Le Rendez-vous*, 9–10.

[6] Ibid.

[7] M. Chavardes, *Une Campagne de presse, la droite française et le 6 février 1934*; S. Berstein (ed.), *Le 6 février 1934*; P. Jankowski, *Cette vilaine affaire Stavisky, Histoire d'un scandale politique*.

[8] S. Berstein, *La France des années 30*, 61–5; P. Machefer, *Ligues et fascisme en France, 1919–1939*; P. Milza, *Fascisme français: passé et present*.

[9] S. Berstein, *Le 6 février*, 247–51.

section of public opinion.[10] The discussion group came to be known as the *Groupe du 9 Juillet*, and Laroque would participate in its activities during the first half of 1934. The existing archival record indicates that he participated in deliberations which dealt with the state and the economy,[11] though nothing is known of the precise nature of his contribution. It is interesting to note, however, that the *Groupe du 9 Juillet* did come to advocate a form of corporatism, thus suggesting that Laroque might have exercised some influence on the final result of the group's work.

Over a four-month period, the members of the *Groupe du 9 Juillet* met and developed a plan for the modernization of the French state. They published a final document on 9 July 1934, and the *Plan du 9 Juillet*, as it was called, covered a diverse set of issues, from the moral crisis of society to the necessity of introducing structural reforms in the social, political, and economic spheres.[12] First and foremost, the group outlined its explanation of the sense of malaise which had given rise to the events of February 1934. Its members believed that it was the result of the public's perception that a new plutocracy had arisen under the cover of liberal democracy, and that these interests had corrupted the Third Republic.[13] While these views seemed to evoke the rhetoric of the extreme Right, the *Plan du 9 Juillet* did not necessarily reject liberal, democratic, and republican principles. The group explicitly rejected an authoritarian solution to this lack of confidence in the existing institutions and elites, arguing that national renewal could not betray the principles of liberty, the ideals of public service, and a concern with social solidarity.[14] In other words, the group sought to modernize the terms of the republican covenant and without rejecting its underlying principles.

The *Groupe du 9 Juillet* hoped to transcend traditional ideological cleavages, as demonstrated by its attempt to reconcile the values associated with the Right and the Left. According to the authors, it was necessary to accommodate the necessity of maintaining order with the desire to achieve a greater degree of social justice; these objectives represented the two sides of the same coin, since it was order that made it possible to achieve justice.[15] While these views might have reflected a desire to reach out to previously opposed individuals and parties, it represented little more than a quaint platitude devoid of any practical significance. More importantly, the plan outlined a programme for structural reform aimed at the mod-

---

[10] O. Rony, *Jules Romains ou l'appel au monde*; Dard, *Le Rendez-vous*, 192–200.
[11] MAS, LP, box 66, letter from Jean Henri Adam, 27 April 1934.
[12] See Groupe du 9 Juillet, *Plan du 9 Juillet*.
[13] Ibid. 16.
[14] Ibid. 17–19.
[15] Ibid. 20.

ernization of the French state. It rejected laissez-faire in social and economic policy, advocating the introduction of a *dirigiste* economic system that was to take its place. Like the technocratic and neo-socialist movements of the period, the plan favoured the creation of a planned and mixed economy that would favour the redistribution of economic wealth.[16] The group's corporatist proposals, moreover, would facilitate economic planning while creating a new forum for the conciliation of different social and economic interests. The introduction of corporatism, in its view, would serve to manage industrial relations by providing a framework for the negotiation of working conditions as well as the mediation of industrial conflict.[17] Interestingly enough, these measures echoed Laroque's views concerning the reform of collective bargaining procedures, though the plan went beyond the scope of his own proposals, as demonstrated by its support for the establishment of a council of professional corporations.[18] The latter echoed the reforms which had just been introduced in Fascist Italy, as illustrated by the proclamation of the corporate state. The plan thus advocated a form of corporatist politics, and this undoubtedly contributed to its controversial reputation.

Some historians have claimed that the *Plan du 9 Juillet* represented a form of fascist politics,[19] but the published evidence does not necessarily support this contention. While the plan called for the election of a constituent assembly that would determine the ultimate nature of the state, its authors stated their preference for a parliamentary system of governance with a strengthened executive power, a position which did not denote support for an authoritarian or totalitarian form of politics.[20] The consolidation of the authority and efficiency of the state did not necessarily imply the rejection of republican and democratic principles. The plan, it should be noted, elicited much attention from the media without achieving any tangible results,[21] and Laroque refused to sign the final document out of his opposition to its pacifist tone.[22] In the end, the propaganda value of the *Plan du 9 Juillet* overshadowed its practical significance, but the substance of its proposals did confirm the diffusion of corporatist ideas within the public discourse of the thirties.

[16] Ibid. 44.
[17] Ibid. 44–5.
[18] Ibid. 23–6.
[19] Z. Sternhell, *Ni droite ni gauche: l'idéologie fasciste en France*, 252–3.
[20] Groupe du 9 Juillet, *Plan du 9 Juillet*, 21–3.
[21] P. Andreu, *Les réroltes de l'esprit. Les revues des anunes 30*, 108; Dard, *Le Rendez-vous*, 197–200.
[22] F. X. Merrien, *Étude comparative de l'édification et de l'érolution de l'état-protecteur en France et en Grande-Bretagne*, 242.

L'HOMME NOUVEAU AND NEO-SOCIALISM

While it is impossible to determine the exact nature of Pierre Laroque's contribution to the discussions of the *Groupe du 9 Juillet*, his publications provide us with a public record of his thought and give us some indication of the ideological biases of the circles with which he was associated during the course of the thirties. Most notably, he published articles in *L'Homme Nouveau* and *Les Nouveaux Cahiers*, reviews which were identified with the neo-socialist and technocratic movements. Both publications provided him with the public forum through which he could express his views, namely his conception of social policy and his support for the corporatist organization of industrial relations. Both *L'Homme Nouveau* and *Les Nouveaux Cahiers* were receptive to his corporatist message, since it matched their own stated objectives, namely to promote the reform of the social, political, and economic structures of interwar France.

Laroque's articles were first published in *L'Homme Nouveau*, a neo-socialist publication which was edited by Georges Roditi, a fellow member of the *Groupe du 9 Juillet* who would later attend the Franco-Italian colloquium on corporatism which was to be organized in 1935.[23] Much like the neo-socialist movement as a whole, Roditi and *L'Homme Nouveau* strove to elaborate a revitalized socialist discourse which addressed contemporary problems in a new manner. The iconoclastic spirit of the review was apparent in its first edition, as illustrated by its quotation of Guizot:

> It is not when new ideas are in ferment that there is decadence, but when . . .
> a . . . society which feels oppressed and sick cannot conceive of any great or
> new hope and when, instead of heading towards the future, it only invokes
> the images of the past.[24]

Roditi and his peers were determined to reverse the perceived decadence of the times, and this inspired their search for policy solutions which might address the problems that afflicted the Third Republic.

Roditi believed that a successful reformist politics could not depend solely on the elaboration of a precise political programme. Indeed, he stressed that it was essential to transform the culture of socialist politics, to exhibit an aggressive spirit which would provide socialists with the drive necessary to achieve political power:

---

[23] See Chapter 2; Dard, 192–3; E. Mounier, *Mounier et sa génération: lettres, carnets et inédits*; Andreu, *Les révoltes de l'esprit*, 115–19. Andreu discusses the ideological orientation of *L'Homme Nouveau* and its founder.

[24] *L'Homme Nouveau*, 1 January 1934.

I myself believe that there is today no task that is more urgent than to reconcile socialist idealism and reason with the taste of force. In writing these words, I am not thinking of the phalanxes, the militias, the action groups, nor the young guards, nor of the defence groups that the different parties are organizing in anticipation of civil war. What I have in mind is a different way of thinking and feeling, a style, an attitude towards life.[25]

In Roditi's view, it was essential to abandon a passive and fatalistic approach towards politics, because the ultimate success of this cause was dependent upon a new culture of political activism which did not shy away from the conquest of political power or the exercise of governmental responsibilities.

Georges Roditi and *L'Homme Nouveau* were the proponents of neo-socialism, an ideology that advocated a reformist politics which promoted the positive action of the state in the social and economic spheres. The purpose of neo-socialism, in Roditi's view, was to create a planned economy and establish a new socialist society which would make it possible for the individual to achieve his full potential.[26] These objectives seemed to echo the objectives of others on the political Left, but Roditi argued that mainstream socialism had revealed itself to be a failure. He contended that Marxist doctrine had demonstrated its intellectual bankruptcy, since it had failed to account for the evolution of the capitalist system.[27] The advocacy of a planned economic system, moreover, did not necessarily refer to the public management of a nationalized economy, a traditional objective of the socialist movement, but referred to the creation of a mixed economic system which would be regulated by an interventionist state.[28] Support for a mixed economy, a veritable hybrid of liberal and collectivist principles, was considered to be a form of heresy in many socialist circles, and this position confirmed the ideological specificity of the neo-socialist movement.

Neo-socialism was the product of a revolt against a traditional form of socialist politics which was defined by a belief in a dogmatic form of Marxism and the rejection of the practice of a reformist politics within the framework of a capitalist society. At the time, many had come to believe that Marxist ideology had proved itself to be an inadequate means of analysing capitalism, while the outbreak of the economic crisis of the thirties made it imperative to introduce new policies aimed at reviving economic activity while setting the stage for the introduction of a new

---

[25] Ibid.
[26] Ibid.
[27] *L'Homme Nouveau*, 1 October 1934.
[28] Ibid. 1 September 1934.

socialist order. It was in this context that Hendrik de Man and Marcel Déat emerged as the leading theoreticians and political advocates of a new form of socialism which cast aside an outdated revolutionary rhetoric in favour of a reformist agenda which called for the implementation of new and immediate forms of state interventionism.

Hendrik de Man, a Belgian intellectual and politician, emerged as the leading proponent of neo-socialism, and he had first published his critique of Marxist ideology and practice during the twenties. With *Zur Psychologie des Sozialismus* (1926), translated as *Au delà du Marxisme* in future French editions, de Man questioned the theoretical foundations of orthodox socialism, and his critique attracted the attention of many within the European socialist circles. As Peter Dodge writes:

> In his major theoretical works, de Man attempted to formulate the implications of this disquieting and un-Marxist world for the construction of a theoretically adequate socialist ideology. By the publication of the *Psychology*—his critique of Marxism—he became a figure of international import in socialist circles. The work, aptly re-titled in some later editions as *Beyond Marxism*, was a categorical and comprehensive challenge to the ideological monopoly that Marxism had long maintained on the dominant forms of the continental labour and socialist movements.[29]

The impact of the book can hardly be underestimated, since it would be published in fourteen separate editions and translated into ten European languages.[30] Such success pointed to the fact that many socialists had come to share his qualms concerning Marxist orthodoxy while refusing to accept the permanence of capitalism or the futility of a reformist politics which sought to effect the fundamental transformation of the economic system.

In *Au delà du Marxisme*, de Man argued that socialism was undergoing a prolonged intellectual crisis that had been caused by the discrepancy between the predictions of Marxist theory and the actual evolution of the capitalist system.[31] While orthodox Marxists had long proclaimed the impending collapse of capitalism, their predictions had not come to fruition, thus calling into question the credibility of Marxism ideology. De Man believed that the concept of dialectical materialism, which was central to the Marxist world view, was inherently flawed, since it focused on the study of economics without giving sufficient consideration to the influence of non-economic factors in the process of historical change. He

---

[29] P. Dodge, *Beyond Marxism: the faith and works of Hendrik de Man*, 68.
[30] Ibid.
[31] H. de Man, *Au delà du marxisme*, 2nd edn, 4.

argued that Marx had ignored the importance of culture and psychology in the shaping of human behaviour. In his view, the latter was inspired by deep-seated psychological motivations which had little to do with the rational consideration of economic interest.[32] The evolution of social and political structures might have been influenced by economic forces, but historical development could not be understood by focusing on material factors alone.

The failure of Marxism, de Man argued, could be attributed to the historical context in which Marx had first developed his ideas. Marxist thought was shaped by the dominant intellectual trends of the nineteenth century, and, as such, it was marked by the influence of the progressive and rationalist discourse of the period.[33] Marxism was defined by a linear conception of history: it claimed that the historical process unfolded according to a predictable pattern of social and economic development, and it was this phenomenon that shaped the attitudes of the contending social classes. According to de Man, however, it was essential to focus on the evolution of popular sentiments if one wanted to understand the evolution of European society. He stressed that it was apparent that the cultural values of the working class were still marked by the influence of pre-capitalist mores, an observation which called into question the schematic model of historical development associated with Marxist orthodoxy. Past experience continued to shape collective attitudes, and this implied that one should not overestimate the impact of given economic processes in fostering cultural change. As de Man noted, the aspirations of the working class were defined by a cultural environment that had been shaped by the legacy of feudalism, Christian morality, and the mass acceptance of democratic principles; it was the persistence of these pre-capitalist values which explained popular resentment of social inequality and injustice in the contemporary world.[34] In brief, de Man offered an idealistic interpretation of the historical process, stressing the importance of cultural and psychological factors in the history of social and economic change.

From this perspective, the emergence of class conflict had little to do with any rational recognition of class interest, but represented a practical manifestation of the diffusion of widely shared moral or ideological views. For the working class, their collective espousal of democratic values translated into a reaction against inequality, thus inspiring the struggle for greater social, political, and economic rights.[35] The currency of

---

[32] Ibid. 5.
[33] Ibid.
[34] Ibid. 15–16.
[35] Ibid. 63–7.

egalitarian values explained the rise of progressive politics, and the socialist movement was a perfect illustration of this phenomenon. De Man concluded that socialism could be summarized as the embodiment of a moral revolt against the capitalist system,[36] and it was its ethical dimension that explained both its historical origins and its continued political relevance.

While de Man had redefined socialist doctrine along idealistic lines, he would also come to advocate a reformist politics which sought to effect immediate change while promising to transform the basis of capitalist society. Having criticized the premises of dialectical materialism, he also rejected the belief that capitalism could not be reformed, a view which explained the revolutionary posture of mainstream European socialism. De Man stressed that the constructive action of the state was both possible and desirable as long as society was characterized by the persistence of social injustice.[37] By rejecting the catastrophic predictions of Marxism, he had called into question its brand of revolutionary politics, a position which also explained his advocacy of a reformist politics that drew inspiration from the moral values which had first inspired the socialist movement.

Public policy, from this perspective, had to be determined by practical realities, and de Man's thought was influenced by thinkers who promoted state intervention in the light of contemporary economic difficulties. As Peter Dodge notes, he was influenced by the ideas of John Maynard Keynes, Douglas Cole, and J. A. Hobson.[38] Despite their respective differences, these thinkers tended to interpret the economic crisis of the thirties along underconsumptionist lines. As a result, de Man advocated the introduction of policies aimed at stimulating economic activity, namely the launching of public work projects financed by deficit spending. These ideas were later to be included in the economic plan which he elaborated in response to the economic crisis of the thirties, and which would eventually be adopted by the *Parti Ouvrier Belge* in 1933.

The *Plan du Travail* represented the culmination of de Man's pre-war thinking, since it gave a practical dimension to the theoretical critique of Marxism which he had formulated during the twenties. It was adopted in the midst of the economic depression, and it outlined a pragmatic agenda for state action which was defined by three fundamental objectives: the creation of a mixed economy in which both credit and key industrial monopolies were to be nationalized, the elaboration of public policies aimed at eliminating unemployment, and the introduction of political

---

[36] De Man, *Au delà du marxisme*, 387–9.
[37] Ibid. 348–68.
[38] See the footnote in Dodge, *Beyond Marxism*, 137.

reforms which would extend democratic principles into the social and economic spheres.[39] The plan thus focused upon immediate necessities, while setting the stage for the eventual transformation of a capitalist society into a socialist one.

The plan was defined by the desire to increase the scope of state intervention in the economy. The expansion of state control was to be achieved through a variety of means, including the creation of an institute of state credit which would supervise the financial sector, and the creation of an industrial commissariat which would supervise the activities of a network of industrial consortiums.[40] While the POB might have renounced revolutionary Marxism, its new political programme was radical in its implications, since it called for the introduction of economic planning coupled with the nationalization of key sectors of the Belgian economy.

Neo-socialism achieved its greatest degree of success in pre-war Belgium, but it also found advocates in France, as was illustrated by the schism which divided the French Socialist party. In 1933, a group of dissidents broke from the *Section Française de l'Internationale Ouvrière*, and launched the *Parti Socialiste de France*, a new party committed to a form of reformist socialism.[41] The split was the result of a long-standing dispute over Socialist participation in parliamentary government, a debate that had pitted conflicting interpretations of the role of the SFIO within the existing capitalist system. Within the SFIO, the partisans of the orthodox position had rejected the possibility of assuming political power under current economic circumstances while their opponents called for its participation in government,[42] since they believed that the exercise of power could bring about immediate and enduring social and economic change.

Marcel Déat, a teacher of philosophy and socialist politician, contributed to the debate within French socialist circles during this period, and he had already elaborated a theoretical justification for his own brand of reformist socialism, an intellectual effort which culminated in the publication of *Perspectives socialistes* in 1930.[43] Unlike de Man, however, Déat did not break with the legacy of revolutionary Marxism, since his thought had been influenced by the non-Marxist traditions of the French Left. Indeed, his views were marked by solidaristic principles, the result of his

---

[39] See *Le Plan du travail*, annex to *L'Idée socialiste*.

[40] See section 1 of the *Plan*.

[41] P. Andreu, *Le rouge et le blanc*, 80; M. Déat, *Mémoires politiques*, 275–82; S. Berstein, *Léon Blum*, 377–9; P. Burrin, *La Dérive fasciste: Doriot, Déat et Bergery 1933–1945*, 125–45.

[42] Berstein, *Léon Blum*, 345–81; Burrin, *La Dérive fasciste*, 125–38.

[43] M. Déat, *Perspectives socialistes*.

espousal of a Durkheimian analysis of society. As a consequence, his brand of socialism eschewed confrontation and focused upon the necessity of promoting the moral and functional solidarity of society.[44] These concerns were far removed from the tenets of Marxist thought, and it helped explain his rejection of a class-centred politics and his support for the creation of a wide-ranging coalition which was to assemble all of those who had been marginalized by the capitalist system. Déat believed that capitalism threatened vast segments of French society, including small landowners, artisans, professionals, and bureaucrats; it was incumbent upon the socialist movement to unite these groups in the defence of their common interests.[45] While this strategy might have served an electoral purpose, it also represented a practical application of a solidarist ideology which denied the permanence of class struggle.

While Déat might have been a leading theoretician of neo-socialism, he voiced his impatience with the pursuit of prolonged doctrinal debates which postponed the undertaking of immediate and concrete forms of political action. In his book, he had stressed that it was imperative for socialists to focus on the means for implementing practical change in the current social, political, and economic environment.[46] The pragmatic quality of this reformism was unmistakable, but it should be stressed that he remained committed to a more radical agenda. Déat argued that the creation of a mixed economy in the short run would not postpone or prevent the transformation of capitalist society in the long run, and his ultimate objective remained the creation of a socialist society.[47] From this perspective, short-term reform represented an intermediate measure which did not detract from the long-term goal of the socialist movement.

The objective of the neo-socialist programme, as Déat envisioned it, was the creation of a planned economy which accorded a new and expansive role to the state. While key sectors of the economy, like banking and finance were to be nationalized,[48] the state would supervise national economic activity though industrial boards, corporations in fact, which would include the representatives of both labour and management.[49] These corporatist proposals did not entail sympathy for fascism, since Déat believed that the corporation represented a viable means of introducing

---

[44]　Burrin, *La Dérive fasciste*, 41.
[45]　Déat, *Perspectives socialistes*, 48–64.
[46]　Ibid. 113.
[47]　J.-F. Biard, *Le Socialisme devant ses choix*, 291.
[48]　Déat, *Perspectives socialistes*, 182–4.
[49]　Ibid. 190–1.

some form of democratic control to the management of the economy.[50] In this sense, neo-socialist corporatism echoed the proposals which had been put forward by Durkheim and Duguit during the preceding decades.

As had been the case in Belgium, French neo-socialism became identified with economic planning, and Déat sought to further the *planiste* cause through his involvement with the *Comité du Plan*. The latter had originally been created to promote the plan adopted by the CGT in September 1934, but its efforts soon went beyond the confines of the trade union movement.[51] The committee built upon the ideas of the CGT, and its plan, much like the *Plan du 9 Juillet*, addressed both political and economic objectives. The *Comité du Plan* had elaborated its proposals through a deliberative process which assembled politicians, syndicalists, and veterans; as Déat noted in the preface of the *Plan Français*, its policies were meant to revitalize the economy while uniting a fragmented public opinion.[52] Much like the plan adopted by the POB in Belgium, the *Plan Français* favoured the creation of a mixed economy, namely through the imposition of wage and price controls.[53] These ideas reflected an attempt to develop a practical political alternative to both orthodox liberalism and collectivism, an approach which was consistent with the neo-socialist approach to the economic crisis of the thirties. Whatever its value, however, the *Plan Français* failed to achieve any impact on public opinion as interest in economic planning receded before the growing popularity of the Popular Front coalition which would eventually come to power in the spring of 1936.

Laroque's first contribution to *L'Homme Nouveau* was published in its inaugural number of 1 January 1934, and it outlined what he believed should form the guiding principles of social policy. According to his article, the latter served an overarching moral purpose since it aimed to promote a more equal and fraternal society, principles which evoked both solidarist and socialist thought.[54] Laroque argued that policymakers should avoid enacting paternalistic initiatives, since the purpose of policy was to give the less fortunate a sense of their own worth and independence; this had been achieved by a social insurance system which made it possible for the working class to participate in the management of its

---

[50] *La Vie Socialiste*, 14 March 1934. De Man was similarly interested in corporatism and explicitly referred to the example of British guild socialism. See *L'Homme Nouveau*, July–August 1935.

[51] J. Jackson, *The Politics of Depression in France 1932–1936*, 162.

[52] Comité du Plan, *Le Plan Français*, preface by Déat, 9.

[53] Ibid. 13–15.

[54] *L'Homme Nouveau*, 1 January 1934.

benefit programmes.[55] The encouragement of public participation was central to his conception of social policy, because it addressed the psycho logical dimensions of individual and collective existence. The problems with social paternalism, in his view, lay with the fact that it turned the working classes into the passive recipients of charity.[56] Whatever its intention, a paternalistic approach to social reform had been undermined by its perverse moral and psychological impact.

Public participation was essential to the diffusion of social tensions and the cultivation of social solidarity, and this could be achieved through the use of existing social structures. Part of the appeal of the professional corporation, he noted, lay with the fact that it could be viewed as an outgrowth of existing trade union confederations,[57] a notion that echoed the corporatist proposals which had been promoted by the minimum programme of the CGT. Furthermore, Laroque maintained that it was imperative to consider social policy as the aggregate of a wide array of distinct and complementary measures, and this included the corporatist reform of collective bargaining procedures as well as the introduction of social insurance benefits, all of which aimed to cultivate social solidarity.[58] While this confirmed the solidaristic bias of his views, it is important to note that his conception of policy was also characterized by a consideration of practical realities, namely his analysis of the respective failures of the collective bargaining system and the French labour movement.

Laroque discussed these questions in an article that he published in January 1935. While corporatist structures might serve to enforce the moral discipline necessary for the negotiation and enforcement of collective bargaining agreements, he also stressed that they addressed the inherent weakness of the French labour movement: 'To one and the other there lacks unity and authority, equally indispensable to organizations charged with a distinctive purpose. This unity and this authority can only be given to the corporation by external intervention, and only by the state.'[59] In Laroque's mind, corporatism would compensate for the historic weakness and division of the labour movement. While the logic behind this proposal was clear, it did have controversial implications, since he suggested that the CGT, the largest trade union confederation in interwar France, should be granted the monopoly of representation within these corporatist structures.[60] The proposal called into question the pluralist

<hr>

[55] *L'Homme Nouveau*, 1 Jannary 1934.
[56] Ibid.
[57] Ibid.
[58] Ibid.
[59] Ibid. 1 January 1935.
[60] Ibid.

traditions of the French labour movement, but it did represent an honest and practical response to its collective inability to provide effective representation for its members.

The effectiveness of the *syndicats* also depended on their representative character and this also explained Laroque's support for the compulsory enrolment of workers in an expanded CGT.[61] These corporatist ideas, however, did not signal the wholesale abandonment of liberal and democratic principles, and this form of compulsory membership was reminiscent of the principle of the closed shop which was common to certain Anglo-Saxon countries. Though he remained vague as to the actual mechanism of his proposed corporations, there is no reason to believe that the internal democracy of the labour movement would have been compromised by the establishment of these structures. Laroque's proposals explicitly rejected authoritarian or totalitarian politics, a point which he made clear in the lecture he gave at the *Conservatoire des Arts et Métiers* in April 1935. These policies were influenced by solidaristic principles and an analysis of practical realities, and were intended to create a more effective framework for the resolution of industrial conflict without calling into question the internal democracy of the labour movement.

LES NOUVEAUX CAHIERS AND TECHNOCRACY

While these corporatist ideas appealed to the neo-socialist Left, it should also be mentioned that Laroque found a receptive audience in other circles, as demonstrated by his contributions to *Les Nouveaux Cahiers*. Founded in 1937 by Auguste Detoeuf, *Les Nouveaux Cahiers* was a review associated with the technocratic movement, and its contributors came from a variety of backgrounds, including business, the civil service, and the arts.[62] It was not as explicitly ideological as *L'Homme Nouveau*, and it enjoyed an independent stance with regard to the existing political parties. During its years of publication, it managed to attract an impressive list of contributors, including Guillaume de Tarde, Robert Lacoste, Simone Weil, René Cassin, and Jean Paulhan.[63] This notable achievement mirrored the accomplishments of an unconventional business executive who had been involved in a decade long struggle to promote the modernization of the social and economic structures of interwar France.

---

[61] Ibid., July–August 1935.
[62] G. Lefranc, *Les Organisations patronales en France*, 254.
[63] Ibid.

Auguste Detoeuf was an engineer by training, a product of the elite *École Polytechnique* who had been employed by the state before moving to the private sector, eventually becoming the head of Thomson-Houston in 1925.[64] This academic and professional background contributed to the shaping of his ideological outlook, and his career was representative of the rise of a new class of scientific and managerial personnel, so-called technocrats, who sought to promote new approaches to the social, political, and economic problems of the Third Republic.[65] Detoeuf's activism had begun during the twenties. At the time, he had been greatly impressed by American managerial methods and had joined the neo-capitalist *Redressement Français*.[66] Detoeuf was a firm believer in the virtue of new managerial approaches, an illustration of his faith in technological progress and the notion that it would now be possible to address the social problems associated with the evolution of modern capitalism. Detoeuf, in fact, was a critic of traditional economic liberalism who believed in the possibility and the necessity of reforming the capitalist system as it existed in interwar France,[67] and this explained his support for new and specific remedies for the perceived deficiencies of the economic system.

By the thirties, the advent of the Depression had made Detoeuf even more critical of laissez-faire, and he came to believe that the very survival of the economic system was being undermined by its inherent irrationality.[68] One of the main problems of the system, as he saw it, lay with the rise of speculative activity. The latter made the principle of rational economic choice irrelevant to the functioning of contemporary capitalism, and this had made capitalism both irrational and unpredictable.[69] The evolution of the market system had set the stage for its own destruction, and it became necessary to devise a solution to the economic crisis. According to Detoeuf, the economic depression had made it imperative to make use of state intervention, but his approach also stressed the importance of associating labour and employers in the management of industrial relations. The implementation of corporatist economic structures would serve to assist in the management in the economic system, and it should be noted that his proposals bore more than a passing resemblance to Laroque's ideas on the matter.[70] There is no way to determine, however, whether Laroque

---

[64]   R. F. Kuisel, 'Auguste Detoeuf, Conscience of French Industry: 1926–1947', *International Review of Social History*, 20 (1975), 150–1.

[65]   G. Brun, 'Technocrates et technocratie en France (1918–1945)'.

[66]   Kuisel, 'Auguste Detoeuf', 152–4.

[67]   Ibid.

[68]   A. Detoeuf, 'La fin du libéralisme', in Centre Polytechnicien des Études Économiques, *X-Crise: de la récurrence des crises économiques*, 71.

[69]   Ibid. 76–8.   [70]   *Les Nouveaux Cahiers*, 15 February 1938.

had actually influenced Detoeuf. Furthermore, it is also true that his support for a compulsory form of labour representation did not repudiate democratic principles,[71] a fact which provided another interesting point of comparison between their respective corporatist proposals.

As previously mentioned, the technocratic movement referred to the rise of a new scientific and managerial class, as well as to the emergence of new approaches to the management of the private and public sectors.[72] The ideology of technocracy owed much to the evolution of managerial science as well as the experience gained through the introduction of interventionist policies during the First World War. Technocracy was a product of an eclectic set of influences, including Fordism, Taylorism, and the political experimentation of Total War.[73] On the whole, it was identified with the call for the modernization of contemporary social, political, and economic structures, and this concern gained widespread currency during the inter-war period. The technocrats believed in the virtues of a reformed and interventionist state which would serve as a catalyst for the transformation of French society, a notion which found support throughout the political and ideological spectrum of the twenties and thirties.[74]

Henri de St Simon, the famed utopian thinker, was seen by many to be the ideological forerunner of the technocratic movement. St Simon had been an ardent believer in scientific and technological progress, and this same bias would later define the technocratic discourse.[75] These views also explained technocratic attitudes towards the capitalist system, and this was especially true in the context of the economic crisis of the thirties. The technocrats did not believe in an unregulated marketplace, believing instead that economic activity had to be organized and managed along 'rational lines', thus leading them to advocate the creation of a planned economic system.[76] The advocacy of *planisme* reflected a distinctly statist approach to social and economic policy.

Auguste Detoeuf and *Les Nouveaux Cahiers* were representative of the technocratic movement, but it should also be mentioned that the leading vehicle for the diffusion of technocratic ideas was to be found in a

---

[71] Ibid.

[72] Brun, *Technocrates et technocracie en France*, 15.

[73] C. S. Maier, 'Between Taylorism and Technocracy: European ideologies and the vision of industrial productivity in the 1920s', *Journal of Contemporary History*, 5, 2 (1970), 27–61; M. Fine, 'Albert Thomas: a reformer's vision of modernisation 1914–1932', *Journal of Contemporary History*, 12 (1977), 545–64; M. Fine, 'Hyacinthe Dubreuil: le témoignage d'un ouvrier sur le syndicalisme, les relations industrielles et l'évolution technologique de 1921 à 1940', *Le Mouvement Social*, 106 (1979), 45–63.

[74] M. O. Baruch, *Servir l'état français*, 22–6.

[75] Brun, *Technocrates et technocracie en France*, 63–7.

[76] Ibid. 107–8.

discussion group founded by students and graduates of the *École Poly-technique*. Launched during the early thirties, *X-crise* was dedicated to the search for practical solutions to the economic crisis, and both Detoeuf and Laroque participated in its activities.[77] The group's approach to social and economic questions owed much to the history and traditions of the *École Polytechnique*. Founded in the aftermath of the French Revolution, *Polytechnique* was France's most prestigious engineering school, and it enjoyed a privileged status as a *grande école*. During the second half of the nineteenth century, the school had come under the sway of reformist thought, and figures like Le Play, Le Chatelier, and Lyautey would increasingly influence its students and staff.[78] These influences would also contribute to the evolution of the school's teaching curriculum, as had been demonstrated by the introduction of a course on social econom-ics in 1906.[79] The launching of *X-crise* might have coincided with the onset of the economic crisis, but it also confirmed the reformist spirit exhibited by many of the students and graduates of the *École Poly-technique*.

As we have seen, Detoeuf believed that capitalism was in the midst of a profound crisis, and this view was shared by other members of *X-crise*. According to Jean Coutrot, one of the group's most prominent members, economic liberalism had been rendered obsolete by contemporary events.[80] It is therefore unsurprising that the reformist agenda of *X-crise* focused upon the notion of economic planning. Unlike the neo-socialists, however, the group's support for economic planning was an outgrowth of their pseudo-scientific faith in the virtues of new scientific and managerial techniques, and this was not necessarily linked to a desire to elaborate a new and practical form of reformist socialism.[81] The interventionist bias of *X-crise* reflected the views of the technocratic movement as a whole, and those of *Les Nouveaux Cahiers* in particular, considerations which provide us with a more precise understanding of the context in which Laroque had elaborated and disseminated his ideas during the thirties.

By the latter part of the decade, Pierre Laroque had come to believe that France was undergoing a period of radical transformation, a view which he outlined in an article published in *Les Nouveaux Cahiers* in October

---

[77] Centre Polytechnicien des Études Économiques, *X-crise*; P. Miquel, *Les Polytechni-ciens*; Kuisel, 'Auguste Detoeuf'; *Témoignage* Laroque.

[78] A. Petit, 'L'Impérialisme des géomètres à l'École Polytechnique. Les critiques d'Auguste Comte', in B. Belhoste et al. (eds.), *La Formation polytechnicienne 1794–1994*, 61.

[79] Picot, 'Les années d'enlisement. L'École Polytechnique de 1870 à l'entre-deux-guerres', 175–7, in Belhoste et al., *La Formation polytechnicienne*.

[80] O. Dard, 'Les Novations intellectuelles des années breate: l'example de Jean Coutrot', 125.

[81] Dard, 'Les Novations intellectuelles des années trente', 127–31.

1937.[82] The nationwide strikes of 1936, followed by the electoral victory of the Popular Front coalition, had signalled a fundamental change in the social and political climate. Most importantly, he looked favourably upon the reforms introduced by the Blum government. The Matignon accords of 1936, which had assembled the representatives of government, workers, and industrialists in an unprecedented three party summit, had seemed to mark the beginning of a new era in French industrial relations.[83] The accords paved the way for the reform of the collective bargaining system, and Laroque proved sympathetic to this initiative, as well as to the other measures introduced by the Blum government.[84] Nevertheless, he believed that the relations between labour and management continued to be defined by a climate of tension and mistrust. Numerous reports suggested that they often refused to abide by the new procedures instituted for the arbitration and conciliation of industrial disputes, thus calling into question the effectiveness of these reforms.[85] These results demonstrated that the Blum government had not radically transformed social relations, illustrating the fact that the latter were influenced by cultural and psychological factors that could not be resolved by legislative action alone.

The shift in French public policy was confronted with deeply ingrained attitudes and well established practices which had not disappeared despite the introduction of new legislation. Despite these reforms, Laroque noted that employers sought to preserve their authority in the workplace while the trade unions attempted to exercise control of employment and working conditions.[86] The solution to these problems lay in a spirit of compromise, and this had little to do with legislative initiatives and had more to do with the culture and practice of industrial relations. Laroque offered suggestions which, he believed, might improve the social climate. For example, he proposed that labour be consulted in the matter of firing, an initiative which he thought would contribute to the establishment of a climate of goodwill and cooperation in the workplace.[87] The most effective means of class collaboration lay beyond the scope of legislative action

---

[82] *Les Nouveaux Cahiers*, 15 October 1937.

[83] Ibid.

[84] Ibid. MAS, LP, box 4, letter from Henri Caillemer, 30 July 1936. Letter from Pierre Olivier Lapie, 15 May 1936. Letter from Léo Lagrange, 18 June 1936. His correspondence suggests that he was a supporter of Blum and the Popular Front government.

[85] *Les Nouveaux Cahiers* 15 October 1937. See É. Gout, P. Juvigny, and M. Moussel, 'Politique sociale', in P. Renouvin et al., *Léon Blum, chef de gouvernement 1936–1937*, 241–76, for a discussion of Blum's social policy, namely in the matter of collective bargaining agreements.

[86] *Les Nouveaux Cahiers*, 15 October 1937.

[87] Ibid.

alone, since it had to be accompanied by a corresponding shift in individual and collective attitudes.

The ideological preferences of *Les Nouveaux Cahiers* became more apparent in 1938, during its second year of publication. At this point, the review professed its support for the Swedish approach to the management of industrial relations.[88] These views were the result of its exposure to the Swedish experience in this area, and *Les Nouveaux Cahiers* organized a joint Franco-Swedish conference on the topic in June 1938. During the course of a three-day meeting held at Pontigny, the representatives of Swedish business and labour organizations explained to their French hosts the manner in which they negotiated working conditions and resolved industrial disputes.[89] The French responded enthusiastically to these presentations, and they even subjected their foreign guests to a barrage of questions which extended over a twelve-hour period.[90] The Franco-Swedish colloquium made a strong impression on its organizers, and it instilled in their minds a lasting admiration for the Swedish model of industrial relations, an experiment which demonstrated that it was possible to effect the profound transformation of industrial relations while remaining committed to democratic principles.

The Pontigny conference led to the publication of a special edition of *Les Nouveaux Cahiers* which provided readers with a detailed account of its proceedings, and the following edition discussed how the lessons of the Swedish model of industrial relations might be harnessed in order to address the lingering problems of industrial relations in France. These lessons did not necessarily refer to specific policies, but touched upon the importance of cultural and psychological factors in the shaping of the relationship between employers and employees. For example, one article stressed that the success of the Swedish model owed much to the spirit of respect and tolerance which characterized the relations between labour and management.[91] Such a climate stood in marked contrast to the persistent tensions that defined industrial relations in contemporary France. As Lucien Laurat noted, the size and strength of the labour movement also proved essential to Swedish achievements, since it was this tradition which made it possible to achieve lasting social reforms.[92] This provided another contrast with the weak and divided French labour movement which had not proven itself to be as effective in representing

---

[88] *Les Nouveaux Cahiers*, 15 August 1938; Dard, *Le Rendez-vous*, 259–61.
[89] Ibid. 15 July 1938.
[90] Ibid.
[91] Ibid. 15 August 1938.
[92] Ibid.

the interests of its members. These differences might have rendered some pessimistic about the situation in France, but Detoeuf concluded that the Swedish model was worthy of admiration, since it demonstrated that much could be achieved if labour and management demonstrated a willingness to compromise, exhibited goodwill, and shared a sense of solidarity.[93] These sentiments might have been well founded, but they did not provide the readers of *Les Nouveaux Cahiers* with specific or practical solutions to the problems raised by the persistence of social tensions in interwar France.

THE EVOLUTION OF PIERRE LAROQUE

Pierre Laroque's growing reputation in the field of social policy led to his employment as a lecturer at the *École Libre des Sciences Politiques*, and he was entrusted with the teaching of a course on industrial relations in 1936. Within a couple of years, this course would form the basis of a new book entitled *Les Rapports entre patrons et ouvriers*.[94] The structure of both the course and the book reflected the influence of his collective bargaining report of 1934, as well as the articles he had published in *L'Homme Nouveau* and *Les Nouveaux Cahiers* during the intervening years. Most notably, *Les Rapports entre patrons et ouvriers* confirmed that his views had evolved over time as he became sceptical of the claims of Fascist corporatism and ceased to promote the corporation as a panacea for the failings of the collective bargaining system.

This ideological shift can be evaluated by looking at the book reviews which Laroque published in the *Revue Française de Science Politique* during the mid to late thirties.[95] They provide the reader with a useful snapshot of his views, and make it possible to evaluate how his thinking changed during the years that followed his submission of the report on collective bargaining. For example, his enthusiastic account of Marcel Prélot's study, *L'Empire fasciste. Les origines, les tendances et les institutions de la dictature et du corporatisme italiennes*,[96] published in 1936, suggested that his sympathy for Fascist corporatism had started to wane, though it is also true that he had already taken pains to distinguish his variant of corporatism from its Fascist counterpart. In reviewing the book, Laroque

---

[93] Ibid.

[94] P. Laroque, *Les Rapports entre patrons et ouvriers*.

[95] MAS, LP, box 66, copies of various book reviews submitted to the *Revue Française de Science Politique*.

[96] Ibid.

mentioned that he was impressed by Prélot's objectivity; he noted that the author defined Fascist corporatism as a means for exercising state control over the population and the economy.[97] At the very least, Laroque had become more sensitive to the totalitarian objectives of Fascist social policy.

In February 1940, another review further confirmed this shift in Laroque's appraisal of Fascist corporatism, as revealed by his response to Piero Sacerdoti's study, *Le Corporatisme et le régime de la production et du travail en Italie*.[98] In his mind, the author's analysis left an important question unanswered:

> There is nonetheless one question upon which this book does not satisfy our curiosity: the extent to which Fascist corporative organization gives autonomy to businesses and individual initiative, from an economic angle, and the extent to which, from a social angle, the subjection of workers to tasks of collective interest affects their liberty, affects their material situation.[99]

The raising of this question was revealing in its own right, given the nature of his own corporatist views. The review further confirmed that he had become sceptical of the claims made by the Fascist regime, an attitude which stood in marked contrast to the conclusions of his collective bargaining report. If anything, Laroque had become somewhat less naïve during the intervening years.

In 1938, the publication of *Les Rapports entre patrons et ouvriers* confirmed Laroque's status as a rising expert in the field of social policy. This study examined the history and evolution of industrial relations from the French Revolution to the present day, discussing both French and foreign approaches to this question. As had been the case with his CNE report, his interpretation of industrial relations remained defined by a linear conception of history; he believed that the events of 1936, characterized by the outbreak of nationwide strikes, the election of the Popular Front and the conclusion of the Matignon accords, had to be understood as the culmination of a prolonged historical process.[100] This historical perspective was central to his conception of social policy, since Laroque believed that the development of policy was contingent upon a consideration of long-term social and economic trends.

---

[97] MAS, LP, box 66.
[98] Ibid.
[99] Ibid.
[100] MAS, LP, box 67, manuscript of *Les Rapports entre patrons et ouvriers*, 2–3.

According to *Les Rapports entre patrons et ouvriers*, the history of French social and economic development had been defined by the revolutions of 1789 and 1848. The French Revolution had resulted in the rejection of the corporatist traditions of the *Ancien Régime*, and this entailed the application of the liberal and individualist principles associated with laissez-faire economics. In legal terms, employment was now regulated by the contractual relationship of free and consenting individuals.[101] The conditions of employment depended upon the mutual agreement of these parties, but the egalitarian principles which influenced the law ignored the inequality which accrued from existing social and economic conditions. This discrepancy led to the evolution of the legal system during the course of the nineteenth century, and the introduction of new forms of legislation gradually compensated for the limitations of the contract system.[102] These changes were important, since they reflected increased public concern with the social question.

Les Rapports entre patrons et ouvriers noted that the onset of industrialization and the rise of the working class raised a new set of challenges for succeeding French governments.[103] The birth of modern capitalism and the emergence of a new class system had revolutionary implications for French society, and the accelerating pace of these changes accounted for the outbreak of the revolution of 1848.[104] Laroque presented a narrative which described French social history as a succession of class conflicts shaped by economic forces, an approach which echoed the Marxist conception of history. Laroque stressed, however, that both conflicting and conciliatory tendencies coexisted during any given phase of historical development. The conflict between opposing social and economic forces could thus be managed, and it was possible for policymakers to pursue reformist politics as a viable alternative to revolutionary action.

The end of the nineteenth century had witnessed the transformation of social relations as laissez-faire receded before the growth of an organized labour movement and the implementation of various forms of state interventionism. This phenomenon was reflected in the evolution of the law, as demonstrated by the recognition of the right of workers to form their own *syndicats*, a reversal of the anti-union bias which had defined the law since the French Revolution.[105] The law had begun to move away from a dogmatic liberalism which had justified the prohibition of the

---

[101] Ibid. 38.
[102] Ibid. 44.
[103] Ibid. 100–2.
[104] Ibid. 97.
[105] Ibid. 118.

syndicats ouvriers, but this change was by no means accidental since it reflected the changing reality of French industrial relations. The granting of the right to organize was all the more important given the persistence of conflict between management and labour, as reflected by the recurring outbreak of strikes and lockouts throughout the latter part of the century.[106] These tensions confirmed the fact that social relations were shaped by the strength of the contending parties, but this did not imply that these conflicts were permanent or inevitable. Laroque observed that the same period had witnessed various initiatives to find a peaceful solution to these problems, and this included attempts at mediating labour disputes.[107] Over the next few decades, the evolution of French labour legislation would gain in momentum, culminating in the collective bargaining legislation which would be introduced in 1919 and 1936.

The First World War, according to the narrative presented in *Les Rapports entre patrons et ouvriers*, had ushered in a new era of promise. During the conflict, the representatives of management and labour had cooperated under the aegis of an interventionist state, an experience which had been defined by a climate of trust and goodwill, thus marking a break with the pre-existing pattern of industrial relations.[108] The collaboration of labour and management was abetted by an increase in government regulation, a lesson which was not lost on an author who had a bias against laissez-faire and state minimalism. Furthermore, Laroque maintained that the transformation of the social environment had affected the early post-war years, and that the minimum programme of the CGT had reflected this new atmosphere.[109] The experience of the Great War had shown that class cooperation was indeed possible, and that this could be achieved through a greater degree of state intervention in the social and economic spheres. French labour legislation, moreover, seemed to reflect these new attitudes. The law of 25 March 1919 provided a new framework for the negotiation of collective bargaining agreements, an initiative which promised to transform industrial relations in peacetime France.[110] The state thus provided legal recognition to a mechanism which served to promote a process of negotiation in the workplace, but the law proved unable to pacify industrial relations since it lacked the constraints which would have made its application more effective. In any case, the interwar period soon witnessed the revival of industrial conflict, as the patriotic spirit of wartime

---

[106] MAS, LP, box 67, manuscript of *Les Rapports entre pabrous et ouvriers*, 143–6.
[107] Ibid. 155.
[108] Ibid. 269–70.
[109] Ibid. 281.
[110] Ibid. 279.

receded before the revival of past attitudes and approaches towards the management of industrial relations.

The return to peacetime conditions and the revival of industrial conflict did not mean that the lessons of the First World War had been forgotten. The role of the state had been fundamentally altered during this period, and reformist policies continued to be promoted by both politicians and labour leaders. For Laroque, the creation of the CNE, in 1925, was a prime example of the legacy of wartime, and it demonstrated what an alliance of the state and organized labour could actually achieve.[111] As we have seen, the CNE was a consultative body which formalized the public consultation of various social and economic interests, and it had been inspired by the *Conseil Économique du Travail* which had been promoted by the minimum programme. While Laroque applauded this development, he also stressed that the persistence of a narrow conception of economic interest made it difficult to reconcile the demands of business and labour organizations. The main problem, in his view, lay with the fact that employers sought to preserve their authority within the workplace and continued to exhibit a paternalistic attitude towards their workforce.[112] It was this mentality that explained the revival of industrial conflict, a phenomenon which illustrated how cultural and psychological factors remained critical to the evolution of industrial relations.

By the mid thirties, it seemed that a new era was dawning in the field of French industrial relations. The Matignon accords of 1936 and the ensuing legislation of the Blum government had resulted in the introduction of important and historic reforms. Most notably, Laroque focused on the reform of the collective bargaining mechanism which had been introduced in 1919. The government's initiatives in the field of industrial relations were based on three fundamental principles: independence of the unions, a strengthened collective bargaining process, and a new system of workshop delegates.[113] These measures were significant, but they fell short of what Laroque deemed was necessary for the transformation of industrial relations. As Laroque noted, conflict between labour and management persisted despite these achievements. The business community remained sceptical of the collective bargaining process, and this outlook could only undermine the practical impact of the government's legislation.[114] French business leaders still refused to acquiesce to the limitation

---

[111] Ibid. 319–20.
[112] Ibid. 300–25.
[113] Ibid. 333–4; See Renouvin et al, *Léon Blum, chef de gouvernement 1936–1937*.
[114] Ibid. 343–4.

of their authority within the workplace, and this paternalistic mindset
made it impossible to achieve lasting social peace.

These experiences demonstrated that legislation alone could not transform industrial relations. *Les Rapports entre patrons et ouvriers* stressed the
importance of psychological and cultural factors in influencing the latter,
and it was this particular insight that represented the book's most interesting contribution to the analysis of the relationship between labour and
management.[115] Though Laroque did not deny the importance of various
social, political, and economic factors in fuelling social tensions, he
believed that their underlying cause was of a psychological nature:

> Whatever the importance of the economic causes of class conflict, the latter
> is mainly due to the existence of an inferiority complex among the workers in
> heavy industry, a sentiment that he is socially inferior to his employers; it is a
> reaction against this inferiority.[116]

The desire for respect lay at the root of working class grievances. This
interpretation of class conflict was reminiscent of Hendrik de Man's views,
and the archival evidence suggests that Laroque had indeed read the works
of de Man and Déat, not to mention the writings of Durkheim and
Bouglé.[117] Laroque believed, moreover, that different groups were defined
by their own specific attitudes. In contrast to their working class counter-
parts, the artisans did not suffer from the same sense of inferiority. He
explained this difference by the fact that the individual artisan could
always aspire to the ownership of a workshop, and that this gave them a
sense of relative equality with the more prosperous elements of society.[118]
This portrait of the artisan class was uncanny in its prescience, given the
difficulties that he would encounter in the years that followed the introduction of French social security. During the post-war years, a wide-
ranging coalition, which included the representatives of the artisan trades,
would oppose the attempt to implement a universal system of old age
insurance in light of its rejection of the solidarist rhetoric and the redistributive objectives of social security.

Les Rapports entre patrons et ouvriers expanded upon the comparative
dimension of his CNE report by examining previously ignored models of
collective bargaining. Laroque now considered the Swedish model to be
the most interesting variant of the liberal system of industrial relations. He
noted that Sweden had benefited from the existence of strong labour and

---

[115] Renouvin et al., *Léon Blum.* 369–73.
[116] Ibid. 373.
[117] MAS, LP, box 140, copies of various bibliographies used for his class and book.
[118] Laroque, *Les Rapports.*

management organizations, and that this had facilitated their attempts at negotiating working conditions and mediating industrial disputes.[119] Both parties favoured the peaceful resolution of industrial conflict. The representatives of labour and business were equally committed to a system which combined an attachment to liberal freedoms with a belief in social conciliation.[120] Sweden thus demonstrated that industrial relations could be managed in a mutually beneficial manner within a liberal and democratic framework. At the same time, the book confirmed the evolution of his views concerning Fascist corporatism; he openly acknowledged reports of the violation of collective bargaining agreements and the failure of class cooperation.[121] Laroque's exposure to such information readily explained his critical stance towards Fascist social policy, and this skeptical outlook had already been suggested by his various book reviews.

The expression of such praise for the Swedish model of industrial relations was probably influenced by Laroque's involvement with *Les Nouveaux Cahiers*. The Franco-Swedish conference of June 1938 had decisively influenced the review's attitudes towards the Swedish approach, but it is impossible to determine whether Laroque actually attended this event. Materials contained in his private papers suggest that he was aware of the information that was made available to the organizers and participants. Furthermore, a paper found in his personal archive suggests that his sympathy for the Swedish model had increased after the publication of *Les Rapports entre patrons et ouvriers*.[122] It reads like a synopsis of the information presented at the conference, and it concludes that the Swedish model was the most 'perfect' example of a liberal conception of industrial relations.[123] In marked contrast with his collective bargaining report of 1934, Laroque seemed no longer convinced of the necessity of imposing a *dirigiste* approach to the management of these relations.

Les Rapports entre patrons et ouvriers was a useful book of reference for those interested in the study of industrial relations. The limited sales of the book, which totalled 814 copies for both 1938 and 1939, did not do justice to the widespread attention that it garnered in the press during this period.[124] Two dozen book reviews were published in various papers, and these accounts were almost unanimously positive. The reviewers generally

[119] Ibid. 260.
[120] Ibid. 265.
[121] Ibid. 196–7.
[122] MAS, LP, box 67. This document probably served as lecture notes for his industrial relations class at *Sciences Po*.
[123] Ibid. 8–9.
[124] MAS, LP, box 63, relevé de Fernand Aubier-Éditions Montaigne, 15 March 1940.

acknowledged the author's mastery of the subject, his objectivity, and his scholarly contribution to a field which had been neglected by academic research.[125] The critical response to the book confirmed the fact that Laroque had become a recognized expert in the field of industrial relations, and this success marked the end of an intellectual journey which had first begun with the research that he had conducted for the *Conseil National Économique*, an assignment that had turned him into a one-time advocate of corporatist politics.

By the end of the decade, Laroque had become less naive about the nature of social problems and the ability of the state to effect radical change. In an April 1940 lecture entitled *L'Évolution de la legislation ouvrière depuis 1936*,[126] he reiterated the observations presented in his book while offering new insights about the French national character. Laroque argued that the French were beset by contradictions, since they exhibited a temperament that was both conservative and revolutionary in nature. The French were mindful of protecting the status quo but were also prone to revolutionary outbursts when a regime proved unable to adjust to new social and economic conditions.[127] This analysis explained the history of French industrial relations. Conservative attitudes made it difficult to introduce reformist policies, thus contributing to the accumulation of social frustrations which often culminated in revolutionary disturbances. French policymakers had to learn to manage change while respecting the desire for social stability, a difficult balancing act that would prove relevant to the fate of social security in post-war France.

CONCLUSION

Pierre Laroque believed that it was imperative to develop new policies which addressed the challenges which confronted interwar France. The advocacy of the corporatist management of industrial relations was a response to the persistent tensions which characterized the relationship between labour and management, and it held the promise of creating a new era of class cooperation defined by a heightened sense of social solidarity. The corporation was an instrument of state interventionism which also sought to limit the extent of state control by granting the

---

[125] MAS, LP, box 63, clippings from various papers including *La Tribune des Fonctionnaires*, 13 May 1939, *Le Populaire*, 25 December 1938, *Le Peuple*, 1 August 1938.

[126] MAS, LP, box 22, notes for a lecture entitled *L'Évolution de la legislation ouvrière depuis 1936*, April 1940.

[127] Ibid. 2.

representatives of labour and management a key role in the negotiation of working conditions and the mediation of industrial conflict. The inherent ambiguity of corporatism was well attuned to the ambivalent posture of those who sought to develop policy solutions that were neither liberal nor collectivist, and which reflected a willingness to promote a practical *via media* between existing political and ideological alternatives. Both neo-socialists and technocrats promoted corporatists policies because they seemed consistent with their own respective political objectives. Neo-socialists believed that corporatism would make it possible to introduce socialism through the implementation of reformist measures, while technocrats could argue that it would provide a new framework for the management of industrial relations which might discipline an irrational and dysfunctional market system.

By the end of the decade, Laroque had become less sanguine about the claims of Fascist corporatism, and this knowledge compelled him to reappraise his advocacy of a democratic variant of corporatism. The public response to the reforms instituted by the Blum government made him realize that policymakers had to contend with deeply ingrained attitudes and practices, and that this made it difficult to effect change through legislation alone. These cultural and psychological considerations limited what governments could achieve, and there was no obvious solution to this social and political dilemma. The success of the Swedish model of industrial relations only comforted this line of analysis, since its achievements were the outcome of a cultural environment which put a premium on cooperation and compromise, principles which could not be enforced by any given set of policies. Laroque's understanding of industrial relations had matured, but there was no indication that his underlying views concerning the nature of society and the role of the state had undergone any fundamental change. While he might have reconsidered the value of the professional corporation, he remained committed to a belief in the virtue of a state interventionism which was mitigated by administrative decentralization. As his later career would demonstrate, he remained convinced that social policy served to promote social solidarity, an objective which could only be achieved by fostering the participation of those destined to benefit from the introduction of new forms of progressive legislation.

4

Vichy, the Resistance, and Free France

The rise of the Vichy regime following the conclusion of the armistice of June 1940 ushered in a new and unexpected phase in Pierre Laroque's career which led him to assume important responsibilities far removed from the concerns of social policy. Until the autumn of 1940, he contributed to the elaboration of the policies of the Ministry of Labour, but his work was cut short by his dismissal from the civil service, a consequence of anti-Semitic legislation of the Vichy regime. During this period, Laroque participated in the development of important and sometimes controversial initiatives, such as the drafting of the legislation which introduced the *comités d'organisation*, the elaboration of a corporatist scheme for the management of industrial relations as well as an aborted attempt to reform social insurance. In late 1940, he gained employment in the private sector and joined the Resistance, a prelude to his departure for London and his stay at the headquarters of the Free French movement. These experiences provided him with new opportunities to exhibit his wide-ranging talents, but his contribution to the struggle against Vichy and the Axis powers bore no relationship with the development of social policy. Upon his return to the Ministry of Labour in 1944, however, he finally revisited the issue of social insurance, and this set the stage for the introduction of social security in postwar France.

LAROQUE AT VICHY

The armistice of June 1940 brought an end to the participation of France in the war against Nazi Germany, but it also set the stage for a political revolution of sorts, as illustrated by the collapse of the Third Republic and the rise of the Vichy regime. Led by Marshal Pétain, a national hero who had achieved fame as a result of his service during the First World War, the new state was committed to an anti-republican politics, and it sought to purge France of a political legacy which it blamed for the decadence of the pre-war years and disastrous military campaign of the spring and summer of 1940. As a consequence, the government initiated a vast array of reforms in different fields, and this activity touched upon the area of social policy. The highest circles of the government did not necessarily share the same views or objectives, and these internal divisions would eventually have an impact on its various initiatives. The policies developed by Pierre Laroque and his colleagues at the Ministry of Labour became a source of some of these tensions, as became increasingly apparent during the coming months.

By the late summer, Pétain proclaimed the advent of the National Revolution,[1] a slogan which summarized the anti-democratic and anti-republican prejudices of the Vichy regime. This reactionary bias was apparent in the Marshal's speeches, inspired as they were by the counter-revolutionary thought of René de La Tour du Pin and Charles Maurras.[2] These ideological influences explained the authoritarian, organicist, and corporatist world view of a government which condemned the ideas and institutions associated with the defunct Republic. According to Pétain, the main task which befell the government was primarily a moral one, a necessary reaction to the internal divisions and national decline which had supposedly characterized interwar France. On 25 June 1940, he had called for the moral and intellectual renewal of a society which had lost its sense of purpose and duty, and had been subjected to the degrading pressures of capitalism and socialism which had fostered the social and political fragmentation of French society.[3] These themes were typical of a reactionary tradition which rejected both the free market and state collectivism, invoking the natural harmony of a society whose members were to be united in a new sense of common purpose. Illiberal and anti-individualistic in its assumptions, the rhetoric of the regime denounced a capitalist system which had generated class conflict and bred revolutionary agitation, and it proclaimed the advent of a new social order which was to be free of all social tensions. The National Revolution thus promoted a reactionary utopia based upon a cherished family, an extensive corporatist structure, and a strong yet decentralized state, themes which had long been part of the discourse of the extreme Right.[4] While vague and schematic, these ideas were nonetheless important, since they defined the rhetoric of the government and influenced its internal debates over the course of public policy.

---

[1] J.-P. Azéma, *1940: L'Année terrible*, 255–64; J.-P. Cointet, *Histoire de Vichy*, 134–51.
[2] H. du Moulin de Labarthète, *Le Temps des illusions*, 159–62.
[3] P. Pétain, *Appel du 25 juin 1940*, in *Discours aux Français*, 66–70.
[4] P. Pétain, 'La Politique sociale de l'avenir', in ibid.; P. Pétain, *Actes et écrits*, 491–4.

The *État Français* was permeated by acute personal and ideological rivalries at the highest levels, and this ultimately affected the policy process. The government brought together a diverse collection of individuals and ideologies, and while they shared a common reformist impulse, their basic assumptions and approaches often differed and were sometimes downright antagonistic.[5] These internal tensions accounted for the eclectic nature of Vichy-ite policies. While some advocated the pursuit of a modernizing agenda influenced by technocratic ideas, others favoured a return to an idealized pre-industrial age. This conflict was best illustrated by the debate surrounding the *Charte du Travail*, a labour charter introduced in 1941 which was characterized by its corporatist ambitions. Jean-Pierre Le Crom has argued that the development of the charter pitted opposing strands of French corporatism, namely its traditionalist and neo-syndicalist tendencies: the former sought to organize the professions while abandoning any recourse to any form of *syndicalisme*, while the latter sought to establish *syndicats* for both labour and management, thus providing a syndicalist basis for the corporatist organization of industrial relations.[6] This debate reflected the fundamental ambivalence of corporatist politics. Both traditionalists and neo-syndicalists sought to eliminate class conflict through the corporation, but the latter sought to institutionalize conventional structures of social and economic representation while the former denied the value of organizations which they blamed for exacerbating the social tensions of the defunct republic.

The advent of the Vichy regime resulted in the renewal of the nation's political leadership, and new figures were appointed to various government ministries, as would be the case at the Ministry of Labour. In July 1940, René Belin, one of the leaders of the pre-war CGT, accepted the post of Minister of Labour in the Laval government, later explaining that he felt compelled to serve out of deference to the Marshal and in order to defend the interests of working people.[7] Before the war, Belin had come to prominence as a leader of the anti-Communist wing of the CGT and had promoted the agenda of *planisme* within the labour movement; he had also participated in the deliberations of *X-crise* during the course of the thirties.[8] Belin was anything but a typical leader of the CGT; being interested in ideas and policies, his intellectual curiosity accounted for his activism as Minister of Labour during the first two years of the Vichy

---

[5] R. Paxton, *La France de Vichy, 1940–1944*, 2nd edn., 180–5.

[6] J.-P. Le Crom, *Syndicats nous voilà!*, 16.

[7] IHS, BP, *Rapport sur l'activité du ministère de la production industrielle et du travail du 15 juillet au 15 Novembre 1940*, 2.

[8] R. Belin, *Du secrétariat de la CGT au gouvernement de Vichy*, 78–9.

regime. In July 1940, however, the appointment of Belin shocked many observers,[9] and the new minister would soon have to contend with the sustained opposition of cabinet colleagues who were hostile to his various policy initiatives.

While the nomination of a one-time leader of the CGT might have surprised some, it did prove consistent with the government's attempt to transcend traditional ideological cleavages. It also reflected the widespread appeal which the regime had garnered throughout all segments of society during the summer months. The swift and spectacular collapse of the French armies had resulted in mass psychological shock, and it was this context of confusion and bewilderment that had made it possible for Marshal Pétain to come to power.[10] Pétain became a source of hope and inspiration to many, and this popular support was to be exploited by the architects of the National Revolution. At the same time, the tragic outcome of the military campaign resulted in the re-evaluation of past assumptions in many quarters of public opinion, and this process of self-examination led to the repudiation of the principles and institutions associated with a discredited Third Republic.[11] This loss of confidence translated into a willingness to consider anti-democratic and anti-republican forms of politics. The labour movement was not immune to this climate of doubt and experimentation. During this period, in fact, the *Bureau Confédéral* of the CGT called for the creation of a new community of labour uniting all of the social classes,[12] an initiative which demonstrated its willingness to forsake the language of class conflict and participate in the creation of a new social and political order.

René Belin was presented with daunting social and economic challenges, since the German invasion and occupation had disrupted the normal patterns of social and economic life. While the German advance into French territory had sparked the mass evacuation of the civilian population, as refugees fled before the advance of the enemy, the armistice divided the country into occupied and unoccupied zones, thus complicating transport and communications from one zone to the next. French industrial production had come to a standstill, and this economic downturn led to an increase in unemployment during the summer months,[13] a reality that compounded the chaos that had ensued from the onset of the German advance into France. Furthermore, the Germans began to impose

---

[9] Ibid. 129.

[10] Paxton, *La France de Vichy*, 15–58.

[11] Ibid.

[12] J. Julliard, 'La Charte du Travail', in R. Rémond and J. Bourdin (eds.) *Le Gouvernement de Vichy 1940–1944*, 158; G. Lefranc, *Les Expériences syndicales en France de 1939 à 1950*, 37–9.

[13] Belin, *Du secrétariat de la CGT*, 140.

their will upon industries located within the occupied zone, thus implementing a form of economic control which threatened both national sovereignty
as well as the ability of the economy to provide for the needs of the
French population.[14] Given these developments, it was imperative for the
government to act rapidly and decisively if it was to revitalize the economy,
provide employment, and resist the demands of the occupation forces.

Notwithstanding the Vichy regime's ultimate objectives, its first obligation was to address these difficult circumstances, and it was in this context
that Pierre Laroque joined Belin's personal staff. While little is known of
the details of his contribution to the work of the Ministry of Labour, it is
altogether clear that his efforts focused on three main areas of policy: the
creation of a system of economic planning, the development of a corporatist structure for the management of industrial relations, and the elaboration of a plan to reform the social insurance system.[15] These activities
harkened back to the ideas which he had formulated during the thirties,
but they also anticipated his subsequent work as the architect of post-war
social security. At this point, however, his service in the Ministry of
Labour was somewhat incongruous, since he contributed to the drafting
of the domestic policies of an authoritarian regime despite his rejection of
its politics. In his memoirs, Belin would later recall how Laroque first
responded to his ideas concerning the objectives of the ministry:

> He accepted, at my behest, to provide me with his invaluable assistance.
> I still remember the first conversation which we had in my office of the rue
> Alquié. I outlined before him, in necessarily schematic terms, the projects of
> social and industrial reorganization that were slowly taking shape in my
> mind. I discussed the necessity of strict economic controls, which would
> require an institutionalization of the labour movement. 'But, this is fascism',
> he said. 'Let's not refer to any "isms"', I responded, 'because we would lock
> ourselves in . . . Do you think that we can actually do anything else in the
> present circumstances?' 'No', he answered, 'I don't see how'. 'So would you
> be willing to help me prepare and draft these projects which cannot be
> entrusted to the regular administration?' He accepted.[16]

While these recollections might have been committed to paper over three
decades after the fact, they do shed light on Laroque's political inclinations

---

[14] Belin, *Du secrétariat de la CGT*, 141–4.

[15] P. Laroqne, *Au service de l'homme et du droit: souvenirs et réflexions*, 124–6;
P. V. Dutton, *Origins of the French Welfare State*, 192–4. Dutton states that Laroque played
a central role in the attempt to reform social insurance in 1940, but Laroque's memoirs are
rather vague on this point, and the recollections of Francis Netter, as recorded in the oral
history conducted by the *Comité d'Histoire de la Sécurité Sociale* (*Témoignage* Netter),
provide another explanation for the reform effort of 1940.

[16] Belin, *Du secrétariat de la CGT*, 134.

in the aftermath of the armistice. Though he had once admired Fascist social achievements, Laroque had never forsaken his belief in a democratic and republican state, but now he was compelled to revisit the issue of corporatism in an explicitly authoritarian context.

The government's first priority lay with the revitalization of the French economy, but the end of the fighting did not imply a return to the practice of laissez-faire. Indeed, it intended to pursue interventionist policies aimed at maintaining its control of the economy, an objective that could be explained by the Occupation and the prospect of German control of French industrial production. It was in this spirit that the government introduced the law of 16 August 1940, legislation that set the framework for a planned economic system. According to the law, both human and physical resources were to be coordinated by so-called *comités d'organisation*, which were to be set up in each sector of industrial activity.[17] Belin and Laroque, two veterans of the *planiste* movement of the thirties, put their *dirigiste* ideas into practice, though they could not have foreseen the context in which these principles would finally be turned into public policy.

According to a report which he submitted to the Marshal on 16 August 1940, Belin believed that it was imperative for the state to intervene in the economy. The minister did not believe that the short-term revival of French industry could be assured by market forces:

> The situation of French industry is serious. Since the last month of September, the entire economy has been dominated by the absolute priority accorded to military production. The cessation of hostilities led to the end of these orders. And the adaptation of the factories to the new conditions created by the armistice is rendered particularly difficult after the separation of the occupied and non-occupied zones, after the near impossibility for France to import raw materials or export its products. In these circumstances, an immediate effort must be made to reorganize the economy in terms of the new situation, to get from the means of production maximum profit out of our manpower and material resources. This effort must be made to provide work, and the means of existence, to thousands of workers; it is essential to the material and moral revival of our country.
>
> It would be vain to wait for the adjustment of market forces. While admitting that the action of economic laws can, under certain circumstances, re-establish a disrupted equilibrium, this process can only be a slow one. One cannot depend upon the organizational effort of our industrialists. Whatever their goodwill, their potential cannot be compared with the problems which must be resolved. The state alone disposes of the means of actions which are effective immediately. It must act energetically and without delay.[18]

[17] MAS, LP, box 41, *Rapport à Monsieur le Maréchal de France*, 16 August 1940.
[18] Ibid. 1–2.

While sheer necessity might have compelled the government to pursue interventionist policies, the situation also provided it with the opportunity to rationalize the economic system with the cooperation of business leaders. Belin proposed that new committees, staffed by the representatives of business and government, be charged with directing the supply of human and material resources in each economic sector.[19] The law of 16 August 1940 thus reinforced the power of the state and management at the expense of French labour, an ironic development given the Minister's background as a leader of the pre-war CGT.

Belin was fully aware of the implications of his proposal, but he stressed that it was important for the government to act rapidly before addressing other contending social issues.[20] It was more important to revitalize industrial production before dealing with the status and role of organized labour in this changed environment. Furthermore, his subordinates, including Laroque, had already started working on a plan for the corporatist management of industrial relations, an initiative that bore some resemblance to Laroque's pre-war views. By the beginning of September, these ideas had taken form with a project to establish a network of social committees that were meant to organize the members of each sector of economic activity.[21] From the outset, this initiative provoked much opposition within the government, and this controversy illustrated the existence of conflicting interpretations of corporatism at the highest levels of the Vichy regime.

Belin made good use of Laroque's background as a lawyer, civil servant, and social policy expert. In an ironic twist of fate, his past work in the field of collective bargaining now proved useful during his tenure at the Ministry of Labour. While Belin would later acknowledge his debt to the ideas of Auguste Detoeuf in the field of industrial relations, it should be recalled that Detoeuf's proposals closely resembled Laroque's one-time corporatist views.[22] In any case, Detoeuf had conceived the corporation as an outgrowth of existing forms of social and economic representation. The implementation of corporatist structures would serve to consolidate the representative role of the *syndicats* while including them in the management of industrial relations. Belin and his subordinates thus pursued a corporatist agenda which acknowledged the reality of class conflict; this neo-syndicalist perspective sparked the opposition of traditionalists who believed that the natural harmony of society had been disturbed by the

---

[19] MAS, LP, box 41, *Rapport à Monsieur le Maréchal de France*, 16 August 1940, 3–6.
[20] Ibid. 6.
[21] *Institut d'Histoire Sociale*, Belin Papers, letter to Marshal Pétain, 21 December 1940, 2.
[22] Belin, *Du secrétariat de la CGT*, 78–9.

excesses of industrialization.[23] The Ministry of Labour, it should be noted, also suffered from its marginal status within the councils of government. Belin was never an intimate of the Marshal; the head of state and his entourage, not to mention the deputy prime minister and the minister of finance, were definitely hostile to his various initiatives in the field of social policy.[24] This personal and political isolation accounted for Belin's inability to promote his most ambitious projects, namely those which sought to reorganize industrial relations and rationalize the social insurance system.

The Ministry of Labour thus advocated the corporatist management of industrial relations, and its plan evoked the ideas that Laroque and Detoeuf had promoted during the thirties. In the current context, however, corporatism was harnessed to the objectives of the National Revolution. According to existing archival records, the Ministry sought to organize workers and management under the aegis of a compulsory trade union organization.[25] It should be recalled that Laroque had originally promoted this measure in response to the weakness and fragmentation of the labour movement. Furthermore, the implementation of corporatist policies had been intended to strengthen the collective bargaining process and promote the cultivation of a new sense of social solidarity. The authoritarian potential of Laroque's thought had been mitigated by the fact that the internal democracy of the labour movement would have been left untouched by his proposals. At Vichy, however, Laroque was involved in the elaboration of a corporatist network of industrial organization that was meant to replace, and not strengthen, the trade union confederations which were to be disbanded by the Vichy regime,[26] a decision which went against the very logic of his pre-war views.

René Belin eventually submitted his proposed legislation for the approval of the cabinet, and this sparked a debate which would last throughout the autumn of 1940. From September through November, a special cabinet committee formed of Belin, Darlan, Alibert, Caziot, and Baudouin modified the plan according to the recommendations made by various government ministries.[27] By the end of November, a modified version of the project was submitted for approval by the cabinet. It sought to transform the very nature of industrial relations

[23] Le Crom, *Syndicats nous voilà!* 65–8.

[24] du Moulin de Labarthète, *Le Temps des illusions*, 152; Belin, *Du secrétariat de la CGT*, 177–81.

[25] MAS, LP, box 41; IHS, BP, dossier B.

[26] Paxton, *La France de Vichy*, 209. All management and labour associations were disbanded on 9 November.

[27] IHS, BP, letter to Pétain.

by creating a new administrative framework for class collaboration, thereby addressing the social concerns which had been left unaddressed by the law of 16 August 1940:

> Liberal capitalism has split all communities, pitted increasing numbers of the masses against one another; it has divided the nation into classes where men get together only in terms of what opposes them to others. It has even weakened the national sentiment by extending into the international sphere the conflict of interests between classes. The goal which we propose is, in reaction against this regime of division, to create, between all men who collaborate to the country's economic life…a sense of their solidarity, to group them into conscious communities. The result can only be attained by a profound reform of the economic system, by the abandonment of the primacy attributed to capital over the other factors of production, by a distribution of new responsibilities and profits. This reform will only be achieved by a reorganization of the structure of industry.[28]

This rationale was anti-capitalist and redistributionist in nature, and its radical character undoubtedly contributed to the controversial reputation of the Ministry of Labour.

Despite the changes introduced by the cabinet committee, the scheme was still based upon a compulsory system of labour representation. The entire working population was to be organized according to their membership in given vocational categories.[29] Furthermore, it did not abandon a class-centred approach to the management of industrial relations. The plan advocated the creation of a dual organizational structure which would assemble both labour and management.[30] Its most interesting feature lay with its creation of a network of social committees. Set up at the local, regional, and national levels, these committees were to include an equal number of representatives of labour and management, and they were to be entrusted with the negotiation of working conditions and the mediation of industrial disputes.[31] In other words, this structure would provide for the negotiation and enforcement of collective bargaining agreements in each industrial sector.

During his pre-war career, Laroque had sought to empower a working class which had long been marginalized under the capitalist system, but the current proposal reflected a desire to strengthen the authority of the state in social and economic affairs. Little reference was made to the enhancement of working class participation in the management of

---

[28] IHS, BP, *Rapport à Monsieur le Maréchal de France*, 19 November 1940, 1–2.
[29] Ibid. 2–3.
[30] Ibid. 3.
[31] Ibid.

industrial relations, and the Ministry of Labour stressed the importance of consolidating the power of the state in relation to the existing social and economic interests. In fact, an internal memorandum argued that it was important for the state to affirm its authority in light of the demands of both labour and management.[32] It is altogether possible, however, that this rationale served to counter the arguments employed by those who opposed the minister's policies, since these critics were fully aware of the neo-syndicalist dimension of Belin's corporatist project.

For the Minister of Finance, Yves Bouthillier, the proposals put forth by the Ministry of Labour were anathema to the principles of the *État Français*. Bouthillier noted that the plan implicitly recognized an obsolete class structure and empowered economic interests which, he believed, had weakened the defunct Republic. From this perspective, the reform threatened to revive the social tensions of the past:

> As I pointed out in my letter of November 22, far from organizing on a new basis a real corporatist regime, this project will revive separate labour and business organizations, and their rivalry, but with this difference: as official organizations benefiting from a recognised monopoly, these groups will express the opinion of all producers and, to a certain extent, of the government.
>
> The social committees, formed of representatives having received a mandate from their respective organizations, cannot play a more effective role than that of the old commissions formed of labour and management representatives, that is, of a structure of compromise. But they would have the power to make collective bargaining agreements compulsory, and this makes me fear a return to the inflation of social costs, which would have once more the most serious repercussions on the finances of the country.[33]

The Minister of Finance argued that the social committees would have too much power, implying that that had been the result of the Blum government's reform of collective bargaining procedures. Bouthillier feared that the committees would provide labour with the means of controlling industrial activity, and it was this prospect which explained his hostility to the project.[34]

These fears were shared by others within the government, and this opposition explained the fact that the plan was never implemented, despite

---

[32] IHS, BP, *Les Fédérations nationales dans l'organisation professionelle*, 22 November 1940, 2.

[33] IHS, BP, *Lettre du ministre secrétaire d'état aux finances à monsieur le ministre secrétaire d'état à la production industrielle et au travail*, 4 December 1940, 4.

[34] Ibid. 4–5.

its approval by the cabinet.[35] This failure did not signal the end of corporatism, since the government would revisit the issue at a later date and in an altogether different manner. A new committee, the *comité d'organisation professionelle*, was established in March 1941, and its deliberations would result in the introduction of the *Charte du Travail* later that same year.[36] While the charter established the framework for a future corporate state, its content confirmed the government's inability to address its internal contradictions. In an unsigned article published in *Droit Social*, Laroque would provide readers with a snapshot of the confused political and intellectual climate which had given rise to the *Charte du Travail*. In his view, the latter highlighted opposing interpretations of corporatism, the one syndicalist and the other communitarian, and combined both statist and liberal approaches towards the development of social policy.[37] In other words, the charter was the product of a political compromise, and this called into question both its internal coherence and its ultimate effectiveness.[38] The ambivalent character of the *Charte du Travail* might have reflected the ideological divisions of the government, but it also produced an unworkable piece of legislation.

Belin's attempt to reorganize industrial relations had provoked much hostility within the government, thus demonstrating that the very meaning of corporatism was subject to debate among its various advocates. The Ministry of Labour, however, had elicited controversy in other areas of policy, as had been reflected in its attempts to reform the social insurance system. Laroque, in fact, was involved in the drafting of a proposal which had been elaborated in the summer of 1940.[39] This was unsurprising, given his background and expertise, but it should also be mentioned that one of his future subordinates would also play a key role in developing this plan for social insurance reform. Francis Netter, a government actuary, was intimately involved in this initiative, not to mention a subsequent proposal that was submitted in 1942. The backgrounds of Pierre Laroque and Francis Netter bore some interesting similarities. An engineer by training, Netter had graduated from the *École Polytechnique* in 1931, and he had then become an actuary with the Ministry of Labour.[40] Like other civil

---

[35] IHS, BP, *Rapport à monsieur le Maréchal de France*, 6 December 1940. IHS, BP, letter to Pétain, 21 December 1940, 2.

[36] MAS, LP, box 41, typescript of *Genèse et tendances de la Charte du Travail*, anonymous article published in *Droit Social*, January (1942). See also Julliard, 'La Charte du Travail 172–80.

[37] MAS, LP, box 41, *Genèse*, 2.

[38] Ibid. 3–4.

[39] Laroque, *Au service*, 126; Dutton, *Origins of the French Welfare State*, 192–4.

[40] *Témoignage* Netter; J.-P. Launay, *Francis Netter: une vie pour le développement du progrès social*, 11.

servants of his generation, including Laroque himself, he had come to believe in the necessity of reforming the social and economic structures of interwar France. During the thirties, he had been a member of the SFIO and had participated in the activities *X-crise*.[41] Netter believed in the virtues of an interventionist state, and he now contributed his actuarial expertise to the attempt to rationalize social insurance.

As Netter later recalled, the director of social insurance had entrusted him with the task of developing a plan for the reform of social insurance benefits in the summer of 1940.[42] Though little is known about the details of his work, it seems that his proposals were incorporated into the plan adopted by the Ministry of Labour. Accordingly, the latter sought to reform the actuarial basis of old age insurance, substituting redistribution for the capitalization of resources while extending benefits through a unified administrative infrastructure.[43] The reform sought to rationalize the actuarial and administrative bases of social insurance, thus providing for a more streamlined and effective system of coverage. Its bureaucratic structure would simplify the chaotic administration of the existing system. A network of 800 regional *caisses* would manage the existing social insurance programme as well as the family allowance and industrial accident benefit schemes.[44] The proposed reform would thus have an impact on other social programmes, and it held out the promise of a more coordinated approach towards the development and management of the relevant policies.

While these objectives might have seemed laudable, they aroused the hostility of groups that played a key role in the administration of the existing social insurance system. Most notably, the mutual aid societies were intent on stopping a proposal that threatened their privileged status. In the autumn of 1940, the *Fédération Nationale de la Mutualité Française*, the organization which represented these societies, made its disapproval of the impending reform public and pressed the Ministry of Labour to abandon its plans.[45] This opposition, it should be stressed, was abetted by the ideological and political intrigues of the Vichy regime. Once more, Belin encountered serious internal opposition, a situation which served the interests of his external critics.

While the existing archives are far from complete, it would seem that the criticisms which emanated from within government circles were

---

[41] Ibid.

[42] *Témoignage* Netter.

[43] AN, 2 AG 499, *Projet du travail-loi portant réforme de la législation sur les assurances sociales*, articles 4 and 5.

[44] Dutton, *Origins of the French Welfare State*, 192–4.

[45] Mutualité Française, FNMF, *p-v du conseil d'administration*, 28 September 1940, 14.

galvanized by efforts of the *Direction de la Famille*, an office of the *Secrétariat à la Famille et à la Santé*. Its services produced a series of hostile reports which were distributed to various government ministries and services.[46] Its hostility towards the reform of social insurance was based upon its analysis of the financial and administrative aspects of the proposed legislation. Most notably, the *Direction* argued that the latter represented an exercise in statism that defied the corporatist and decentralizing objectives of the Vichy regime.[47] These fears proved consistent with the rhetoric of the National Revolution, but they also reiterated the arguments that had been raised in opposition to the social insurance project that had been developed by Georges Cahen-Salvador in the aftermath of the First World War.

The reports of the *Direction de la Famille* explicitly denounced the solidaristic and redistributive character of the project and defended the interests of the lower middle class. According to a report submitted on 15 October 1940, only those who earned 42,000 francs or less would be deemed eligible for the receipt of social benefits.[48] As a consequence, the plan would not benefit the most skilled elements of the workforce. This was deemed unacceptable, and the report argued that the proposed reform represented nothing more than a form of social assistance.[49] This critique was not based on financial considerations alone, since it also gave voice to the social paternalism which was commonplace in Vichy-ite circles.

The reform of the financial basis of social insurance also drew criticism on moral and psychological grounds. The redistribution of resources, in the view of another memorandum, severed the relationship between individual contributions and benefits, and this could only encourage the multiplication of new and demagogic demands on the part of the insured population.[50] This rather naive interpretation of the mechanism of redistribution was based upon a belief in the virtue of capitalization. According to this view, the latter served to maintain the financial probity of the social insurance system. Finally, the fear of statist bureaucracy translated into a defence of the existing network of social insurance *caisses*. Another report stressed that while the unification of the administrative

[46] It is impossible to determine with absolute certainty who authored all of these reports; they were generally repetitive in their arguments, thus suggesting a common author. André Lavagne, a member of the *Conseil d'État* who had been assigned to the Direction, had known Laroque since childhood and had signed the report dated October 24 1940.

[47] AN, 2 AG 499, *Observations sur le projet de loi portant réforme de la législation sur les assurances sociales*, 15 October 1940, 1–2.

[48] Ibid.

[49] Ibid.

[50] AN, 2 AG 499, *Note sur le projet de réforme des assurances sociales*, 30 October 1940, 2.

infrastructure might be justified in the name of functional simplicity, it threatened the personal rapport that had developed between the insured and those who managed the distribution of benefits.[51] Whatever the value of this line of argument, the combination of internal and external opposition would condemn the proposed legislation, and it was eventually abandoned by the Ministry of Labour. Both cabinet colleagues and the Marshal's personal staff would effectively block Belin's initiative.[52] The lobbying of concerned pressure groups, coupled with the persistence of conservative attitudes at the highest levels of the government, had demonstrated that it was exceedingly difficult to reform the social insurance system.

Pierre Laroque's participation in the development of Vichy-ite social policy was cut short by his dismissal from the civil service in October 1940, but Francis Netter, his future subordinate, would continue to play a role in the development of social insurance policy. In February 1942, René Belin submitted a new proposal, and it elicited a similar response from the same combination of internal and external critics that had frustrated the plans submitted in 1940. Once more, the Ministry of Labour sought to rationalize the administrative infrastructure by establishing a network of *caisses territoriales* which would replace the *caisses* run by the mutual aid societies.[53] As had been the case in 1940, the project sought to simplify the management of the administrative infrastructure of social insurance and increase its financial resources.[54] As could be predicted, this new initiative was met by the hostile reaction of both internal and external opponents.

The Marshal's staff considered the reform to be contrary to the doctrine of the National Revolution and they feared that it would create serious political difficulties for the government.[55] The sceptical position of Pétain's entourage was based on a conservative interpretation of the regime's corporatist and decentralizing rhetoric, not to mention concern about the public opposition to the plan. Both the mutual aid societies and the *Fédération Nationale Catholique*, a leading Catholic pressure group, urged the Marshal to abandon a plan that negated, in their view, the spirit

---

[51] AN, 2 AG 499, *Examen du projet portant réforme de la législation des assurances sociales*, 18 October 1940, 5.

[52] Belin, *Du secrétariat de la CGT*, 155–7; du Moulin de Labarthète, *Le Temps des illusions*, 148–9; Y. Bouthillier, *Le Drame de Vichy*, vol. 2, 363.

[53] AN, 2 AG 499, *Rapport au Maréchal Pétain*, 28 February 1942, 1–2.

[54] AN, 2 AG 499, *Nouvelle note sur le projet de loi relatif aux assurances sociales*, 16 March 1942, 2–3.

[55] AN, 2 AG 499, notes, undated and unsigned (referring to a two-hour discussion between Belin and the director of social insurance).

of the *Charte du Travail*.[56] As had been the case in 1940, the tacit alliance between internal and external critics would halt this attempt to reform social insurance. Indeed, the archives of the Marshal's staff suggest that they were in fundamental agreement with the arguments presented by these aforementioned interests.[57] Much like the discredited Third Republic, the *État Français* proved itself to be amenable to pressure group politics.

THE RESISTANCE AND FREE FRANCE

Pierre Laroque's participation in the development of these policy initiatives was cut short by the regime's anti-Semitic policies. As a result of the law of 3 October 1940, he was classified as a Jew and dismissed from the *Conseil d'État* and the Ministry of Labour.[58] Laroque's career as a public servant had abruptly ended, but this dismissal proved to be a blessing in disguise, since he would no longer be involved in the elaboration of the social policies of the Vichy regime. Within a few weeks, moreover, he obtained a job in the private sector through contacts he had made during his military service, and he began work in the textile industry in the vicinity of Lyons.[59] Having found an alternative source of income, he became involved in a host of activities, some of which were of an illegal and subversive nature. During his stay in Lyons, he wrote and lectured about social policy questions and joined the Resistance movement of the unoccupied zone.[60] While he became involved in the struggle against the Vichy regime, he remained interested in the study of social and economic questions. In a series of lectures he delivered at various local institutions, he exhibited an approach towards social policy which proved consistent with the evolution of his thought during the interwar period.

[56] AN, 2 AG 499, correspondence preserved in the relevant file, e.g. the letter of the *Fédération Nationale Catholique*, 20 March 1942. The preceding letter also refers to its lobbying effort against the aborted reform of 1940. Letter of the *Fédération des Unions Mutualistes de la Seine Inférieure*, 6 April 1942.

[57] AN, 2 AG 499, *Note sur la loi relative à l'organisation des caisses d'assurances sociales*, 19 March 1942; letter from the *chef du cabinet civil* to the president of the *Familiale de Périgueux*, 29 April 1942.

[58] Laroque, *Au service*, 126–7; Interview of Mme Colette Laroque, 5 November 1998; MAS, LP, box 140, *curriculum vitae*. His employment officially ended on 14 December 1940. Belin had tried to have Laroque exempted from the new legislation, see Belin, *Du secrétariat de la CGT*, 134.

[59] *Au service*, 127–9.

[60] Ibid. 129–30; Interview of Mme Colette Laroque.

Despite his involvement with the corporatist projects of the Ministry of Labour, Laroque had not reverted to the corporatist ideas which he had professed during the thirties. He continued to espouse reformist views which were neither authoritarian nor totalitarian in nature, and he expressed these views in public forums, a risky undertaking given the context of the time. On 19 November 1941, for example, he gave a lecture on the various economic systems of the contemporary world to the students of the *École de Service Social*.[61] The surviving lecture notes suggest that he did little to mask his own ideological sympathies, despite the repressive atmosphere of the unoccupied zone. During this particular lecture, he argued that the world was defined by the rivalry of liberal and authoritarian forms of economic organization.[62] Laroque obviously referred to market-based systems and their collectivist alternatives, but his lecture also evoked a 'liberal-corporatist' model, which he distinguished from the two preceding systems.[63] One can surmise that this model best described his own views, since it referred to the existence of a third way of sorts, which lay between liberalism and collectivism.

Laroque did not believe in untrammelled laissez-faire or state minimalism, but this did not turn him into an advocate of authoritarian or totalitarian forms of social and political organization. As he noted, liberalism in Great Britain, the United States and Scandinavia was now characterized by the public coordination of different social and economic interests, an approach which highlighted the abandonment of a strict conception of laissez-faire.[64] While this analysis might have been accurate, it also described his personal inclinations in the matter of social and economic policy. Laroque remained interested in the management of industrial relations. In another lecture, he argued that collective bargaining, conciliation, and arbitration were essential elements in the effort of liberal states to organize industrial relations.[65] Laroque still believed that it was possible to pursue reformist policies within the social and economic framework of the market system. Furthermore, he revealed, at least in a tacit sense, his hostility towards fascism, an attitude which could be surmised by his definition of the latter. Laroque stressed that fascism entailed the complete subjugation of the individual in the interest of an all-encompassing state,

---

[61] MAS, LP, box 48, notes entitled *Les Principales formules étrangères d'organisation économique et sociale*, 19 November 1941.

[62] Ibid. 1.

[63] Ibid.

[64] Ibid. 2–3.

[65] MAS, LP, box 48, notes of *Les Problèmes du travail*, 20 May 1942, 5.

while liberalism and socialism promoted the freedom of the individual.[66] Given his past statements and writings, there could be little doubt as to the nature of Laroque's own ideological inclinations.

During this period, he became a member of the Resistance, and he participated in high-level meetings with the leaders of the underground movement.[67] While his involvement in the Resistance might have seemed unsurprising, it should be noted that this decision was not commonplace in the context of the time. Throughout the occupation of France, the Resistance would remain the affair of an activist minority that was subjected to repression enforced by the French police, German forces, and other auxiliary organizations.[68] Opposition groups had emerged in the aftermath of the French defeat, but their membership was limited and their activities were uncoordinated. As the war dragged on, however, these movements increased in size, as did the scope of their activities, which ranged from the production of propaganda material to the gathering of intelligence and the pursuit of guerrilla operations directed at the Germans and their local allies.[69] The growth of the Resistance was felt in both the occupied and the unoccupied zones, but the division of France accounted for the local peculiarities of the underground movements which operated in northern or southern France.

The Resistance was characterized by the extreme diversity of its membership, and its constituent movements were inspired by different ideologies; furthermore, different groups advocated distinct strategies with regard to the pursuit of the struggle against the Vichy regime and the Axis powers.[70] In the unoccupied zone, the absence of a German military presence until November 1942, coupled with the administration of the Vichy regime, played an important role in the ideological evolution of the movements which had become active in southern France. As Roderick Kedward has pointed out, the dogmatic attitudes and repressive policies of the government engendered an ideological reaction of sorts; by 1941, it had become apparent that the underground movements increasingly identified with a republican tradition which had been repeatedly denounced by the French government.[71] Laroque's participation in the

---

[66] MAS, LP, box 48, notes of *Les Problemes du travail*, 20 May 1942, 5. 6.

[67] Laroque, *Au service*; Interview of Colette Laroque. Laroque joined *Combat*, the organization set up by H. Frenay. Moreover, he met with leading figures such as A. Parodi, J. Moulin, A. Philip, Frenay, and G. Bidault.

[68] See F.-G. Dreyfus, *Histoire de la Résistance*; J.-F. Muracciole, *Histoire de la Résistance en France*; H. Noguères et al., *Histoire de la Résistance en France*.

[69] Ibid.

[70] Ibid.

[71] H. R. Kedward, *Resistance in Vichy France: a study of ideas and motivation in the Southern Zone 1940–1942*, 237–9.

underground movement thus coincided with a revival in support for the republican and democratic principles which had been associated with a discredited Third Republic.

Until the occupation of the southern zone, the local resistance focused on the production of propaganda, and this took the form of leaflets and newspapers.[72] This material was directed against both the Germans and the Vichy regime, and it sought to influence public attitudes in a country which was subjected to intense police surveillance and the censorship of the conventional media. Whatever their ideological biases, these publications were characterized by the recurrence of common themes, namely the denunciation of the domestic policies of the French government and its subservience to the Germans, as well as voicing support for Free France and the Allied war effort.[73] The efforts of the underground, however, was not limited to the distribution of propaganda, since it also pondered the challenges that France would face after the collapse of the Vichy regime and the defeat of the Axis powers.

These concerns with the future led to the creation of the *Comité Général d'Études* in July 1942, a think tank set up by Jean Moulin, de Gaulle's personal representative before the leaders of the underground movements.[74] The CGE served in an advisory capacity, producing analyses of the main problems that would confront a liberated France, and it outlined potential solutions to these challenges. Laroque was involved in the activities of the CGE, although little is known of the nature of his work for the committee.[75] It is unlikely that his contribution involved any substantial examination of the issue of social insurance. While the CGE discussed various social and economic policy questions, as well as a host of legal and administrative issues, it never dealt with the issue of social insurance in any substantive form.[76] At this time, neither Laroque nor the Resistance were excessively concerned with a question which remained of marginal importance in the context of the German occupation of France.

After the invasion of the unoccupied zone in November 1942, Laroque's involvement with the underground would change in nature, and he assumed new responsibilities outside metropolitan France. Alexandre Parodi and Jean Moulin, two of the senior leaders of the Resistance, asked Laroque to assure the liaison between the CGE and Free French headquarters

---

[72] Dreyfus, *Histoire de la Résistance*, 91–105 and 423; Muracciole, *Histoire de la Résistance*, 28.

[73] H. Michel, *Les Courants de pensée de la résistance*.

[74] D. de Bellescize, *Les Neufs sages de la résistance* 51–74.

[75] Laroque, *Au service*; Interview of Mme Colette Laroque; de Bellescize, *Les Neufs sages de la résistance*, 38.

[76] de Bellescize, *Les Neufs sages de la résistance*, 76–8. The author does not allude to any discussion of social insurance or security.

in London,[77] a posting which meant that he had to leave France and his family. After a few false starts, he finally arrived in the British capital in April 1943.[78] For the following sixteen months, Laroque was destined to play a significant role in the history of the Free French movement.

The Free French movement had been created by General de Gaulle in June 1940, in the midst of the defeat of the French armies and the launching of the armistice negotiations at the behest of the French government. De Gaulle had been an exponent of armoured warfare during the interwar period, and he had been named undersecretary of war by Paul Reynaud in the days preceding the fall of his cabinet.[79] On 18 June 1940, de Gaulle called upon his compatriots to join him in London in order to continue the struggle against Nazi Germany, thus rejecting Marshal Pétain's intention of concluding an armistice agreement with the German government.[80] The *Appel du 18 juin*, as it came to be known, became the founding moment of a movement committed to the pursuit of a French military effort against the Axis powers, but its purpose was not limited to military questions alone, since de Gaulle believed that Free France served an overarching political objective.

As de Gaulle saw it, the ultimate goal of Free France was the protection of the French national interest,[81] and this objective coloured his relations with both the British and the American governments. The relationship between de Gaulle, Churchill, and Roosevelt was a complicated one, defined as it was by succeeding episodes of support and suspicion of the motives which drove each respective party.[82] The attitudes of the Roosevelt administration proved to be most problematic, since the President of the United States was wary of the pretensions of the Free French movement. While Roosevelt remained sceptical of de Gaulle, a man whom his advisors portrayed as a potential dictator, he was also keen to obtain the support of French leaders who might facilitate the pursuit of Allied military and political objectives in the European theatre.[83] As a consequence, the President was unwilling to offer de Gaulle his unequivocal support, as was demonstrated by the political manoeuvring which

---

[77] Laroque, *Au service*, 131; de Bellescize, *Les Neufs sages de la résistance*, 21.

[78] Laroque, *Au service*, 134.

[79] J. Lacouture, *De Gaulle*, i, 322–46.

[80] J.-L. Crémieux-Brilhac, *La France Libre: de l'appel du 18 juin à la Libération*, 48–50; C. de Gaulle, *Mémoires de Guerre: l'appel 1940–1942*, 87–9.

[81] de Gaulle, *Mémoires de Guerre*; Michel, *Les Courants de pensée*, 53–5.

[82] Crémieux-Brilhac, *La France Libre*, chaps. 18, 19 and 20; Lacouture, *De Gaulle*, 523–46.

[83] Ibid.

surrounded the Anglo-American landings in French North Africa in November 1942.

The British and the Americans had not bothered to warn de Gaulle and the Free French of their impending landings in Morocco and Algeria, and this refusal to disclose their intentions was matched by a desire to approach other figures who might further Allied goals in North Africa. These considerations explained American support for General Giraud and Admiral Darlan, since it was believed that they had the potential to rally the local French forces to the Allied cause.[84] While there might have been some justification for the recourse to Giraud and Darlan, it fuelled Gaullist insecurities concerning the Anglo-Americans. In the view of de Gaulle and his main subordinates, the Americans had sought to impose their will without being obstructed by Free French concerns with the protection of French national sovereignty.[85] These fears would remain a leitmotif of Free French attitudes towards the Allied powers, and Laroque would come to play a role in the evolution of the uneasy relationship between Great Britain, the United States, and the Free French movement.

While he was first assigned as chief of staff to the commissariat of the interior of the *Comité Français de Libération Nationale*,[86] a quasi-government in exile set up by the Free French, Laroque soon became involved in the preparations for the Allied invasion of occupied France. It was in this area, in fact, that he made his greatest contribution to the war effort. As the head of the *Service Militaire d'Études Administratives*,[87] he trained a cadre of French officers who were to supervise the administration of the liberated territories, and he helped negotiate an inter-Allied entente that oerved to protect national sovereignty once the Allied forces landed on French territory.

Laroque was entrusted with these tasks in the summer of 1943, and his role transcended the administrative realm, since it touched upon rather sensitive political questions. In fact, he was now at the centre of the complicated relationship between Free France and the allied powers.[88] Laroque's new assignment had been the result of a proposal he had made to his superiors. According to his wartime journal, he had first proposed the creation of a corps of French military liaison officers that would serve with the Allied forces, and this suggestion led to creation of

---

[84] M. Cointet, *De Gaulle et Giraud: l'affrontement*; H. Michel, *François Darlan*.

[85] de Gaulle, *Mémoires de Guerre: l'appel*, 225–6; de Gaulle, *Mémoires de Guerre: l'unité 1942–1944*, 87–123.

[86] Laroque, *Au service*, 143.

[87] Ibid. 150–1.

[88] Crémieux-Brilhac, *La France Libre*; Laroque, *Au service*, 146–80.

the *Mission Militaire de Liaison Administrative*.[89] This idea made perfect sense: one had to maintain public services once Allied forces began military operations on French territory. At the same time, the MMLA served a higher purpose. It sought to avert the imposition of Allied control over the liberated territories and to protect French national sovereignty in the aftermath of the Allied landings in France.[90] The creation of this group was a product of the tensions which had erupted between the Free French and the Anglo-Americans. As the North African campaign had demonstrated, the Americans were more than willing to sideline de Gaulle and the Free French in the pursuit of their own interests, and this only exacerbated the concerns of the Free French leadership. The establishment of an Allied Military Government of Occupied Territories in Italy, more-over, had done little to alleviate these fears of Anglo-American domin-ation, and it was this context that explained the political significance of the work undertaken by Laroque and his colleagues.[91]

The work which Laroque undertook under the aegis of the *Mission Militaire de Liaison Administrative* overshadowed his past assignments with the domestic Resistance and the Free French movement, and his efforts garnered positive reviews on the part of his superiors. In the estimate of his commanding officer, he had managed to establish a positive working relationship with his British and American counter-parts.[92] Whatever the nature of Laroque's abilities, the struggle to main-tain an independent French administrative presence proved to be a long and difficult task. The first edition of the *Field Handbook of Civil Affairs*, published by the Supreme Headquarters of the Allied Expeditionary Forces in May 1944, had caused much consternation amongst the Free French. In a letter to the Free French military headquarters in London, Lieutenant Colonel de Boislambert characterized the handbook as a direct infringement upon French sovereignty; according to the book's guide-lines, Allied officers of civil affairs were to become the administrators of the occupied territories.[93] Whatever the intentions of SHAEF, it is clear that this publication confirmed Free French fears concerning the future of liberated France. In response to this challenge, Laroque pursued his talks

---

[89] Laroque, *Au service*.

[90] AN, F1a 3726, *Rapport sur la Mission Militaire de Liaison Administrative*, 15 March 1944.

[91] Crémieux-Brilhac, *La France Libre*, 686–98.

[92] AN, F1a 3726, *Rapport sur l'activité des Services des Affaires Civiles* (annex to the preceding).

[93] AN, F1a 3840, *Lettre du lieutenant colonel de Boislambert au commandement supérieur des forces françaises en Grande Bretagne et délégation militaire du CFLN*, 18 May 1944. AN F1a 3840, *Note on the Field Handbook of Civil Affairs*; Laroque, *Au service*, 172–8.

with his Allied counterparts and prepared a Free French counter-proposal to the handbook.[94] In a strange succession of events, he had become implicated in the political manoeuvres which had mobilized the attention and efforts of the Free French community in London. The foreboding concerning Allied intentions would later prove unfounded, however, as would become apparent during the Allied campaign in Normandy.

Pierre Laroque returned to France in the days following the launch of Operation Overlord. Like the officers he had helped select and train, he was assigned new administrative duties within the newly liberated areas. On 14 June 1944, after arriving in Normandy with General de Gaulle, he assumed the direction of public services in the vicinity.[95] Laroque was now given a mass of contending responsibilities, an assignment which was all the more complicated given the pursuit of military operations in the area. Most importantly, he had to appoint civilian officials and arrange for the distribution of foodstuffs to the local population.[96] The rapid advance of the Allied forces signalled the end of this appointment, and he was reunited with his family and readmitted to the civil service in the autumn of 1944. It was at this time that he was named director of social insurance in the Ministry of Labour of the provisional government of the French republic.[97] Laroque thus resumed a promising career that had been interrupted by the Vichy regime, and the stage was now set for his most enduring contribution to the development of French social policy.

CONCLUSION

Pierre Laroque's involvement with the Vichy regime might have been short-lived, but it proved significant for a variety of reasons. While he had grown weary of the potential of corporatism to transform social relations and promote social solidarity, his recruitment by René Belin forced him to revisit the question, albeit in a radically transformed social and political climate. Belin might have been committed to a syndicalist variant of corporatism, but his initiatives were wedded to an anti-democratic and anti-republican political agenda, in marked contrast to Laroque's one-time support for a democratic variant of corporatism. In any case, the corporatist proposals submitted by the Ministry of Labour provoked prolonged

---

[94] Laroque, *Au service*, 176–9.
[95] Ibid. 183–9.
[96] Ibid. 185.
[97] Ibid. 191–2; *Témoignage* Laroque.

internal debates, thus highlighting the ideological contradictions of the French government.

During this period, Laroque also became involved in an attempt to reform the social insurance system, an effort which owed much to the work of Francis Netter, an actuary who would become one of his key subordinates in the aftermath of the Liberation. The Ministry of Labour was committed to streamlining its administrative structure and reviewing the financial basis of its benefits programmes. Its proposals faced internal and external opposition, and these critics employed arguments that evoked both the rhetoric of the mutual aid societies as well as the decentralizing objectives associated with the National Revolution. Furthermore, the redistributive aspects of the plan found little echo among those who exhibited paternalistic attitudes towards the working class. In 1942, Belin would revisit the issue of social insurance, and this second attempt at reform achieved a similar result. These failures demonstrated that the overhaul of the system was a difficult undertaking, and that it required a great deal of political resolve in light of the pressures exerted by the concerned interest groups.

After his expulsion from the civil service, Laroque found employment in the private sector and soon became involved with the Resistance and Free French movement. While he remained interested in social and economic policy, as confirmed by his participation in the activities of the CGE, his contribution to the struggle against Vichy and the Axis powers would soon take a new direction. By 1943, he had arrived in London to take up new responsibilities with the CFLN, and he became involved in training the personnel who were to administer public services in a liberated France. The assignment placed Laroque at the centre of the political and military intrigues which defined the complicated relationship between the Free French movement and the Anglo-American powers. The recruitment of this administrative cadre served a political purpose since these officers would protect French sovereignty in the midst of a projected Allied invasion of metropolitan France. While these experiences were far removed from the interests that had marked his career as a civil servant and social policy expert, they undoubtedly confirmed the multifaceted nature of his intellectual and administrative abilities.

5

The Genesis of the Laroque Plan
(1944–1945)

As the newly appointed director of social insurance, Pierre Laroque initiated a policy review which culminated in the passing of the social security ordinances of October 1945. The Laroque Plan, as it was called, sought to rationalize the administrative infrastructure of social insurance while incorporating the family allowance and industrial accident programmes into a unified system of benefits. In sharp contrast to the failed initiatives of the Vichy regime, Laroque was able to implement his reformist agenda despite the opposition of various interest groups. The conjunction of a unique set of circumstances made this outcome possible. While the diffusion of the ideals of the Resistance and Free France had created an environment that was receptive to social reform, the appointment of Alexandre Parodi as Minister of Labour also proved decisive, since he came to wield much influence within the provisional government and wholeheartedly supported Laroque's efforts. French social security was a product of Laroque's long-standing critique of the social insurance system, but it also reflected his views concerning the state, society, and social policy. The Laroque Plan was shaped by his belief in a form of state interventionism that provided the means for the participation of the insured in the management of social security. The introduction of a rationalized and decentralized administrative structure served to achieve this purpose, thus making it possible to promote a new sense of social solidarity among those who were to receive its benefits. These ideas proved consistent with Laroque's past work in the fields of administrative law and industrial relations, and social security was meant to serve the solidaristic objectives which he had once conferred upon the professional corporation.

THE LIBERATION: NEW HOPES
AND HARD REALITIES

By the autumn of 1944, the *Gouvernement Provisoire de la République Française*, presided over by General de Gaulle, had assumed the task of governance in liberated France. Most of the country had been liberated by the Allied armies, but much of the national infrastructure had been damaged by the pursuit of military operations on French territory. It was thus incumbent upon the provisional government to provide for the war effort while beginning the process of national reconstruction.[1] While these goals might have seemed reasonable, the government faced budgetary difficulties which made it difficult to pursue these objectives. The problem was best illustrated by its own budgetary projections. On 18 October 1944, the Minister of Finance declared that the operating budget was of 200 billion francs with a deficit estimated at 120 billion francs.[2] These estimates had taken into account new spending commitments, such as the creation of new ministries and the financing of the *Forces Françaises de l'Intérieur*.[3] These budgetary considerations could only constrain the ambitions of French policymakers, and the bureaucrats of the Ministry of Labour were well aware of these harsh financial realities.

The opening of the Western Front had significantly aggravated an already difficult domestic situation. Military operations had adversely affected industrial production, damaged the transportation network, and impeded the distribution of foodstuffs to the civilian population.[4] While most Frenchmen might have celebrated the Liberation, the retreat of the German forces did not lead to an immediate improvement in living standards. During the Occupation, food rations had barely met subsistence levels, while inflation had led to an increase in the cost of living.[5] The problems of the average Frenchman were matched by the lacklustre performance of French industrial production. By April 1945, total industrial output reached only 60 per cent of the level attained in 1938.[6] The persistence of these domestic difficulties, coupled with the disrepute which befell both the Third Republic and the Vichy regime, fuelled an intellectual climate which promoted the diffusion of utopian ideals focusing upon the creation of a new social order.

The idealistic spirit of the Liberation owed much to the legacy of the Resistance and the Free French movement. While their ideas had been rather vague and schematic, they did express a belief in the necessity of social and economic change.[7] The notion of social justice

---

[1] F. Bloch-Lainé and J. Bouvier, *La France restaurée 1944–1954*, 17.

[2] Assemblée Nationale, *p-v de la commission des finances*, 18 October 1944, Lepercq.

[3] Ibid.

[4] R. Kuisel, *Capitalism and the State in Modern France: renovation and economic management in the twentieth century*, 315–16.

[5] A. Sauvy, 'Démographie et économie de la France au printemps 1944', in Comité d'Histoire de la Deuxième Guerre Mondiale, *La Libération de la France*, 291–302.

[6] M. Margairaz, *L'État, les finances et l'économie*, i, 793.

[7] H. Michel, *Les Courants de pensée de la Résistance*, 392–403.

came to permeate the rhetoric of the Resistance and Free France, thus explaining their support for the introduction of reformist policies once the task of national liberation had been completed.[8] The emergence of this reformist discourse was by no means accidental, since it testified to the ideological dimension of the struggle against Vichy and the Axis powers. From 1942 onwards, General de Gaulle made a number of public pronouncements which reflected a heightened awareness of this aspect of the conflict. On 18 June 1942, he declared:

> For France, in particular, where disaster, treason, and opportunism have disqualified many leaders and the privileged, and where the masses of the people have, on the contrary, remained more courageous and loyal, it would be unacceptable that this terrible trial would leave untouched a social and moral regime which has served against the nation. The France that is fighting believes that the final victory should be of benefit to all of her children. Once independence, security, and national greatness have been recovered, she wants liberty, security, and social dignity to be assured to each Frenchman.[9]

The struggle of Free France was identified with the unflinching patriotism of the French masses, and the prospect of social reform was conceived as a reward of sorts for an idealized majority which had been supposedly betrayed by its social, political, and economic elites. As Jean-Louis Crémieux-Brilhac has noted, the reformism of the Free French movement was influenced by different ideological traditions, including Christian democracy and democratic socialism,[10] and it would exert a lasting influence among its veterans, not to mention the leadership of the *Gouvernement Provisoire de la République Française*.

Neither the Resistance nor Free France had developed any comprehensive agenda for the reform of social insurance or the introduction of social security. The work that had been produced before the Liberation was scattered, schematic, and devoid of any influence upon the shaping of the Laroque Plan.[11] The Resistance had looked at the question of social reform, but its efforts did not focus upon the question of social security. The think tank of the Resistance, the *Comité Général d'Études*, had ignored the issue, choosing to focus on other problems, such as the need to increase industrial production and the necessity of preserving monetary

---

[8] Ibid. 744–7; J.-L. Crémieux-Brilhac, *La France Libre: de l'appel du 18 juin àla Liberation*, 369–70.

[9] C. de Gaulle, *Discours et messages*, 204.

[10] Crémieux-Brilhac, *La France Libre*, 372–82.

[11] B. Valat, 'Résistance et sécurité sociale 1941–1944', *Revue Historique*, 292, 2 (1995), 315–46.

stability after the Liberation.[12] When social security was discussed, it represented little more than a wishful afterthought, as confirmed by the fact that it had been one of the last objectives included in the common programme of the *Conseil National de la Résistance*.[13] While this might have illustrated a general lack of interest in the issue, it is also true that the circumstances of wartime had made it difficult to develop any plans concerning this matter. In February 1944, one leading member of the CFLN had declared:

> As an emergency measure, the provisional government should limit itself to validating the legislation which shall exist at the Liberation, with the exception of certain amendments of a political nature ... But it is impossible to develop a French Beveridge plan before the return to France because we do not possess any information concerning the actual situation of French social insurance and most notably on its financial situation. Vichy no longer publishes anything.[14]

These practical considerations made it difficult to develop any comprehensive agenda in the field of social security, and this question could only be addressed after the collapse of the Vichy regime.

There was much support for the principle of social security, but much work had to be done before it could be transformed into a legislative reality. This problem was resolved upon Laroque's return to the Ministry of Labour, since he possessed the expertise required for the task of drafting the relevant legislation, not to mention access to information which had been unavailable to the services of the CFLN.[15] Laroque's appointment as director of social insurance proved all the more significant, since his success in promoting the Laroque Plan owed much to his excellent relationships with both superiors and subordinates. The new director was ideally suited for his new role, and he was able to give substance to the reformist rhetoric of the Resistance and Free France, a somewhat ironic twist of fate given his involvement with the failed policy initiatives of the Vichy regime.

These failures were highly instructive, since they demonstrated that any attempt to reform social insurance required the exertion of sustained political leadership. As we have seen, there had been no indication that Marshal Pétain had been committed to the reform of social insurance, while his aides and senior ministers were hostile to the proposals which had been submitted

[12] Archives Nationales, F1a 3733, CGE report of May 1943; AN F1a 3733, *Les Cahiers politiques*, 4, (1943); *Témoignage* Parodi: oral history interview conducted by the Comité d'histoire de la sécurité sociale.

[13] See C. Andrieu, *Le Programme commun de la résistance*.

[14] AN F60 909, *communication du commissaire des affaires sociales au CFLN, séance du 8 février 1944*.

[15] *Témoignage* Parodi; Netter interview, *Actes du 105ième Congrès National des Sociétés Savantes*, (1980), annex, 231–63 (CHSS).

by the Ministry of Labour in 1940 and 1942. René Belin had failed in light of his relative isolation and lack of influence within the cabinet. In the autumn of 1944, the situation had changed dramatically, and the provisional government would soon demonstrate its resolve in pursuing its own reformist agenda. The Ministry of Labour would play an important role in the coming months, and it would introduce a variety of social and economic reforms during the course of the following year. This newfound influence was by no means accidental, since it owed much to the personality of the minister who had assumed office in the aftermath of the Liberation.

Alexandre Parodi, a leader of the wartime Resistance, had been appointed Minister of Labour by de Gaulle, and his political success owed much to his personal rapport with the founder of the Free French movement. Furthermore, Parodi was ideally suited to his new ministerial responsibilities. A member of the *Conseil d'État,* he had served in the Ministry of Labour and had risen to the post of director of labour and manpower before the outbreak of war.[16] These experiences had made him intimately familiar with the workings of the Ministry, but his success in the civil service paled in comparison with his accomplishments as a leader of the Resistance. Indeed, he was one of the founding members of the CGE and eventually replaced Jean Moulin as de Gaulle's representative before the underground movements.[17] These experiences became the source of much personal prestige, and Parodi had become personally acquainted with de Gaulle. Parodi would later acknowledge that this background accounted for his success at the Ministry of Labour; in his view, it explained the fact that he was able to implement the majority of his proposals during his tenure in office.[18] While these recollections might indeed be accurate, it would be unfair to underestimate the minister's personal abilities. According to his former chief of staff, Parodi proved himself to be an able and effective member of the provisional government.[19] In any case, the achievements of the Ministry of Labour would prove impressive, and it would usher in, a series of important reforms which included the establishment of the *Comités d'entreprise* and the introduction of a new social security system.[20] It should be noted that Parodi was a man of strong ideological convictions, and that these principles influenced his work as Minister of

---

[16] H. Noufflard-Guy-Loé, P. Laroque, O. Raffalovich, J. Cahen-Salvador, et al., *Alexandre Parodi*, 17–23.

[17] Ibid. 48–9; O. de Bellescize, *Les Neufs sages de la résistance*, 57–8.

[18] *Témoignage* Parodi. Laroque and Parodi, in fact, were old friends who were part of the same social and professional circles, see P. Laroque, *Au service de l'homme et du droit: souvenirs et réflexions.*

[19] Noufflard-Gny-Loé et al., *Alexandre Parodi*, 61–70.

[20] Ibid.

Labour. Parodi believed in the ideal of social progress, and this explained his commitment to the pursuit of social justice.[21] These views undoubtedly contributed to the reformist momentum of the period, and they could only encourage Laroque in his attempt to reform the social insurance system.

Pierre Laroque had been exposed to the problems of French social insurance as a member of the *Conseil d'État* and his service on the staffs of ministers such as Adolphe Landry and René Belin. While he might have chosen to focus on other social and economic questions during the course of his pre-war career, he had been well versed in the issues pertaining to social insurance.[22] Indeed, his exposure to the latter had convinced him of the necessity of reforming the system at some later date.[23] The legislation of 1928–1930 had created a complicated system characterized by the chaotic decentralization of its services, a product of the wedding of a compulsory system of benefits with a voluntary network of mutual aid societies. These deficiencies had become apparent during the course of the thirties, and the Ministry of Labour had already attempted to address these difficulties during the early years of the Vichy regime. The failure of these past initiatives had left these questions unresolved, and the intervening years had been marked by the emergence of new challenges.

THE CRISIS OF SOCIAL INSURANCE

By the autumn of 1944, the social insurance system faced new financial difficulties which resulted from the combination of a host of social, political, and administrative developments. The preceding years had witnessed an increase in the disbursement of benefits, but this evolution had not been matched by corresponding adjustments in the levels of revenue required to finance these programmes. These problems had attracted the attention of the Ministry of Labour and the mutual aid societies entrusted with the management of the different social insurance *caisses*. On 6 October 1944, the *Comité Général d'Entente de la Mutualité*, the coordinating body of the latter, sent Parodi a note which outlined their concerns over the financial plight of the system. The CGE stressed that the latter had been characterized by increasing deficits from 1942 onwards, since contributions to the social insurance system had not kept pace with the

---

[21] Noufflard-Guy-Loé etal., *Alexandre Parodi*.

[22] *Témoignage* Laroque.

[23] Laroque, *Supplément au traité des assurances sociales*, 21; *MAS*, Laroque papers, box 50, article on *prévoyance* submitted to the *Encyclopédie Française*, 13.

distribution of benefits.[24] The dilemma was simple and straightforward, and it was imperative to address this financial imbalance. It was in this spirit that the committee suggested an increase in contribution rates, the recourse to a budgetary supplement, and the granting of a delay in the repayment of the system's financial deficit.[25] These proposals represented a logical response to this financial difficulty, and they confirmed the reformist impulse of a Ministry that had already launched a review of the existing legislation.

In September 1944, Laroque had met with Parodi, and he had agreed to become director of social insurance if this entailed the creation of a new social security system.[26] Before embarking on this task, however, it was incumbent upon the new director to evaluate the plight of social insurance. As a result, Francis Netter, the head of actuarial services, was entrusted with the task of examining the financial resources of its various benefits programmes.[27] On 28 October 1944, Netter produced a report which confirmed the dire warnings of the *Comité Général d'Entente de la Mutualité*. Laroque believed that the situation required immediate action, a point which he stressed in his cover letter.[28] He was not oblivious to the difficult economic circumstances of the time, but he was convinced that it was possible to restore the financial equilibrium of the system without imposing a new burden on the budget or the economy.[29] These considerations seemed reasonable, but they had to be understood in the light of the upcoming overhaul of the social insurance system. While Laroque might have favoured taking immediate action to resolve this financial crisis, he viewed it as a preliminary measure which had to be taken before the implementation of social security:

It is possible and perhaps desirable that in the near future the social insurance of wage earners be replaced by a vast system of national insurance extended to the entire population of the country. I am, myself, an advocate of this formula, and I consider that in the current state of affairs this reform implies the stabilization of the finances of social insurance as it exists today and the improvement of the system in order to achieve greater social efficiency. It is in this spirit and in keeping with a more wide-ranging reform in the coming

---

[24] *Fondation Nationale des Sciences Politique*, Parodi Papers, box 17, *Note sur les mesures urgentes à prendre pour rétablir l'équilibre financier des assurances sociales*, 6 October 1944, 4–7.

[25] Ibid. 10–11.

[26] Laroque, *Supplément au Traité des assurances sociales*, 191–2.

[27] Ibid. 213.

[28] FNSP, PP, box 17, covering letter to *Rapport sur la situation financière des assurances sociales*, 28 October 1944, 1.

[29] Ibid.

months that I have put together the report which is submitted to you today.[30]

The reform of social insurance was a foregone conclusion, and Laroque's ultimate objective lay with a universal system of coverage which would replace legislation that benefited wage earners alone.

As we have seen, Francis Netter, the author of the financial review of 28 October 1944, was a career civil servant who had participated in the failed attempts to reform social insurance; furthermore, he had been a member of the SFIO and *X-crise* during the interwar period. The review that he produced provided Laroque and Parodi with a detailed analysis of the financial difficulties of the system, and it estimated that its deficit would exceed the sum of 3 billion 500 million francs for 1944 alone.[31] Short-term strategems had made it possible to deal with this shortfall. For example, both the *caisse générale de garantie* and the *caisses primaires de maladie et maternité* had liquidated their assets to make it possible for them to fulfil their respective obligations.[32] These initiatives provided short-term relief, but they did little to address the underlying problems which had led to this deficit in the first place.

Netter and his team examined the financial history of the different categories of insurable risk, and they determined that it was the health insurance prgramme that had undergone the most sustained growth in spending. Before the war, health insurance spending had cost between 1 billion and 1 billion 500 million francs.[33] The preceding years had led to an explosion in expenditure and spending reached 6.5 billion francs in 1944.[34] A variety of factors explained the increase in health insurance expenditure. According to the report, the law of 6 January 1942 had severed the link between contributions and benefits; according to its guidelines, any individual could claim benefits as long as he had been registered at a labour office for at least three months.[35] The law thus confused social insurance with social assistance, and this called into question the former's ability to maintain its financial viability. The law was not solely responsible for the current predicament; other pressures had also contributed to the increased disbursement of benefits. The preceding years had been characterized by a decline in sanitary conditions, which favoured the outbreak of disease; moreover, there had also been an increase in the national

---

[30] FNSP, PP, box 17, *Rapport*, 28 October 1944, 2.
[31] Ibid. 1.
[32] Ibid.
[33] Ibid. 3–10.
[34] Ibid.
[35] Ibid. *Témoignage* Netter.

birth rate.[36] The growth of expenditure, therefore, was due to questionable legislative practices and the difficult conditions of wartime France, but the problems of social insurance were not limited to the management of the health insurance programme.

The financial resources of old age insurance had been drained by the introduction of a new benefit programme. The *allocation aux vieux travailleurs salariés*, first introduced in March 1941,[37] represented the most problematic component of the social insurance system. A form of assistance and not insurance, the allowance threatened the financial basis of old age insurance, since both allowances and pensions drew on the same financial resources. The review determined that 1,700,000 people received an average benefit of 3,800 francs, and this had cost 6.5 billion francs by 1944.[38] Netter believed that the Ministry of Labour had grossly underestimated the number of people who would qualify for the allowance, and that it was this failure which explained their inability to evaluate its financial cost.[39] Furthermore, an exceedingly generous administration had attributed the allowance to an ever-increasing scope of individuals. The most flagrant abuse was to be found in the agricultural sector, which accounted for 350,000 to 400,000 recipients alone.[40] The decision to distribute the allocation to an ever-increasing number of people, irrespective of their history of personal contributions, had placed much pressure on the financial resources of old age insurance, and it was incumbent on the government to resolve this dilemma.

Netter's financial review provided the Ministry of Labour with potential solutions to the problems of the social insurance system. These measures included the imposition of a contribution rate set at 12 per cent (6 per cent each for workers and employers), the separation of old age allowance from old age insurance, and the attribution of a budgetary subsidy of one billion francs to cover the deficit of social insurance.[41] These proposals ensured that the system would remain largely self-financing, and the budgetary contribution was merely a short-term measure to provide some immediate relief for its depleted resources. Netter, moreover, suggested that an increase in the rates of contribution imposed on employers and wage earners would not impose an excessive burden on

---

[36] FNSP, PP, box 17, *Rapport*.

[37] Law of 14 March 1941, *allocation aux vieux travailleurs salariés*, in P. Leclerc, *La Sécurité sociale: son histoire à travers les textes, Tome II (1870–1945)*, 695–9.

[38] FNSP, PP, box 17, *Rapport*, 14–34.

[39] Ibid. Officials had expected between 1,250,000 and 1,300,000 beneficiaries.

[40] Ibid.

[41] Ibid. 34.

the economy, given the state of current economic projections.[42] Within the following months, the main recommendations of the review would be passed into law, a reflection of the influence wielded by Nettei and Laroque in the area of social policy. On 30 December 1944, two ordinances increased the contribution to 12 per cent while instituting a separate 4 per cent tax, paid by employers alone, for the financing of an old age allowance which was no longer dependent upon the funds of old age insurance.[43] These measures provided the social insurance system with financial relief, and Laroque was now free to pursue the development of the Laroque Plan.

TOWARDS SOCIAL SECURITY

Pierre Laroque, a veteran of the Resistance and Free France, was not immune to the utopian aspects of their wartime rhetoric. Notwithstanding his background as a civil servant and social policy expert, his conception of social security bore the imprint of the idealistic spirit of the Liberation. In January 1946, Laroque declared that social security would establish the foundations of a new social and economic order:

> France has emerged from the war in a particularly difficult situation. The old frames of reference are broken; one must rebuild, one must innovate in the social field, as is the case in the economic field. And it is within the framework of a new collective effort for the construction of a new social order that our social security plan must be considered. This new social order, we consider that it is the result of ideas which make a clean break with the past, erasing the defects of a foregone system, and based on an entirely new set of principles.[44]

The introduction of a new social security system was symptomatic of a desire to transform France, an agenda which reiterated the language of the Resistance and Free France. Of course, Laroque had long sought to transform social relations, as had been demonstrated by his one-time support for the corporatist management of industrial relations. At this time, however, the political climate seemed all the more conducive to the pursuit of an ambitious agenda for social reform.

---

[42] FNSP, PP, box 17, 33 and 35.

[43] *Journal Officiel*, 30 December 1944, 2197–8. B. Valat, *Histoire de la sécurité sociale (1945–1967)*, 48–9.

[44] Laroque, presentation delivered before the *Centre National d'Information Économique*, 10 January 1946, quoted in A. Barjot, *La Sécurité sociale: son histoire à travers les textes, Tome III, 1945–1981*, 14.

Laroque had long been convinced of the necessity of reforming social insurance, and his return to the Ministry of Labour provided him with a unique opportunity to develop and implement his ideas on the matter. After his expulsion from the civil service, his work for the Resistance and the Free French movements did not deal with the issues of social insurance or social security, but he remained attuned to international developments in the field of social policy. During his stay in London, he became familiar with the substance of the Beveridge Report, a study which called for the establishment of a comprehensive and universal system of social insurance within the United Kingdom.[45] Published in 1942, the report had benefited from widespread publicity, and it is therefore unsurprising that Laroque had become familiar with its content. There is no evidence, however, that it served as a blueprint for the policy review which had been initiated in the autumn of 1944. Beveridge had focused on the question of British social services, and any influence that he may have exerted would have been of a general nature. The significance of the Beveridge Report lay with the fact that it had advocated an extensive system of social benefits which would be matched by an ambitious set of interventionist economic policies.[46] Both Parodi and Laroque shared a similar outlook, and the Laroque Plan was associated with a new and expansive role for the state, thus marking a break from state minimalism and the principles of laissez-faire.

French social security was conceived as part of a wider set of public policies, a point which Laroque made clear in January 1945:

> Social security is one element of a wider policy, including: the guarantee to all to find paid employment, thus full employment and the elimination of unemployment; a wage providing the means for subsistence of the individual and of his family in decent conditions; security of employment, thus a guarantee against the arbitrary decisions of his employers in the matter of hiring and firing; medical coverage permitting the protection of one's physical and intellectual integrity, and, more importantly, the prevention of illness and invalidity, notably through hygiene and workplace safety; finally, in all cases when a worker or his family find themselves deprived of all or part of the benefits of work by virtue of unemployment, illness, maternity, invalidity, old age, or sees its living standards diminished by the presence of young children in the home, the attribution of substitute or replacement revenue.[47]

---

[45] Valat, *Histoire de la sécurité sociale*, 51.

[46] J. F. Harris, *Sir William Beveridge: a biography*. See also: Sir William Beveridge, *Social Insurance and Allied Services*, and *Full Employment in a Free Society*.

[47] Laroque, *Au service*, 198. Laroque mentions that his ideas were outlined in a speech delivered on 23 March 1945 as well as in the texts of the ordinances of October 1945. The

These ambitions went far beyond the scope of social insurance, since the establishment of social security was associated with the promotion of public health and the provision of full employment.

In February 1945, Laroque published an article in *La Santé de l'Homme*, and its content outlined the guiding principles of his work to a public audience.[48] The article showcased his extensive knowledge of social policy and reiterated his belief that it was necessary to reform the social insurance system. In Larqoue's view, the latter was exceedingly complex, and its management left much to be desired; by the outbreak of the war, in fact, it had already been clear that the system was ripe for change.[49] Laroque thus remained committed to the recommendations that he had made in his pre-war writings. It was also true, however, that recent financial difficulties further justified the overhaul of the existing legislation.[50] These observations might well have been justified, but the article's most interesting point lay with its consideration of the role which the insured were supposed to play in the management of the social security system.

Laroque focused upon the cultural and psychological dimensions of social policy, concerns which translated into his support for public participation in the administration of the relevant services. In the post-war era, social security would replace the corporation as the chosen vehicle for the promotion of social solidarity. The participation of the insured was deemed essential to the success of the administrative structures of social security:

> They must be a living institution renewing itself through continuous creation, by the effort of the concerned, involved in the management of the system. The education of the insured must be assured. It is a task of first importance. Its completion is essential, to a large extent, to the renewal of social insurance as well as its moral and social effectiveness.[51]

By combining income support with a mechanism for public participation, Laroque sought to address the economic insecurity of the working class while providing it with a new sense of independence and self-worth, objectives which had defined his thought during the thirties.

excerpt from his memoirs reproduces, verbatim, the content of a note which Laroque had submitted to Parodi in January 1945, see FNSP, Parodi Papers, box 18, *note pour M. le Ministre*, 21 January 1945.

[48] Laroque, 'L'Avenir des assurances sociales françaises', *La Santé de L'Homme*, 28 (1945), 25–8.

[49] Ibid. 25.

[50] Ibid.

[51] Ibid. 28.

The Laroque Plan, it would seem, had also been inspired by the Czechoslovak social insurance system, though it is difficult to ascertain the nature of this influence. According to the recollections of Professor Philippe-Jean Hesse, Laroque would later acknowledge this fact, but the existing archives do not provide the means of confirming this claim in any definite manner.[52] Nevertheless, this recollection does provide a plausible, if altogether partial explanation of the context in which the Laroque Plan was developed. Before the war, Laroque had been well acquainted with domestic and international developments in the field of social insurance, and his knowledge of the Czechoslovak system might have arisen out of his consultation of the studies published by the International Labour Office.[53] Moreover, his extensive network of personal contacts matched the scope of his interests in the area of social policy. In 1938, he was corresponding with the director of Czechoslovakia's health insurance system; the latter had invited him to submit an article to an upcoming publication, an offer Laroque appears to have accepted, though this cannot be confirmed.[54] While this correspondence does not provide us with any indication of his attitude towards the Czechoslovak model of social insurance, it is interesting in light of other indications of a possible Czechoslovak angle to the development of social security.

In February 1946, Alfred Costes, a Communist member of the *Assemblée Nationale Constituante*, openly linked the Laroque Plan with the Czechoslovak social insurance system. Speaking in defence of the *caisse unique*, Costes stressed that the latter would encourage public participation while improving administrative efficiency; he argued that the *caisse unique* was based upon the administrative structure of the Czechoslovak system, which, he claimed, had been the most advanced model of social insurance of interwar Europe.[55] A vocal proponent of social security, Costes was anything but a neophyte when it came to the issue of social policy. During the first Blum government, he had served as president of the labour commission of the Chamber of Deputies and had organized a trip to Czechoslovakia; upon its return, the members of the parliamentary delegation had reported their approval of the Czechoslovak system's wide scope of eligibility and the methodical concentration of its services.[56] These experiences provided Costes with a degree of credibility when it came to the matter of social security, and they also suggest that his comments

<hr>

[52] Conversation with Professor P.-J. Hesse, 9 December 1998.

[53] MAS, LP, box 66, book reviews for the *Revue Française des Sciences Politiques* in both 1933 and 1936.

[54] MAS, LP, box 140, letters from Dr J. Pleskot, 21 July and 1 September 1938.

[55] AN, C 15293, *p-v de la commission du travail*, 14 February 1946, Costes.

[56] AN, C 15166, *p-v de la commission du travail*, 3 June 1937, Perrin.

might have had some basis in fact. Such testimony can only lead to the conclusion that the Laroque Plan might well have been inspired by the Czechoslovak experience, though the exact nature of this influence can only be the subject of speculation.

The Czechoslovak model probably demonstrated that it was possible to rationalize the administrative infrastructure associated with the social insurance legislation of 1928–1930. During the interwar period, Czechoslovakia had streamlined its bureaucracy and increased the coordination between its various services.[57] These initiatives stood in marked contrast to the chaotic organization of French social insurance, and they made it possible to maintain the decentralization of services while making it easier for the authorities to maintain control of their activities. Despite these changes, the regional social insurance *caisses* did not become the passive intermediaries of government directives; indeed, they played a key role in the orchestration of public health campaigns at the local level.[58] In brief, the Czechoslovak experience had demonstrated that administrative reform need not necessarily entail the wholesale centralization of services. These lessons were to be incorporated into the Laroque Plan, as illustrated by the *caisse unique*, the lynchpin of the proposed social security system.

While Laroque sought to simplify the bureaucratic infrastructure of the social insurance system, he was also determined to pursue the logic of administrative rationalization beyond the confines of social insurance. Indeed, he sought to incorporate other benefit schemes into an expanded social security system. These ambitions centred on family allowances and industrial accident insurance, programmes which came under the purview of distinct legislation and were defined by the proliferation of structures and services.[59] The coexistence of these separate systems had created a complicated bureaucratic environment that made it difficult to coordinate similar benefit programmes.

The Laroque Plan was developed during a prolonged consultation process. While those consulted voiced their support for the principle of social security, they were divided as to the projected structure of the system. The CGT was loudest in its support of the government's plans, while the *Confédération Française des Travailleurs Chrétiens* and the mutual aid societies were strongly opposed to the prospect of administrative rationalization. The *caisse unique*, which was to administer all benefits in a given geographic unit, elicited the opposition of those who managed the existing network of social insurance *caisses*. For these dissenting voices, the

---

[57] E. Stern (ed.), *Les Assurances sociales en Tchécoslovaquie*, 6–7.
[58] Ibid. 134.
[59] Laroque, *Au service*, 214.

Ministry of Labour was engaged in an authoritarian project that would result in the establishment of a gigantic bureaucratic apparatus. The integration of social insurance, family allowances, and industrial accident insurance into an expanded system provoked additional criticism because certain observers were concerned about the impact of the unification of these programmes. These concerns were most dearly felt by the representatives of natalist opinion, and they would find a receptive ear within the councils of the provisional government.

In June 1945, Parodi established a special consultative commission which was entrusted with the task of examining the Laroque Plan. The members of the Délepine commission, named for the civil servant who presided over its deliberations, included representatives of politics, business, the unions, and the mutual aid societies.[60] It rapidly became apparent that it was the *caisse unique* that provoked the most controversy among the commission's members. The mutual aid societies were particularly aggrieved and they defended the right of the insured to affiliate with the *caisse* of their choice.[61] The societies were defending their own interests, as they had done in response to previous efforts to reform social insurance. The CGT, on the other hand, proved supportive of the government's plans.[62] While the Délepine commission's deliberations only served a consultative purpose, its recommendations illustrated the intractable nature of the debate concerning the *caisse unique*. The commission rejected the administration's proposals by a majority of one vote, with the representatives of the CGT and the Ministry of Labour voting with the dissenting minority.[63] Nevertheless, the commission could not prevent the government from pursuing its objectives, a result which called into question the relevance of the consultative process.

During this time, the provisional government discarded the proposal to integrate family allowances into the social security system. The allowance scheme had long been the subject of a general consensus, and it touched upon a sensitive political issue, namely the problem of demographic decline. On 19 June 1945, the *Haut Comité de La Population et de la Famille*, a consultative body which advised the government on family policy, argued that it was necessary to keep family allowances separate from social security, though it stressed that it was not opposed to the coordination of these benefit programmes.[64] The committee believed that unification

---

[60] Barjot, *La Sécurité sociale*, 19.
[61] Ibid. 20.
[62] Ibid. 23; Valat, *Histoire de la sécurité sociale*, 66–75.
[63] Ibid. 23; Valat, 11, 66–75.
[64] FNSP, PP, box 17, decision of the *Haut Comité de la Population et de la Famille*, 19 June 1945.

threatened the integrity and efficiency of the family allowance system. In its view, the incorporation of family allowances into an expanded social security system would force them to compete for the same financial resources, potentially undercutting their ability to achieve their objectives.[65] These fears found a receptive ear within the government. Laroque would later claim that it was de Gaulle who had vetoed their prospective integration.[66] While nothing is known about the reasoning behind this decision, it is probable that the head of the provisional government was receptive to the arguments presented by the *Haut Comité de la Population*.

In July, the Ministry of Labour presented its social security plan to the members of the *Assemblée Consultative Provisoire*. The latter examined its statement of principles, but the assembly was devoid of legislative power and was thus incapable of preventing the government from proceeding with its project.[67] Nevertheless, its deliberations were important because they provided a public platform for the discussion of the Laroque Plan. The *demande d'avis* submitted by the government mentioned the incorporation of industrial accident insurance within social security, the creation of a new administrative network of regional *caisses*, the management of the latter by the representatives of the existing *syndicats*, and the imposition of a single contribution which would finance the coverage of all insurable risks.[68] At the same time, the *demande d'avis* reflected Laroque's underlying views concerning the nature of social conflict and the purpose of social policy:

> Social security is a guarantee given to all that in all circumstances they will have the means necessary to insure in decent conditions their subsistence and that of their family. Finding its justification in the fundamental concept of social justice, it is a response to workers' uncertainties about the future, of the constant uncertainties which create among them a sense of inferiority which is the real and deep-seated basis of the distinction between classes, between the owners, sure of themselves and their future, and the workers, upon which the menace of poverty weighs at every moment.[69]

The last sentence evoked the theory of social behaviour which Laroque had first presented in *Les Rapports entre patrons et ouvriers*. Laroque had long believed that social relations were driven by the collective manifest-

[65] AN, CAC 860269, letter from Dr Monsaingeon, 15 June 1945.

[66] Laroque, *Au service*, 214. AN, F 60/646, *note sur le projet d'organisation de la sécurité sociale*, 7 August 1945, 1. This decision was approved by the cabinet.

[67] E. Choisnel, *L'Assemblée Consultative Provisoire (1943–1945): le sursaut républicain*, 15.

[68] Barjot, *La Sécurité Sociale*, 24–5.

[69] FNSP, PP, box 17, *Projet de demande d'avis sur une réforme de la sécurité sociale*, 1.

ation of underlying cultural and psychological factors. While he had once believed that corporatism could address these problems, namely through the participation of the workers in the management of the collective bargaining process, this task would now be entrusted to the *caisse unique*, since the insured were to participate in the management of these new administrative structures.[70] The insured would not be the passive recipients of social benefits, and their participation in the administration of the social security system would provide them with a new sense of their independence and self-worth, thus addressing the psychological dimension of these social tensions.

The Laroque Plan, however, was not without its contradictions. One might have thought that the management structure of the *caisses* would provide for the election of those who were supposed to represent the insured, but the *demande d'avis* did not include an electoral mechanism. The Ministry of Labour opted for the delegation of representatives from existing labour and management organizations.[71] Public participation was to be exercised in an indirect manner, and the system was tilted in favour of the *syndicats*. Indeed, two thirds of the administrative boards of the *caisses* were to be filled by the representatives of organized labour.[72] Different explanations have been offered in order to account for the rejection of an elective system. A report produced by the Ministry of Labour outlined the risk of electoral absenteeism as well as the difficulties related to the establishment of such a process; Laroque would later argue that it would have been impossible to provide electoral lists for the administrative boards of the *caisses* in the midst of upcoming elections to the *Assemblée Nationale Constituante*.[73] These explanations seem reasonable, but they do not mitigate the paradoxical character of a social security system which aimed to promote public participation without providing for the election of the representatives of the insured. Within a year, however, legislators would approve the introduction of an elective system which had been rejected by the Ministry of Labour.[74]

The government's main challenge lay with the persistence of opposition to the proposed *caisse unique*. The Ministry of Labour was not oblivious to this controversy, but Laroque was convinced that the exist-

---

[70] FNSP, PP, box 17, *Rapport sur le projet d'ordonnance portant organization de la sécurité sociale*, 6–7.

[71] Barjot, *La Sécurité sociale*.

[72] Ibid.

[73] FNSP, PP, box 17, *Rapport*, 9–10; *Témoignage* Laroque.

[74] P. V. Dutton, *Origins of the French Welfare State: the struggle for social reform in France, 1914–1947*, 215.

ing administrative network was needlessly complicated and inefficient because it led to the proliferation of overlapping services.[75] In fact, many of the existing *caisses* had sought to coordinate their activities in response to this organizational confusion. In some areas, *comités d'entente* coordinated the services of *caisses* within a given geographic area, an initiative which greatly improved the efficiency of those who participated in it.[76] These practices confirmed his appraisal of the system, and similar observations could be made concerning the administration of the family allowance and industrial accident insurance programmes. Both were characterized by a complex organizational structure, and this had resulted in a hotchpotch of different benefit and contribution rates. Laroque noted, for example, that it was private insurance companies that ensured the coverage of industrial accidents, and the competition between these companies failed to guarantee the uniform coverage of risk.[77] These inefficiencies had to be addressed if one wanted to ensure a uniform scope of coverage for all of the insured.

On 11 July 1945, Alexandre Parodi went before the labour commission of the *Assemblée Consultative Provisoire* and presented the rationale which explained the development of the Laroque Plan. According to Parodi, social security was part of an attempt to transform the environment of the workplace, an objective which reflected the reformist rhetoric of the time.[78] He acknowledged, moreover, that social security had aroused the opposition of important interests, and he admitted that it was the outbreak of this controversy which had led to the *demande d'avis*.[79] Parodi also discussed the reasoning behind the *caisse unique*. The latter would reduce operating costs and concentrate services, changes that would increase the efficiency of the social security system.[80] While these arguments were relatively straightforward, they would never convince those who were desperate to protect their own institutional interests.

Parodi convened a press conference the same day, and his statement further elaborated upon his conception of social security:

> What does it represent? It is a term which is in fashion as a result of a plan that was created in England, the Beveridge Plan, and it has attracted attention to this issue in a striking manner. A complete social security plan embraces a whole series of things, notably measures to insure full employment and avoid unemployment. It is a set of measures which is consistent with these ideas and which includes economic policy, because employment is

---

[75] FNSP, PP, box 17, *Rapport*, 4–6.
[76] Ibid.   [77] Ibid.
[78] Ass. Nat., *p-v de la commission du travail*, 11 July 1945, Parodi.
[79] Ibid.   [80] Ibid.

dependent upon economic activity. Social security is, on the other hand, the set of measures that one can consider to deal with the risks incurred by the worker.[81]

French social security could not be divorced from the pursuit of full employment policies by an interventionist state, a position which effectively reiterated what Laroque had outlined in the internal note he had submitted the previous January.

A week later, the *Comité Général d'Entente* offered a rebuttal to the claims made by the minister. Its secretary general stated that most of their members were hostile to the reform; the government threatened the flexibility of the system by confusing the exercise of supervisory control with the actual administration of the *caisses*.[82] The spectre of bureaucratization was invoked in order to defend the pluralism of the existing administrative structure. Despite the decentralizing objectives of the Laroque Plan, the mutual aid societies viewed the reform as an exercise in state paternalism and centralization, a critique which reiterated the arguments which had been made against Cahen-Salvador's social insurance proposals two decades before.

According to another member of the delegation, the social security plan was symptomatic of a passing fashion in public policy, suggesting that it was the pet project of bureaucrats who had become fascinated with the Beveridge Report.[83] The claim was not far-fetched, even if it overstated the latter's relevance. Francis Netter would later recall that the Beveridge Report had made it fashionable to pursue the systematization and expansion of existing social programmes.[84] Sir William Beveridge had set a new standard for social policy, and it might have impressed French policymakers but it did not necessarily influence the substance of their proposals.

The members of the delegation believed that the provisional government was proceeding in an authoritarian manner, and they stressed that it was essential for the government to take heed of the concerns of those who would be affected by the Laroque Plan.[85] There was some truth to this argument, given the fact that the provisional government exercised exceptional legislative and executive powers. It was merely consulting the *Assemblée Consultative Provisoire*, and ultimate authority on the matter of social security lay in its hands. These powers did not ensure the ultimate success of its proposals,

---

[81] FNSP, PP, box 18, press conference, 11 July 1945.
[82] Ass. Nat., *p-v de la commission du travail*, 18 July 1945, Degas. During its May congress, the FNMF had passed a motion which voiced its hostility to the project. See B. Gibaud, *De la mutualité à la sécurité sociale: conflits et convergences*, 129.
[83] Ibid.
[84] *Témoignage* Netter.
[85] Ass. Nat., *p-v de la commission du travail*, 18 July 1945, André.

since the Ministry of Labour had been forced to abandon its attempts to reform social insurance during the Vichy regime. At this point, however, the government was committed to pursuing this policy and this resolve resulted in an altogether different political outcome.

The *Assemblée Consultative Provisoire* began its deliberations at the end of July 1945, and these debates confirmed the divide between the supporters and the opponents of the Laroque Plan. The CGT remained steadfast in its support for the reform. Georges Buisson, the CGT spokesman on social insurance matters, presented the labour commission's report to the members of the assembly. The commission supported the government's project, but Buisson expressed personal disappointment at the fact that family allowances would not be incorporated into the social security system.[86] These comments reflected the position of the CGT. During his service as a member of the Délepine commission and the *Assemblée Consultative Provisoire*, Buisson had emerged as the most dependable ally of the Ministry of Labour.[87] Throughout the coming years, the CGT would become a leading advocate of social security, support which proved invaluable because the confederation was the largest trade union organization in France.

The CFTC represented a different constituency, and it was altogether hostile to the introduction of the *caisse unique*. Catholic organizations had established a network of *caisses* delivering social insurance and family allowance benefits before the war; Gaston Tessier, the secretary general of the confederation, had served as president of the *Union des Caisses Familiales des Assurances Sociales*.[88] It came as no surprise that the CFTC was eager to defend the existing social insurance system, and Tessier largely reiterated the position espoused by the mutual aid societies. Responding to Buisson's presentation, he argued that the government's proposals threatened a pluralistic administrative structure which was synonymous with liberty.[89] The structure of social insurance was presented as a bulwark against excessive bureaucratization and state paternalism. Tessier, moreover, sought to discredit the Laroque Plan by associating it with the ideas promoted in Vichy-ite and collaborationist circles.[90] Of course, these accusations had some basis in fact, as illustrated by Belin's failed policy initiatives. These arguments fell on deaf ears, and

[86] *Journal Officiel*, no. 68, 1 August 1945, first session of Tuesday 31 July 1945, p. 1675.
[87] Barjot, *La Sécurité sociale*; Ass. Nat., 94001, *p-v de la commission du travail*, 29 June 1945, Buisson.
[88] CFTC, boxes 4h 112 and 113.
[89] *Journal Officiel*, 1687–1689.
[90] Ibid.

the *Assemblée Consultative Provisoire* would pronounce itself in favour of the government's project.

The final vote took place on 1 August 1945, and the result was a victory for the advocates of social security. Though many members chose to abstain from voting, as did the representatives of the CFTC, the final tally was indeed impressive, with 194 members voting in support of the measure with only one dissenting voice.[91] The resulting *avis*, however, did not simply reiterate the position of the Ministry of Labour. Interestingly enough, the assembly called for the integration of family allowances into the social security system, thus rejecting the amendments which had been made by the government.[92] Notwithstanding this difference, a representative cross section of public opinion had pronounced itself in favour of one of the most important reforms of the period. Once this hurdle had been passed, it was possible for Laroque to translate his principles into legislation, an objective which was to be achieved with the publication of the ordinances of 4 October and 19 October 1945.[93] These ordinances established the framework of the new social security system, and the latter was to be set up over the coming months.

For Alexandre Parodi, social security was an instrument of positive liberty which would contribute to the emancipation of the working class. On 22 September 1945, Parodi would declare:

> France is emerging from the ordeal of five years of war and occupation. She is trying, in all fields, to re-establish the freedoms for which so many of her sons gave their lives. She wants to go further and extend these freedoms in social affairs. In this area, freedom takes on an aspect and has requirements that it does not have or that it has to a lesser extent in other areas. The independence of the worker exists to the extent that it is insured by legislation that regulates his working conditions. It is also related to legislation that shields him from those risks which are common to all men, but which become catastrophes for those who depend on their wages and have no savings.[94]

The revival of a republican form of politics did not entail a return to the policies of the interwar period, but it signalled the rise of a new consensus that promoted new social rights which built upon the solidarist legacy of the early twentieth century.

---

[91] Barjot, *La Sécuritié sociale*, 33.

[92] Ibid. 33–7. See article 2 of the *Avis sur le projet d'organisation de la sécurité sociale*. The ordinances of October 1945 would not integrate family allowances into social security, though the management of its system would be closely coordinated with that of social security.

[93] Ibid. 37–44, 53–60.

[94] FNSP, PP, box 18, untitled document, 22 September 1945. This was the text of a speech which was broadcast on the radio.

The ordinance of 4 October 1945 confirmed the substance of Laroque's ideas concerning the necessity of rationalizing existing benefits and structures. The bureaucratic infrastructure of the social security system was centred upon three categories of *caisses*: the *caisse nationale*, the *caisses primaires*, and *the caisses régionales*.[95] The *caisse nationale* was responsible for administering the funds of the system as a whole, while the *caisses primaires* and *régionales* were involved in the management of different forms of insurable risk, the former dealing with health related benefits and the latter were entrusted with the management of the remaining programmes.[96] The network of *caisses primaires* and *régionales* took the place of the pluralistic administrative infrastructure of the social insurance system. The insured would not be affiliated with the *caisse* of their choice, and were to receive benefits from the *caisses* assigned to a specific geographical location.[97] The ordinance also provided for the establishment of *conseils d'administration* which would provide the means for the participation of the insured in the management of the *caisses primaires* and *régionales*. The *syndicats* would name two thirds of the members of the *conseils* of the *caisses primaires*, while a majority of the members of the *conseils* of the *caisses régionales* were also to be selected from among the representatives of organized labour.[98] As a result, the *syndicats* were given a pre-eminent role in the management of social security, a choice which was consistent with the social objectives of the Laroque Plan.

While the ordinance of 4 October 1945 led to the implementation of the *caisse unique*, the ordinance of 19 October 1945 was concerned with the increase in the level of benefits pertaining to health and old age insurance; it also increased the number of insured who might benefit from this coverage.[99] The main innovations of the ordinance lay with its treatment of those who might qualify for health insurance. According to its guidelines, the coverage of medical treatment could be extended for a period of three years if the health of the insured had not significantly improved, but it was also possible for coverage to be extended beyond this three-year limit, if the treatment made it possible for the insured to remain employed.[100] These measures were well adapted to those who suffered from chronic or long-term illness. The ordinance of 19 October 1945 was also notable for its review of old age insurance, since it substituted the redistribution of contributions for the capitalization of accumulated financial resources.[101] Those who were gainfully employed would fund the pensions of the elderly and could become eligible for benefits at the age of 60. After 30 years of contributions, the insured could qualify for benefits

[95] Barjot, *La Sécurité sociale*, 37–9.   [96] Ibid.   [97] Ibid. 37.
[98] Ibid. 38.   [99] Ibid. 53–60.   [100] Ibid. 56–7.   [101] Ibid. 59.

equivalent to 20 per cent of the wages that they had earned during the last ten years of their professional life.[102] The redistribution of resources greatly simplified the task of the social security system, but its ultimate success would be contingent upon the ability of the workforce to continue funding the pension system over the long term.

THE AMBIGUITIES OF A CONSENSUS

While the issue of social security had been included in the common programme of the CNR, the debate concerning social security did not attract the attention of the wider public. The deliberations of the *Assemblée Consultative Provisoire* did not detract from the fact that the Laroque Plan had only sparked the interest of a relatively small circle of policymakers and concerned interest groups. Though support for the concept was universal among the political elites of post-Liberation France, few had bothered to consider how this principle might be given a legislative form. Various proposals were developed by the members of the Constituent Assembly and resolutions were drafted by the socialist Albert Gazier and the Christian syndicalist Gaston Tessier, but these proved to be as vague as the political consensus which supported the principle of social security.[103] Those who were actually interested in social policy were divided as to the structure of social security, and this had been confirmed by the consultations which had taken place during the summer of 1945.

The relative indifference of the public can be gauged by the media's coverage of social insurance and social security during the post-Liberation period. While the press paid attention to the initiatives of the Ministry of Labour, its treatment of these questions was lacklustre at best. Newspaper articles were of a cursory nature, and they were usually relegated to the back pages.[104] Oddly enough, this lack of interest seemed to be shared by those who supported the principle of social security. In 1944, the CGT paid little attention to the reform of social insurance. It first raised the issue of social insurance in an article concerning the financial crisis

---

[102] Ibid.

[103] OURS, Albert Gazier papers. *Confédération Française Démocratique du Travail,* CFTC, box 4h 113. These include copies of both draft resolutions. The former, drafted by the Socialists, advocated the introduction of a national social insurance service.

[104] FNSP, PP, box 18, analyses of the press conferences of 4 January 1945 and 11 July 1945. The latter report noted that 13 out of 18 dailies had 'largely' reproduced the minister's statements. An actual review of the mentioned papers reveals, however, that the articles were extremely limited in length and often relegated to the back pages.

bequeathed by the Vichy regime.[105] The leadership of the Confederation addressed the financial problems of the system in mid-November, when the *Bureau Confédéral* called upon the provisional government to address this problem.[106] The delayed response of the CGT reflected the fact that it was preoccupied by other social and economic priorities, an attitude which was ironic given its subsequent role as a leading advocate of post-war social security.

The parties and *syndicats* which claimed to represent working class opinion chose to focus on the task of national reconstruction, and this contributed to the marginalization of the social security issue. Most notably, the *Parti Communiste Français* and the CGT focused upon the 'battle of production', a campaign to revitalize industrial production, and this limited the scope of their demands during this period.[107] The focus on industrial production was a necessity for a country which had to rebuild its infrastructure while pursuing its military effort against Nazi Germany. Furthermore, the reformist spirit of the Liberation was characterized by an obsessive focus on the nationalization of industry, and this became the leitmotif of the public discourse.[108] Paradoxically enough, the development of the Laroque Plan was a product of the same political environment, but the lack of public interest in the issue did not detract from its historical importance.

CONCLUSION

French social security was conceived in a unique political environment, and it was the conjunction of an exceptional set of circumstances which led to its implementation in 1945. The rhetoric of the Resistance and the Free French movement made social reform fashionable, and de Gaulle's provisional government was committed to the renewal of the social and economic institutions of post-Liberation France. Laroque developed the government's project and he benefited from the influence that Parodi wielded within a quasi-authoritarian provisional government. Unlike previous governments, it pursued its objectives despite the opposition,

[105] *Le Peuple*, 30 September 1944.

[106] Ibid. 25 November 1944.

[107] F. Bloch-Lainé and J. Bouvier, *La France restaurée 1944–1954*, 115; B. Frachon, *La Bataille de la production. Nouvelle étape du combat contre les trusts*. Frachon was a Communist *syndicaliste* who became one of the leaders of the post-Liberation CGT.

[108] R. Kuisel, *Le Capitalisme et l'État en France*, 271–314; B. Frachon, *Au rythme des jours, tome premier: 1944–1954*. Social security is not even mentioned in this collection of Frachon's writings and speeches.

though it eventually abandoned its plans to integrate family allowances into a unified administrative structure.

The Laroque Plan was conceived in light of the deficiencies of the social insurance system, and Laroque had been made aware of these problems during the early thirties. The case for reform was a straightforward one, given the chaotic form of decentralization which had been associated with the legislation of 1928–1930. The introduction of the *caisse unique* was meant to address this issue, while the integration of other programmes, like family allowances or industrial accident insurance, served a more ambitious objective, namely the creation of an expanded system of coverage which would cover the entire population of postwar France.

In Laroque's mind, the creation of a universal social security system was not an objective in and of itself, since it represented the means for promoting a new climate of social solidarity in post-war France. French social security would empower the insured by virtue of their participation in the *conseils d'administration* of its *caisses*. Participation in the management of social security was supposed to provide workers with a new sense of their independence and self-worth, thus addressing the underlying cultural and psychological causes of existing social tensions. It remained to be seen whether social security would achieve these objectives, and the relative indifference of the population called into question its ability to transform social relations. The Laroque Plan might have been based upon a practical consideration of various technical and administrative problems, but it also reflected Pierre Laroque's utopian aspirations concerning the impact of the new social security system.

6

The Failure of Universalism
(1946–1948)

From October 1945 onwards, the introduction of a universal social security system seemed to be a foregone conclusion. By 1947, however, the Ministry of Labour was forced to back down from its attempt to extend old age insurance system in light of a public revolt against the pursuit of this policy. *Cadres*, artisans, and business owners were united in their opposition to the expansion of the social security system because they believed that it would impose new financial burdens without providing them with any corresponding advantages. These groups rejected solidarist arguments, and they objected to the universalization of old age insurance because it entailed the redistribution of their income to the less fortunate members of society. Despite Laroque's predictions, social security did not transform social relations, and the legislature would eventually acquiesce to the demands of this anti-reformist coalition. As a consequence, the administration of old age insurance was fragmented along vocational lines, a disavowal of the principle of national solidarity that defined the universalist objectives of the Laroque Plan.

THE OPPOSITION: OLD AND NEW

Throughout 1945, social security had elicited opposition from different quarters, but the arguments presented by these critics had failed to convince the provisional government. The only notable exception lay in the area of family allowances, and de Gaulle had vetoed the integration of the latter into a single administrative structure. The controversy surrounding the *caisse unique* did not attract the attention of the wider public, and the Ministry of Labour was able to rationalize the bureaucratic infrastructure that defined the social insurance system of the thirties and forties. Despite this failure, the *Fédération Nationale de la Mutualité Française* and the CFTC continued to denounce the reforms introduced in October 1945, but the focus on the *caisse unique* would eventually recede before the emergence of a new form of opposition which focused on the economic implications of French social security.

In the meantime, the ordinance of 4 October 1945 did not silence the critics of the *caisse unique*, and they now sought to reverse the course of the government's policy. In December 1945, the members of the general assembly of the FNMF passed a resolution which voiced the displeasure of the mutual aid societies with regard to this *fait accompli*:

> After reiterating their support for the principle of an expanded system of social security, so as to increase the benefits of the insured as well as prevention and improvement of public health, they have expressed once more their great regret that this important reform, which involves virtually all wage earners and considerable funds, representing close to 30 per cent of wages, has been promulgated without being debated by an elected parliament, which violates the democratic sentiments of the country. Those regrets are great because the renewed study of the ordinance reveals, with increasing clarity, that it consists mainly, in fact, of a hasty and incomplete reorganization concerning its administrative and managerial structures.
>
> They remain surprised that the projected reorganization confirms the triumph of the *caisse unique* that they avoided during the Occupation, a nasty innovation which will not bring about the announced financial savings or simplification.[1]

These arguments explicitly rejected the logic of administrative rationalization, and the FNMF denied that the latter would lead towards an improvement of services. Whatever the accuracy of these claims, they did nonetheless express the outrage of groups which had been deprived of their role in the distribution of social benefits.[2] If anything, the resolution represented the *cri de coeur* of mutual aid societies marginalized by the implementation of the Laroque Plan.

Within a couple of years, however, the mutual aid societies obtained an important concession from the Ministry of Labour. On 25 February 1947, the *Fédération Nationale de la Mutualité Française* and the *Fédération Nationale des Organisations de Sécurité Sociale* concluded an accord which provided for the distribution of social security benefits by the mutual aid societies.[3] This agreement gave new hope to the opponents of the *caisse unique*, and they believed that the agreement represented an essential first step in their campaign against the ordinance of 4 October

---

[1] Archives Nationales, CAC 920247, resolution passed by the general assembly of the FNMF (10–12 December 1945).

[2] Ibid.

[3] Confédération Démocratique du Travail, CFTC, box 4h 113, *Accord relatif à la participation de la mutualité à l'application de la sécurité sociale*, 25 February 1947.

1945.[4] While this change might have been a positive development for the mutual aid societies and Catholic *syndicalistes*, this objective was not to be achieved because public opinion and the political establishment remained indifferent to this contentious issue. The frustration of this goal was to be illustrated by the CFTC's repeated efforts to convince the *Mouvement Républicain Populaire* to take a hard line stance on the *caisse unique* and to make its abolition one of its main legislative priorities.

Like the mutual aid societies, the CFTC had not been silenced by the ordinance of 4 October 1945. The confederation continued to voice its opposition to this reform and its persistence was a reflection of the scope of Catholic initiatives in the field of social insurance.[5] It was incumbent upon the CFTC to protect this confessional network of *caisses*, a testimony to the enduring particularism of the Catholic community. In September 1945, in fact, the confederation had passed a resolution that called for the maintenance of the administrative pluralism which, it believed, was a practical manifestation of democratic rights.[6] Though such rhetoric might have appeared extreme, it did reflect a genuine sense of crisis, and this was to be confirmed by the confederation's incessant lobbying of its political allies during the following months.

At the congress of the *Mouvement Républicain Populaire*, held in December 1945, Gaston Tessier, the head of the CFTC, outlined, in stark terms, the threat presented by the *caisse unique*:

> When it comes to the Parodi-Laroque ordinance of 4 October on social insurance, I would like to make two comments: the first is that when it comes to the whole of our movement of ideas and achievements, the application of the ordinances would bring about the destruction of a free network of social security which is of prime importance to our movement. In the *caisses familiales*, there are at this time 1,300,000 insured not to mention the *caisses mutualistes*. This is a network of influence, of social work, of resources of all kinds, which we should not abandon.
>
> Secondly, on the ground of principle, we should make sure that our action remains faithful to its character and remains different from that of the socialists. And what is this great difference? It is the free organisation of our activities. Thus, for us, freedom finds its application in a form of pluralism which is rather fundamental.[7]

---

[4] Mutualité Française, FNMF, *p-v du c.a*, 28 February 1947. Gaston Tessier attended this meeting.

[5] See E. Leriche, *Les Assurances sociales et notre apostolat ouvrier*.

[6] CFDT, CFTC, box 4h 113, *Résolution sur la sécurité sociale adoptée par le XXI congrès de la CFTC*, 15/18 September 1945.

[7] AN, MRP 350 AP 14, *p-v de la commission de politique sociale et familiale*, 15 December 1945, 42–3.

The independence of Catholic social institutions had been guaranteed by the administrative pluralism introduced by the legislation of the interwar period. Furthermore, the existence of this confessional network of *caisses* represented a non-statist alternative to the social policies associated with the political Left.

The CFTC sought to influence the legislative process through the *Mouvement Républicain Populaire*, a strategy which made sense since both shared a common Christian democratic ideology and drew support from the same elements of society. Many of the candidates and deputies of the MRP, including Charles Viatte, its spokesman on social security policy, had been active in the CFTC.[8] It is therefore unsurprising that the confederation pressured the movement to adopt a hard line stance with regard to the administrative structure of social security. The CFTC remained steadfast in its opposition, aligning itself with the mutual aid societies and supporting the MRP.[9] In December 1945, the confederation urged the MRP parliamentary group to introduce legislation that would rescind the ordinance of 4 October 1945.[10] Tessier, in fact, would urge the movement to take a more aggressive stand on the issue of the *caisse unique*. Indeed, he was disappointed with the fact that his demands were not included in the programme of the tripartite coalition which united the MRP, SFIO, and PCF.[11] The persistence of the CFTC was a product of its desire to preserve the independence of the Catholic social institutions, an objective which could be understood in a country marked by a history of anti-clerical struggles. It is also true, however, that Catholic opinion had become concerned with the influence of communism in post-war France.

The CGT, the largest trade union, had come under the sway of Communist *syndicalistes* and its members were to play a critical role in the management of the new social security system through the *conseils d'administration* of the *caisses primaires et régionales*. Tessier thus feared that the Communists would assume control of social security over the coming months.[12] These concerns could not be easily dismissed, given the PCF's emergence as a leading political force in post-Liberation France. These fears would explain the CFTC's initial refusal to participate in the

---

[8] G. Adam, *La CFTC*, 132–3. See B. Béthouart, *Des syndicalistes chrétiens en politique: de la Libération à la Vième République*.

[9] CFDT, CFTC, box 4h 112, *commission confédérale* of 15 December 1945.

[10] CFDT, CFTC, box 4h 112, letter to Albert Gortais (Deputy Secretary General of the MRP), 29 December 1945.

[11] CFDT, CFTC, box 4h 112, letter from Tessier to André Colin (Secretary General of the MRP), 26 January 1946.

[12] CFDT, CFTC, box 4h 112, letter from Tessier to an MRP parliamentarian, 26 June 1946.

administration of the social security system.[13] While this boycott might have been devoid of any impact on public policy, it effectively symbolized the intractable nature of the CFTC's opposition to the ordinance of 4 October 1945.

The mutual aid societies and their Catholic allies had been unable to reverse the implementation of the *caisse unique*, but the Laroque Plan remained vulnerable to other forms of criticism. From 1944 onwards, Pierre Laroque had sought to introduce a universal system of benefits which gave practical form to his belief in social solidarity. The redistributive aspects of social security would become the subject of increasing opposition once the *Assemblée National Constituante* decided to hasten the timetable for the universalization of old age insurance. The revolt against redistribution found its origin in the campaign launched by the representatives of middle management and technical personnel, the so-called *cadres*, who became active in the year that followed the Liberation. The interests of the *cadres* were promoted by the *Confédération Générale des Cadres*, an organization which had been founded in October 1944.[14] The CGC espoused a decidedly conservative outlook when it came to social and economic policy. During the following decades, the confederation sought to defend the economic interests of its membership, advocating a reduction in the levels of taxation and the maintenance of a distinct system of benefits within the social security system.[15] The CGC proved effective in pushing for the latter objective, and its success contributed to the unravelling of the universalist objectives of the Laroque Plan.

From 1945 onwards, the confederation denounced the Laroque Plan, and it invoked arguments which would be adopted by those who opposed the introduction of a universal system of social benefits. In October, it had denounced the fiscal implications of social security, and had called upon its members to join together:

> against the ordinance published on 6 October concerning our being subjected to a totalitarian social insurance, an ordinance that establishes a disguised super-tax which strikes at the *cadres*, without even providing them with benefits which are proportional to their contributions.[16]

---

[13] CFDT, CFTC, box 4h 112, *Bureau Confédéral*, 15 December 1945. This decision was later approved by the *Comité National*, 2–3 February 1946. See the communiqué of 4 February 1946. The CFTC would later change its position on the matter.

[14] A. Malterre, *La Confédération Générale des Cadres, la révolte des mal aimés*, 18–23.

[15] R. Mouriaux, 'La Résistance à l'éclatement: le cas de la CGC', in G. Lavau (ed.), *L'Univers politique des classes moyennes*, 314.

[16] AN, *Centre des Archives Contemporaines* 760228, copy of the CGC motion of 16 October 1945.

The *cadres* defined the issue of social security in economic terms, and this focus proved more effective in mobilizing public opinion than the question of the *caisse unique*. The persistence of economic difficulties during the post-war period provided this critique with an increased public resonance, and it pointed to the existence of a form of class consciousness which could not be reconciled with the solidaristic objectives of the Laroque Plan.

The *cadres* refused to participate in the social security system because they believed that their contributions would not provide them with a corresponding level of benefits. These apprehensions expressed an implicit but unequivocal critique of the redistributionist objectives of social security.[17] A narrow conception of economic self-interest thus explained their opposition to universalization. Their campaign against the latter would gradually gain in momentum, and it benefited from the creation of a new organization which publicized their efforts: the *Comité de défense des intérets du personnel et des cadres*.[18] By 1947, these efforts resulted in the creation of a complementary system of coverage that addressed their specific grievances. The success of the *cadres*, in fact, would anticipate the fragmentation of the old age insurance system, a result of the widening opposition to the universalization of social security benefits.

The artisans, like the *cadres*, were apprehensive with regard to their prospective inclusion within an expanded social security system. They were determined to maintain their social and economic status, a task that was complicated by the diversity of the artisan trades.[19] The artisans embodied an ideal of small ownership, and many believed that they were a living example of the possibility of social advancement.[20] The progress of industrialization, however, represented a challenge to their survival, as did the prospect of increased levels of taxation. Throughout 1946, various artisan periodicals argued that the imposition of the new social security contribution would result in the extinction of the artisan trades.[21] While these claims might have seemed excessive, similar concerns were voiced by the representatives of small- and medium-sized business, an unsurprising development since artisans were often entrepreneurs.

The members of the artisan trades had long been wary of new forms of taxation and regulation, and this had been apparent during the interwar period. They had largely been opposed to the policies of the Popular Front

---

[17] *Cadres de France*, November 1945; ibid. 1 July 1946.

[18] A.-M. Guillemard, *Le Déclin du social*, 84; *Cadres de France*, 15 July 1946; ibid. 1 August 1946.

[19] *Qu'est-ce que l'artisanat?*, préface d'André Siegfried, 21.

[20] M. Debré, *L'Artisanat classe sociale*, 320. *Qu'est-ce que l'artisanat?*, 18–19.

[21] *L'Artisan Comtois*, 15 May 1946. *L'Artisan d'Aunis et Saintonge*, December 1946.

government because the limitation of working hours and the introduction of paid vacations had made it difficult for many artisans to remain in business.[22] The universalization of social security promised to compound these problems, further hindering the ability of artisans and small business owners to survive in a difficult economic climate. While this line of argument was undoubtedly important, it only provided a partial glimpse into the mentality of the artisans, since they were also influenced by a heightened sense of class consciousness. Before the war, one of their leading spokesmen had proclaimed that his colleagues were proud of the fact that they had emancipated themselves from the proletarian condition.[23] Economic concerns alone did not explain the desire to protect the social status of these tradesmen; it was also due to a refusal to be assimilated with the working classes. These considerations explained their rejection of a social security system which redistributed their contributions and their support for an independent old age insurance programme, thus echoing the demands which had been made by the *cadres*.[24]

The leaders of business were hostile to the Laroque Plan, and various chambers of commerce had voiced their opposition to this initiative on a number of occasions. The Paris Chamber of Commerce expressed concern that a universal social security system would impose a new burden upon the middle classes and small businesses.[25] The business community, moreover, had been aggrieved by the prospective integration of family allowances into a single administrative structure.[26] This objection was unsurprising as the family allowance system had been promoted by private enterprise during the preceding decades.[27] Over the coming months, the chambers of commerce would become more strident in their opposition to social security, and this evolution was due to the decision to extend old age insurance benefits to the entire population. In December 1946, the presidents of the chambers of commerce denounced the legislation passed by the *Assemblée Nationale Constituante*.[28] The presidents objected to the

---

[22] N. Metton, *Brève histoire de l'artisanat en France 1925–1963*, 11.

[23] Ibid. 4–5. This declaration was made in 1922 by the leader of the *groupe artisanal* in the Chamber of Deputies.

[24] *L'Artisan d'Aunis et Saintonge*, January 1947. *La Voix Artisanale*, 5 April 1947.

[25] Chambre de Commerce de Paris, CCP, III, 5.70 (1), *Le Projet d'unification et d'etatisation des institutions de sécurité sociale*, 2 June 1945, 19; CCP III, 5.50 (13), *Extension du régime de sécurité sociale aux chefs des petites entreprises*, 22 March 1945.

[26] AN, CAC 920247, letter from the Chambre de Commerce de Cambrai to the Minister of Labour, 12 March 1946. Letter from the Chambre de Commerce de Douai, 11 March 1946.

[27] Pedersen, *Family, Dependence and the origins of the Welfare State*, 224–88.

[28] CCP III, 5.50 (7), *La Généralisation de l'assurance viellesse*, 23 December 1946.

imposition of a new fiscal burden on their members, and they united their efforts with those of the artisan trades. At the same meeting, they decided to work with the *Chambre des Métiers de France*, a decision which reflected the emergence of a widespread anti-reformist coalition.[29]

By the end of 1946, there was no shortage of groups willing to participate in the campaign against social security, and the *Confédération Générale des Petites et Moyennes Entreprises* became a particularly active and outspoken critic of universalization. The confederation was founded on 6 October 1944 and it sought to promote the interests of small- and medium-sized businesses.[30] The CGPME was hostile to all forms of state interventionism and feared the influence of the trade union movement. Under the charismatic leadership of Léon Gingembre, it voiced the anxieties of a conservative lower middle class, and played a central role in the anti-reformist coalition which came into being during the autumn of 1946.[31] Claiming to represent over three thousand organizations, Gingembre exerted his social and political influence through his ceaseless activism and impressive oratorical abilities.[32] Such dynamism was matched by a well-honed strategic sense, and he hastened to develop links with other like-minded organizations, as demonstrated by his participation in the establishment of *Comité National de Liaison et d'Action des Classes Moyennes*.[33] The latter coordinated the efforts of the artisans, the *cadres*, and the liberal professions, and it heightened the effectiveness of the campaign against old age insurance.[34]

These activities would culminate in a wave of civil disobedience aimed at preventing the implementation of the legislation passed by the ANC. During a rally held on 10 March 1947, the CGPME signalled the refusal of its members to register with the authorities, a move which would make it impossible to collect contributions and distribute benefits.[35] Throughout this period, the confederation called for the creation of a system of old age insurance which discriminated between different socio-economic groups and was financed by a reduced rate of contributions. According to Gingembre, his constituency refused to participate in a social security system which escaped its control while imposing an

[29] CCP III, 5.50 (7), note for the president, 20 December 1946; Letter from the *Assemblée des Presidents des Chambres de Métiers de France*, 21 December 1946.

[30] S. Guillaume, *Confédération Générale des Petites et Moyennes Entreprises* 19–20.

[31] H. Ehrmann, *Organised Business in France*, appendix, table iv.

[32] Ibid. 172–7.

[33] Guillaume, *Confédération Générale*, 28; Ehrmann, *Organised Business in France*, 178.

[34] J. Montaye and P. Bony, 'Le Refus par les commerçants et industriels de la loi du 22 mai 1946', *Actes du 112ième Congrès National des Sociétés Savantes*, Lyon, 1987, 395.

[35] *L'Artisan d'Aunis et Saintonge*, March 1947.

excessive contribution rate; he estimated that a differentiated system could greatly reduce administrative costs, thus reducing the burden imposed by social security.[36] The confederation, however, did not limit its critique to the consideration of economic issues, and its propaganda also focused on the increased influence of the CGT. In its view, social security not only wasted financial resources, but it placed the Communist-dominated CGT in control of a bureaucratic monolith which would be unresponsive to the concerns of the insured.[37] Much like the CFTC, the CGPME was mindful of the increase of Communist influence in post-war France.

The representatives of big business would play a supporting role in the campaign against the extension of old age insurance. Established in 1946, the *Conseil National du Patronat Français* sought to cultivate its support among small- and medium-sized businesses, a strategy which could only benefit those who were at the forefront of the struggle against universalization.[38] The CNPF followed a pragmatic strategy in order to achieve this objective. In June 1946, its president, Georges Villiers, stressed his support for social progress, but argued that new social policies could only be implemented in a slow and gradual manner.[39] The moderate stance of the big business lobby reflected its lack of credibility with the French public. During the Occupation, many French firms had collaborated with the Germans, and this had tarnished the reputation of big business in the aftermath of the Liberation. This explained its relative timidity in promoting a clear programme which catered to its specific interests.[40] Unlike the CGPME, the CNPF eschewed any direct assault upon the social security system. Its role was of a supporting nature, and it backed the position of the *cadres* in the course of their negotiations with the representatives of the Ministry of Labour. Indeed, the CNPF would eventually contribute to the conclusion of an agreement which met the demands that had been submitted by the *cadres* during the preceding months.

The collective agreement of March 1947 anticipated the fate of the rest of the old age insurance system. It was the CNPF which submitted the proposal that formed the basis of a separate pension system designed for

[36] *Le Figaro*, 2 April 1947. AN, F 60/671, *Note technique sur le coût de l'assurance-vieillesse*, (CGPME).

[37] CFDT, CFTC, box 4h 113, CGPME propaganda leaflet of early 1947. AN, F 60/671, *Note remise au Ministre du Travail, au sujet de l'extension aux non-salariés de la sécurité sociale*, undated and unsigned, (CGPME).

[38] H. Weber, *Le Parti des patrons. Le CNPF 1946–1990*, 99. G. Villiers, *Témoignages*, 117–18.

[39] AN, 72 AS 835, *Assemblée générale du 12 juin 1946, discours de Georges Villiers*.

[40] AN, 72 AS 835, *Assemblée générale du 7 décembre 1946, p-v de la commission sociale*, Villiers; Weber, *Le Parti des patrons*, 114.

middle management and technical personnel.[41] Big business thus contributed to the fragmentation of old age insurance along vocational lines, a trend which would gain momentum over the coming months. The role played by the CNPF illustrated its subtle and pragmatic advancement of a conservative social and economic agenda. Throughout these years, it conveyed the social and economic concerns of the business community while avoiding direct confrontations with the government. Interestingly enough, it paid little attention to the question of social security. Its president, Villiers, usually ignored the issue, focusing instead on inflation, wage and price controls, budgetary restraint, and the limitation of state interventionism.[42] It was the lower middle classes and the representatives of small business that formed the backbone of the anti-reformist coalition, and big business was reduced to a secondary role in the drama which unfolded in the first few months of 1947.

THE PARTIES AND SOCIAL SECURITY

From 1945 onwards, the main parties represented in the *Assemblée Nationale Constituante*, namely the PCF, MRP, and SFIO, were united in their support for the principle of social security. Differences arose over the administrative structure of social security, with both Communists and Socialists supporting the *caisse unique* while the MRP sought to postpone or reverse its implementation. The future of the Laroque Plan was contingent upon a rather complicated social and political environment. The Socialists and the Communists were not particularly interested in the issue of social security, and this relative indifference was confirmed on more than one occasion. The Socialist members of the *Assemblée Consultative Provisoire* had promoted an ambitious counter-proposal to the project submitted by the provisional government, but it was rather vague and the SFIO never bothered to elaborate upon its ideas.[43] In January 1947, one of its leaders would acknowledge this fact, arguing that the party had never been interested in the issue and that this explained the relative paucity of their thought regarding social policy.[44] Like the rest of the political establishment, the Socialists had been concerned with

[41] Villiers, *Témoignages*, 141.
[42] AN, 72 AS 835, *Discours; Les Leçons du passé. Réponse de M. Georges Villiers à des declarations de M. Guy Mollet* (Paris, 1957).
[43] *Le Populaire*, 1 August 1945.
[44] OURS, SFIO, *p-v du comité directeur*, 8 January 1947, Capocci.

other questions, namely the economic situation and the constitutional debates surrounding the foundation of the Fourth Republic.

The attitude of the SFIO could be explained by a variety of factors. The issue of social security had never captured the public imagination, despite its inclusion in the common programme of the CNR and the diffusion of the reformist rhetoric of the Resistance. After the war, the Socialists stressed the necessity of implementing the structural reform of the capitalist economy, and their electoral propaganda ignored social security altogether, focusing instead on the nationalization of key industries and financial institutions.[45] Fixated by the panacea of nationalization, the SFIO dismissed a policy which did not have the same ideological significance, a direct result of its commitment to the radical transformation of the capitalist system. The revolutionary traditions of the SFIO thus contributed to the marginalization of the issue of social security within Socialist circles. When the question was raised, it was discussed in a strictly partisan context which made little reference to its actual substance or historical significance. It is also true that the tripartite coalition formed by the MRP, PCF, and SFIO was subjected to various strains, and the Socialists came to be exasperated with their Communist allies. Some even expressed concerns over the prospect of Communist control over the administrative infrastructure of social security,[46] a position which echoed the fears which had been voiced by the CFTC and the CGPME.

In the year that followed the Liberation, the PCF had emerged as the leading party of the French Left. Communist participation in the Resistance had given the party an aura of legitimacy that was confirmed in the elections to the *Assemblée Nationale Constituante*. Like the SFIO, the PCF had been an advocate of social security, but it remained committed to the pursuit of other objectives. In 1945, the creation of a social security system was not one of its main priorities; it preferred to focus on the campaign in favour of 'the battle of production'.[47] The commitment to the 'battle of production' was consistent with a political strategy which eschewed sectarian and extremist rhetoric in the aftermath of the Liberation. In fact, Communist support for social security was merely the outcome of support for the policies outlined in the common programme of the CNR.[48] By the end of 1945, the positions of the PCF and SFIO were remarkably similar: the issue of social security remained of marginal importance to their public

---

[45] OURS, SFIO, *p-v du comité directeur*, 24 October 1945 and 7 May 1946.

[46] OURS, SFIO, *p-v du comité directeur*, 10 July 1946 and 8 January 1947.

[47] *Parti Communiste Français*, *p-v du comité central*, 21 January 1945; communiqué entitled *Salut aux combattants et aux vainqueurs de la production*, 1 September 1945.

[48] PCF, *p-v du comité central*, 3–4 November 1945, resolution entitled *Pour la défense du peuple-Pour le triomphe de la démocratie*.

discourses. The appointment of Ambroise Croizat to the Ministry of Labour, however, would signal a shift in Communist attitudes, and the PCF then became an aggressive proponent of the *caisse unique* and universalization.

This evolution was not an altogether automatic one, and the party had hesitated with regard to the introduction of the *caisse unique*. In the autumn of 1945, Jacques Duclos, the interim leader of the PCF, had considered supporting the Christian syndicalists in their campaign to rescind the ordinance of 4 October 1945.[49] The PCF rapidly changed course, and its leadership came to realize the importance of the new social security system. The creation of a new administrative structure provided the PCF with a remarkable opportunity to extend its influence, considerations which probably contributed to the change in its outlook. By July 1946, the Communists emerged as aggressive proponents of the *caisse unique* and universalization, and they invited the Socialists to participate in a *comité d'entente* which would develop a common strategy in support of these policies.[50] From this point onwards, *L'Humanité*, the party newspaper, provided extensive coverage of Communist support for the new social security system. Nevertheless, Benoît Frachon, a leading Communist *syndicaliste*, would argue that few of his colleagues seemed to be aware of the social and political significance of social security.[51] The shift in political strategy, therefore, did not imply that the PCF had truly grasped this reality and this was to be confirmed by the party's ultimate response to the anti-reformist revolt of 1946–1947.

The PCF proved willing to change its position in the light of subsequent social and political developments. Once the breadth of the opposition to the universalization of old age insurance had become clear, the party decided to support the creation of a system based on the principle of occupational solidarity; in March 1947, the *Bureau Politique* instructed Croizat, the Minister of Labour, to prepare legislation which would serve this objective.[52] For the PCF, political expediency proved more important than remaining steadfast in it support for the Laroque Plan. While Ambroise Croizat and Alfred Costes had been consistent and vocal advocates of social security, the rest of the party's leadership did not share the same commitment to the pursuit of this policy. Though the CGT might have been more conscious of the practical relevance of the

---

[49] CFDT, CFTC, box 4h 113, copy of note from Duclos (interim leader of the PCF).

[50] PCF, *décisions du secrétariat*, 8 July 1946.

[51] PCF, *p-v du comité central*, 27 November 1946, Frachon; H. Raynaud, *La Défense de la sécurité sociale*, 1–19.

[52] PCF, *p-v du bureau politique*, 9 January 1947. In the meeting of 27 March 1947, Duclos argued that the middle classes should not be compelled to join the general regime.

caisse unique, the positions adopted by the PCF reflected the fact that the issue of social security was not central to the conduct of its political strategy, an attitude which explained its willingness to support the fragmentation of old age insurance along vocational lines.

The MRP, on the other hand, had aligned itself with its allies of the CFTC. The movement had been unable to reverse the implementation of the ordinance of 4 October 1945, but its subsequent efforts were abetted by the rise of middle class resentment towards the redistributive aspects of social security. Initially, its position was defined by its opposition to the *caisse unique*. The MRP stressed that it supported the principle of social security but was opposed to its rationalization of the administrative structure of the social insurance system.[53] As a consequence, the movement sought to postpone the application of the ordinance of 4 October 1945. In February 1946, the Socialist- and Communist-dominated labour commission of the *Assemblée Nationale Constituante* rejected its proposal to postpone the introduction of the *caisse unique*.[54] The fate of this proposal reflected the political impotence of a party that was unable to prevent the rationalization imposed by the Laroque Plan. In April 1946, an MRP deputy would acknowledge the failure of its efforts in his correspondence with Gaston Tessier.[55] This outcome could be explained by Socialist and Communist support for the *caisse unique*, not to mention the fact that the issue had not attracted the attention of the population at large.

The MRP was faced with a political *fait accompli*, and it chose to reiterate its support for of a universal system of benefits. During the parliamentary caucus meeting of 25 April 1946, Charles Viatte advised his colleagues to support the bill which called for the universalization of social security in the absence of any viable alternative.[56] Unanimously adopted by the ANC, the law of 22 May 1946 provided for the extension of social security benefits, and it ignored the issue of the *caisse unique*. The redefinition of the question of social security along fiscal lines, however, would lead to a change in the MRP's position, and it became the advocate of a tax weary middle class.[57] The reference to the themes of the anti-

[53] CFDT, CFTC, box 4h 113, letter from Charles Viatte to *La Familiale du Jura et de la Côte-d'Or*, 11 December 1945. Newly appointed in his position as spokesman on social security matters, Viatte voiced his support for the mutualist system.

[54] AN, C 15293, *p-v de la commission du travail*, 14 February 1946.

[55] CFDT, CFTC, box 4h 112, letter from Dupraz (MRP deputy) to Gaston Tessier, 15 April 1946.

[56] Fondation Nationale des Sciences Politiques, MRPS, box 50, parliamentary group minutes, 25 April 1946.

[57] FNSP, MRPS, box 11, 'MRP à l'action', 15 February 1947.

reformist coalition proved ironic given the movement's attempt to forge a progressive image, but it reflected an awareness of an important change in public attitudes. In the spring of 1947, the movement would even call for the creation of a benefit system adjusted to the needs of various social and economic groups.[58] Like the PCF, the MRP would back away from its support for the principle of social security, but it had always remained consistent in its criticism of the bureaucratic implications of the Laroque Plan.

FRENCH SOCIAL SECURITY: SUCCESS AND FAILURE

By 1947, the failure of universalization marked a sharp contrast with the momentum which had characterized the efforts of the Ministry of Labour in the months that followed the Liberation. In the aftermath of the promulgation of the October ordinances, the political environment seemed favourable to the pursuit of the Laroque Plan's ultimate objective, namely the introduction of a universal system of benefits covering the entire population. In early 1946, the labour commission of the *Assemblée Nationale Constituante* would devote much of its time to the issue, though its discussions were noteworthy for their confusion of various principles and policies. More importantly, the election of the ANC had shifted the dynamics of the social security debate, since the assembly was entrusted with legislative power. The Ministry of Labour, and Pierre Laroque, could no longer determine the parameters of the legislative process, as had been the case during the course of the provisional government, and this would contribute to the unravelling of their policy objectives.

The roots of this failure could be found in public concern for the plight of the elderly in post-war France. By January 1946, a multiparty consensus had emerged in support of the extension of the allowance for aged workers, and various parties had submitted proposals promoting this goal.[59] The concern with the elderly led to a modification in the timetable for the universalization of old age insurance. Political pressure made it imperative to address this question, but this led to a hasty attempt at introducing universal benefits, a measure which outraged those who rejected the redistributionist aspects of social security. Laroque was not responsible for this miscalculation, and it simply confirmed the institutional shift

---

[58] FNSP, MRPS, box 11, motion approved by the third national congress of the MRP, 13–16 March 1947.

[59] AN, C 15293, *p-v de la commission du travail*, 24 January 1946, Costes. AN, C 15293, *p-v de la commission du travail*, 31 January 1946.

which had taken place since the autumn of 1945. Ultimate control for the development of social policy now lay with the ANC, and the latter proved sensitive to the evolution of the social and political climate. In the short term, however, the Ministry of Labour had remained in control of the policy process, and the labour commission had focused on its legislative proposals.[60] During this period, Laroque was able to maintain some influence, a reflection of a level of knowledge and expertise which dumb-founded his critics within the *Assemblée Nationale Constituante*.[61] Fot the time being, the director of social security wielded a level of influence which was inversely proportional to the ignorance and indifference of the public and its elected representatives, but it would soon recede when the ANC chose to exercise its legislative power.

On Wednesday 27 March 1946, Croizat and Laroque made a joint appearance before the members of the labour commission. The minister stressed that income support for the elderly should come under the form of an extension of old age insurance.[62] This approach was based on practical considerations, since alternative forms of assistance would require the disbursement of budgetary funds, and this was impossible given current circumstances.[63] Support for the elderly could only be assured through a self-financing social security programme. This position was consistent with the gradualist strategy which Laroque had advocated since the autumn of 1944.[64] Political realities, however, made it difficult to pursue this approach, and the labour commission sought immediate action for this social problem. The government now faced a dilemma, because the cost of a premature extension of social security would be prohibitive and might have an adverse impact on the economy. As Laroque noted, the impact of such a move would be brutal, and it would strain the administration of the social security system.[65] A universal system of benefits entailed an increase in the fiscal burdens to be borne by employers. Indeed, the short-term expansion of social security would result in a tenfold increase in the number of employers liable to contribute to its finances.[66] The persistent economic difficulties of the post-war period called into question the wisdom of such an initiative, and there was no guarantee that the system would be able to achieve self-sufficiency in the short term. Laroque argued that social security would only become self-supporting after an extended period because of the

---

60 AN, C 15293, *p–v de la commission du travail*, 21 March 1946.
61 *Journal Officiel*, Débats ANC, no. 78, 9 August 1946, Brunhes, 3065.
62 AN, C 15293, *p–v de la commission du travail*, 27 March 1946, Croizat.
63 Ibid.
64 AN, CAC 760228, *Note pour le Ministre*, 1 April 1946, 2.
65 Ibid. 3–4.
66 Ibid. 3.

difficulties involved in the setting up of a universal system of coverage.[67] Unless the state heavily subsidized this expansion—an unlikely outcome—a hasty extension would be doomed to failure. Laroque concluded that universalization should only be implemented over a prolonged period of time.[68] This gradualist approach was thus based upon a consideration of economic and administrative realities. Unfortunately, this analysis did not take into account contemporary political pressures, namely the desire to implement some measure designed to address the plight of the elderly.

By April 1946, the extension of social security benefits had come to the fore of the political debate, but its implementation raised the concerns of both the Ministry of Labour and the Ministry of Finance. André Philip, the Socialist Minister of Finance, was fearful of the macroeconomic impact of universalization. Fearing that it would have an inflationary effect on prices, he expressed his approval of universalization, but his support was conditioned upon the alignment of its date of implementation with the revival of French industrial production (upon reaching 120 per cent of the levels of production recorded in 1938).[69] The expansion of social security was predicated upon an improvement in national economic performance, a solution which was consistent with the strategy which had been adopted by the Ministry of Labour in the aftermath of the Liberation.

The combined efforts of the labour commission, the Ministry of Labour and the Ministry of Finance resulted in the elaboration of a bill which reflected these concerns. The studies of the Ministry of Labour were subjected to the amendments submitted by the members of the labour commission which, in turn, responded to the qualms of the Ministry of Finance.[70] The law of 22 May 1946 would include a conditional application date, as had been suggested by the Minister of Finance. By virtue of its article 33, the extension of given benefits would depend upon the state of specific economic indicators: old age insurance would be implemented upon the attainment of 110 per cent of the levels of industrial production which had been recorded in 1938, while the introduction of the remaining benefits would depend upon reaching 125 per cent of the same pre-war figures.[71] The law thus postponed the implementation of a universal system of benefits. Oddly enough, the bill had been approved without the benefit of a parliamentary debate, and it received the unanimous

---

[67] Ibid.

[68] Ibid. 4.

[69] AN, C 15293, *p-v de la commission du travail*, 17 April 1946, Peeters.

[70] Netter interview, *Actes*.

[71] H. C. Galant, *Histoire politique de la sécurité sociale française 1945–1952*, 76.

support of the departing members of the ANC.[72] The universalization of social security benefits had not been the subject of public debate, a rather peculiar outcome given its historical significance.

By the late summer of 1946, the legislators resumed their lobbying in favour of the provision of support for the elderly. On 22 August, the labour commission contacted the ministries of Finance and Labour requesting the immediate allocation of benefits, an initiative which called into question the timetable set by the law of 22 May 1946.[73] The government acquiesced to this demand, and this led to the elaboration of new legislation that provided for the implementation of a universal system of old age insurance. The law of 13 September 1946 called for the levy of contributions from 1 January 1947 onwards, with the distribution of benefits beginning on the first of April.[74] Within a few weeks, however, the implementation of the law resulted in a fiasco which must have embarrassed its advocates. A wave of mass resistance swept through the country, with much of the population refusing to register with the authorities, a move which made it difficult to collect contributions and deliver benefits.[75] The outburst of such public hostility could be attributed to the economic difficulties of the time. In January 1947 alone, the Blum government had introduced wage and price controls in response to the threat of inflation.[76] The economic problems of the period heightened the financial anxieties and social resentments of a vast cross section of French society. Many viewed social security as an additional form of taxation which compounded their difficulties without providing them with any corresponding advantages, and it was the diffusion of this sentiment which explained the revolt against old age insurance.[77] While universalization might have been inspired by solidaristic objectives, its implementation revealed the deep-seated social divisions of post-war France.

In a sense, this outcome was predictable, given the results which had been achieved by the *cadres*. For over a year, the CGC had campaigned

---

[72] Galant *Histoire politique*, 78.

[73] AN, C 15313, *p-v de la commission du travail*, 22 August 1946.

[74] A. Barjot, *La Sécurité sociale: Son histoire à travers les textes, Tome III*, 1945–1981, 85.

[75] B. Faure, 'Généralisation de l'assurance viellesse à l'ensemble de la population', *Droit Social*, 12, 1 (1949), 25–8; R. Jambu-Merlin, 'Le Problème de la sécurité sociale des travailleurs non-salariés au lendemain de la Libération', *Droit-Social*, 3 (1970), 11–16. AN, C 15409, *p-v de la commission du travail*, 27 February 1947, Viatte. He noted that a demonstration had taken place in his department; it rallied 5,000 people in a town of 15,000. See also *Le Figaro*, 21 March 1947.

[76] M. Margairaz, *L'État, les finances et l'économie. Histoire d'une conversion*, ii, 867; *Témoignage* Netter.

[77] *Le Figaro*, 12 February 1947.

against their inclusion within the social security system. In August 1946, Croizat appointed a commission to examine the demands of the *cadres*.[78] The search for an acceptable political compromise proved difficult, because the solidaristic bias of the Ministry of Labour was incompatible with the position defended by the *cadres*, and this was confirmed by the commission's deliberations.[79] The Ministry of Labour was faced with an intractable conflict, and there was no easy solution to this political impasse. The *cadres* simply rejected the solidaristic objectives of universalization and they refused to believe that social security would provide them with generous benefits. According to Henry Lespès, an MRP deputy and *cadres* spokesman, the contributions of the *cadres* would be increased in exchange for reduced levels of benefits if they were compelled to abandon their existing retirement programmes.[80] Perhaps the advocates of social security had failed to promote the virtues of social solidarity, but it was also true that the economic climate of the post-war years contributed to the revival of social tensions.

The negotiations progressed slowly, and their conclusion coincided with the outbreak of mass resistance to the universalization of old age insurance. The *cadres* actually walked out of the proceedings and the CIDC convened a new mass rally, developments which compelled the government to accept the proposals which had been submitted in January 1947.[81] The Ministry of Labour had capitulated, and this result foreshadowed the fate of the rest of the old age insurance programme. The final agreement was based upon proposals submitted by the CNPF, and it confirmed the special status of the *cadres*. While the latter were technically affiliated to the social security system, they now benefited from a supplementary pension scheme that preserved their financial position by abandoning any pretence to redistribution.[82] The collective agreement of 14 March 1947 demonstrated the virtual impossibility of achieving a uniform and universal system of old age insurance, and it was unsurprising that the government would soon acquiesce to the demands of the other elements of the anti-reformist coalition that had emerged during the preceding months.

The opposition to the universalization of old age insurance was anything but homogeneous, but its representatives were united in their belief that the old age insurance system had to be divided along occupational

---

[78] AN, C 15313, *p-v de la commission du travail*, 1 August 1946, Croizat.

[79] P. Baldwin, *The Politics of Social Solidarity*, 169–72; PBP, *p-v de la commission paritaire d'étude des régimes complémentaires de sécurité sociale*, 16 September 1946.

[80] *Journal Officiel, Débats* ANC, no. 78, 9 August 1946, Lespès, 3075–6.

[81] Baldwin, *The Politics of Social Solidarity*; BDP, *p-v*, 4 January 1947.

[82] Ibid.

lines and it was this principle which guided the efforts of the labour commission of the *Assemblée Nationale*.[83] Viatte, the MRP deputy, produced a report which adopted this approach, and it was approved by his parliamentary colleagues on 20 March 1947.[84] The government was presented with a *fait accompli* which made the creation of a vocational system all but unavoidable. The Minister of Labour then appointed a commission to examine the issue of old age insurance. The commission assembled the representatives of a wide array of interests, and its debates reflected the social particularism of its members. Officially created on 29 April 1947, the Surleau commission brought together members drawn from the CGT, the CFTC, the CNPF, and a variety of other professional organizations.[85] First convened on 4 June 1947, its deliberations illustrated the intellectual confusion which surrounded the question of social security. While opposition to the extension of old age insurance had been widespread, it did not result in the development of a coherent and comprehensive agenda for social policy and reflected instead the diverse interests of given social and economic groups. Of course, this represented a significant problem, since the commission was supposed to advise the Ministry of Labour on the forthcoming reform of old age insurance.[86] Its discussions would simply reflect the biases of those who rejected the principle of social solidarity and the prospect of economic redistribution.

The members of the Surleau commission could not agree upon a common set of guidelines concerning the means and rates of contributions which were to finance old age insurance.[87] The opposition to universalization was entirely negative; there was little which united the groups which had succeeded in blocking the implementation of the law of 13 September 1946. The depth of their anti-solidarist prejudices, moreover, was confirmed by the work of the sub-commission that was entrusted with the task of elaborating a new old age insurance system. Its recommendations were based upon the principle of occupational solidarity, thus rejecting the more wide-ranging conception of social solidarity which

---

[83] AN, C 15409, *p-v de la commission du travail*, 6 March 1947, Loygue and Stefannelli.

[84] AN, C 15409, *p-v de la commission du travail*, 20 March 1947.

[85] AN, CAC 760228, *Note pour M. le Ministre*, 19 May 1947. Laroque questioned the credentials of the *Comité National d'Action des Classes Moyennes* and did not select anyone from the CGC in deference to sentiments of the CGT and the CFTC.

[86] AN, CAC 760228, *p-v de la commission chargée d'étudier les modifications à apporter à la loi du 22 mai 1946*, 4 June 1947, Mayer.

[87] AN, CAC 760228, *p-v de la commission chargée d'étudier les modifications à apporter à la loi du 22 mai 1946*, 4 June 1947, de Lagarde; CAC 760228, *p-v*, 12 June, Montaye; CAC 760228, *p-v*, 17 June, Surleau; CAC 760228, *p-v*, 25 June, Surleau.

was synonymous with a universal system of social security.[88] The sub-commission's work also reflected the economic concerns of its members, since it advocated modest benefits reminiscent of current levels of social assistance, a result that called into question the potential effectiveness of its recommendations.[89]

The sub-commission called for the creation of a fragmented old age insurance system characterized by the establishment of distinct *caisses* for the artisans, industry and commerce, the liberal professions, and the agricultural sector.[90] While this position was consistent with the rhetoric of the anti-reformist coalition, it created a new set of difficulties for the Ministry of Labour. As the *rapporteur* observed, the fragmentation of the pension regime would increase administrative costs without providing for those whose occupations did not fall into the prescribed vocational categories.[91] Such criticism might have been warranted, but the actual significance of the sub-commission's recommendations lay with their explicit rejection of the solidaristic objectives of the Laroque Plan. Indeed, its report called for the introduction of flexible rates of contribution adjusted to the needs of the aforementioned vocational categories.[92] At the same time, the *rapporteur* noted that some members advocated funding through taxation, a method of financing which had already been rejected by the Ministry of Finance.[93] The work of the sub-commission thus expressed the contradictory aspirations of its members, but the Ministry of Labour had little choice but to try to make sense of its guidelines.

On 19 July 1947, Pierre Laroque responded to these proposals in a report that he submitted to the Ministry of Labour. In his mind, they entailed the creation of a complex system that would be difficult to implement, and they discarded the solidaristic principles central to his conception of social security. First and foremost, the complexity of the social fabric made it difficult to establish a system based on occupational categories. For example, Laroque noted that 80 per cent of artisans were both artisans and merchants, thus complicating their classification.[94] Secondly, the principle of occupational solidarity would lead to the establishment of a new bureaucratic infrastructure, resulting in increased administrative costs

---

[88] AN, CAC 760228, *Rapport sur les travaux de la commission d'études nommée par la commission chargée d'étudier les modifications à apporter à la loi du 22 mai 1946*, 1.

[89] Ibid.

[90] Ibid. 2.

[91] Ibid.

[92] Ibid. 4.

[93] Ibid. 5.

[94] MAS, LP, box 40, *Rapport à Monsieur le Ministre du Travail sur le projet de loi instituant une allocation de vieillesse pour les personnes non-salariées*, 19 July 1947, 2.

while making it difficult to supervise its activities.[95] The implications of this reform represented a denial of the logic of administrative rationalization which had been central to the development of the Laroque Plan. Furthermore, Laroque stressed that these recommendations left certain questions unanswered, because they failed to account for those who did not fall into the prescribed occupational categories, such as taxi drivers and tugboat operators, and this might lead to their exclusion from the old age insurance programme.[96] The commission's proposals served the interests of the organized professions, thus discriminating between these groups and those who did not benefit from the same level of representation.[97] In his view, therefore, the project negated the principles which had inspired his work since the Liberation, because it would produce a fragmented social security system that discriminated between different segments of French society.

Laroque concluded that these guidelines confirmed the persistence of middle class prejudices in post-war France:

> They are totally without any sentiment of solidarity with the other segments of the population. Their particularism is pushed to the extreme and their anarchic individualism is incompatible with the principles upon which any system of social security must be based. Reason requires us, in these conditions, to abandon the attempt, under current economic circumstances and the psychological atmosphere of the categories of which we are talking, from including them in a social security system. I believe that what is needed today, in common sense terms, is the pure and simple adjournment of the law of 22 May 1946. It was, it is wise to remember, the formally expressed intention of the authors of the law to suspend its application until the day when the index of industrial production would have reached 110 or 125 compared to 1938. This meant that the universalization of social security was to be subordinated to a substantial improvement in the economic situation, and to a delay sufficient to provide for the education of the interested parties and to make them understand the scope and importance of the given reform.[98]

While bitter in tone, these lines provided an accurate assessment of the factors which had led to the failure of universalization. The economic conditions of post-war France contributed to the revival of social tensions which made it difficult to pursue solidaristic policies, a problem which was compounded by the irresponsibility of the political establishment which had prematurely extended old age insurance benefits. The law of 13 September 1946 was the product of political myopia and it played into

---

[95] MAS, LP, box 40, *Rapport*, 19 July 1947, 2.
[96] Ibid. 3.   [97] Ibid.   [98] Ibid. 5.

the hands of those who were hostile to the principle of social solidarity, a notion which lay at the root of a universal system of coverage.

The work of the Surleau commission led to the drafting of the law of 17 January 1948, legislation which provided for the fragmentation of old age insurance into separate systems designed for the artisans, industrialists and merchants, the liberal professions, and the agricultural sector.[99] The law might have proved consistent with the recommendations which had been submitted to the Ministry of Labour, but it was subjected to criticism from the Ministry of Labour and various political parties, including the PCF, SFIO, and MRP.[100] The *Assemblée Nationale*, however, had been forced to respond to public pressure, and policymakers had to contend with the outcome of the legislative process. The pursuit of a universal system of social security had ended in failure, and the attempt to introduce a practical instrument of social solidarity had resulted in the creation of a system which reflected the social fragmentation of post-war France.

CONCLUSION

In 1945, Pierre Laroque had elaborated a social security plan which had not captured the public imagination, despite its noble rhetoric and its vast ambitions. Such indifference would give way before an expanding anti-reformist coalition assembling artisans, business owners, and *cadres* which rejected the redistributive aspects of social security. These groups were unreceptive to solidarist rhetoric, and their focus on a narrow conception of occupational solidarity reflected the revival of social tensions in a climate of persistent economic difficulties. These considerations made it difficult to implement a universal social security system, and they highlighted the fact that Laroque had been naive in believing that social security could effectively promote social solidarity in the first place. The pursuit of this objective was dependent upon the actual implementation of the system, but these tensions made it impossible to achieve this outcome.

The initial success of the Laroque Plan was the product of a unique set of circumstances and this was to be confirmed by later political developments. The election of the *Assemblée Nationale Constituante* in October 1945 signalled the end of this exceptional period, since it entailed the gradual reassertion of legislative control over the development of social policy. The development of relevant legislation would now be subjected to an expanding set of influences. The political parties were amenable to

---

[99] Barjot, *La Sécuritié sociale*, 97.　　　[100] Ibid. 95–8.

public pressure and this contributed to the unravelling of the gradualist strategy which Laroque had promoted since the autumn of 1944. By April 1946, a multi-party consensus had emerged in order to provide the elderly with some form of financial assistance, and this hastened the timetable of universalization. The law of 13 September 1946 provoked a widespread social revolt, and the Ministry of Labour had to abandon its attempt to extend old age insurance. The Surleau commission promoted the notion of occupational solidarity, an explicit rejection of the universalist ambitions of the Laroque Plan. Despite Laroque's reservations, this principle led to the fragmentation of old age insurance, a result which was finally achieved with the introduction of the law of 17 January 1948. The redistributionist objectives of social security were abandoned, and the social particularism of the anti-reformist coalition now found its expression in a system which no longer reflected the aspirations of its main architect.

The failure of universalization was the product of a particular set of social and economic circumstances. The implementation of the law of 13 September 1946 coincided with the *prise de conscience* of an alienated middle class.[101] They perceived the new social security contribution as a new form of taxation which heightened their anxieties about the preservation of their status and the maintenance of their standard of living. These insecurities were compounded by the fear of excessive CGT influence. As Francis Netter later recalled, those groups which opposed the extension of old age insurance were hostile to the redistribution of their financial resources by a system which was to be administered by the Communist-dominated CGT.[102] Communist and CGT support for social security had some unforeseen consequences, since their domineering methods not only reinforced the hostility of their critics but also managed to irritate their Socialist allies.[103] While opposition to social security gained in momentum, the relationship between its main political advocates would deteriorate as time progressed.

While the failure of the law of 13 September 1946 might be attributed to a combination of social, political, and economic circumstances, it demonstrated the fact that the political consensus which had supported the principle of social security had been an altogether shallow one, since neither the public nor the political establishment had really focused on the issue. Laroque had conceived social security as an instrument to empower the working classes and promote social solidarity, but the attempt to

---

[101] *Le Figaro*, 29 January 1947.
[102] Netter, 'L'Histoire des retraites: les non-salariés', *Droit Social*, 1 (1967), 46.
[103] *Journal Officiel*, Débats ANC, no. 89, 10 September 1946, 3584.

extend old age insurance had the opposite effect, inspiring the activism of an anti-reformist coalition which rejected the ideological premises and economic costs of universalization. The Laroque Plan had been marked by a degree of utopianism, and the harsh realities of the post-war period confirmed the lesson that Laroque had learned during the preceding decade: legislation alone could not erase ingrained prejudices or transform public attitudes.

Conclusion

The Laroque Plan was developed in the months that followed the Liberation, and while its content had been influenced by the inefficiencies of the social insurance system, its ambitions reflected the idealistic spirit of the times. Pierre Laroque believed that social security would transform social relations by cultivating among the insured a new sense of social solidarity, an objective that would be achieved through their participation in the management of its administrative infrastructure. The purpose of social security proved consistent with his long-standing views concerning social policy, and his past writings in the fields of administrative law and industrial relations had expressed a particular conception of the nature of society and the role of the state. Laroque had always been an advocate of state interventionism, but he also promoted the creation of decentralized structures which provided for public participation. These concerns had been central to his advocacy of the corporatist management of industrial relations, and they similarly inspired his work in the field of social security.

As a student, Laroque had been exposed to the legal doctrines of Léon Duguit and Maurice Hauriou, and this had turned him into a proponent of solidarism and a decentralized state. Nevertheless, it was his work as a civil servant which sparked his interest in social policy, namely his assignments with the Ministry of Labour and the *Conseil National Économique*. While he became acquainted with the problems of social insurance during this period, he came to focus on the study of collective bargaining legislation during the course of the thirties. Laroque was initially impressed with Fascist corporatism, and he became an advocate of the corporatist management of industrial relations. The corporation, in his view, would facilitate the negotiation of working conditions and favor the enforcement of the ensuing agreements. The corporation would incite the representatives of business and labour to resolve their differences in a peaceful and cooperative manner. The working classes would be empowered by this process, thus diffusing social tensions and contributing to the cultivation of a new spirit of social solidarity among the respective parties.

These views found a receptive audience during the thirties, as both technocrats and neo-socialists responded favourably to the promise of a new form of industrial organization which transcended existing liberal and collectivist alternatives. Laroque promoted his corporatist proposals though a variety of means, participating in the meetings of organizations such as the *Groupe du 9 Juillet* and *X-crise* while contributing articles to reviews such *L'Homme Nouveau* and *Les Nouveaux Cahiers*. This enthusiasm for corporatism did not last, a result of his growing awareness of its practical limitations, not to mention his realization that the Fascists had made exaggerated claims concerning their achievements while denying basic democratic freedoms. Furthermore, his analysis of the collective bargaining reforms introduced by the Blum government had led him to conclude that public attitudes could not be transformed by legislation alone. Nevertheless, he remained committed to the principles which had driven him in the first place, and the consistency of his approach towards social policy would become all the more apparent when he came to elaborate the Laroque Plan.

By the time he was appointed director general of social insurance in 1944, Laroque had been an advocate of the system's reform for over a decade, an outgrowth of his early exposure to the social insurance legislation of 1928–1930. The latter had been the product of political compromise, and he believed that this had resulted in an exceedingly complex and ineffective social insurance system. These conclusions were shared by other observers, and the Ministry of Labour attempted to reform social insurance during the first two years of the Vichy regime. These failures testified to the influence wielded by groups such as the mutual aid societies, but also confirmed the limited influence of René Belin, a minister who was unable to garner support for his initiatives within the highest circles of the government. After the Liberation, Alexandre Parodi would succeed where his predecessor had failed, but this achievement could be attributed to the conjunction of a unique set of political circumstances. Parodi was able to achieve most of his policy objectives as a result of his influence within the provisional government, a result of the prestige that he had gained as a leader of the Resistance.

Pierre Laroque made the most of this environment, and he devised a plan which succeeded in rationalizing benefits and services, reforms which were incorporated into the ordinances of 4 October and 19 October 1945. The Laroque Plan became a legislative reality, despite opposition to the *caisse unique*, the lynchpin of the administrative structure of the new social security system. Neither the FNMF nor the CFTC were able to reverse this policy, and their campaigns to rescind the ordinance of 4 October 1945 did not attract the attention of the wider public. While the provisional government and the main political parties were committed to the principle of social security, there was little evidence that the population was interested in this question, but this would change when the issue of social security was redefined along fiscal lines. The potential cost of a universal system of coverage provoked the hostility of a wide array of socio-economic groups, and it was this phenomenon which put an end to the reformist momentum of the post-Liberation era.

The failure of universalization was due to the revival of social tensions within a climate of persistent economic difficulties, and it translated into a rejection of the solidarist principles and redistributive mechanisms of the social security plan. The public reaction to the law of 13 September 1946 resulted in a political fiasco, but this outcome could be explained by the abandonment of the gradualist strategy which Laroque had advocated since the Liberation and had been incorporated into the law of 22 May 1946. The reversal of the legislature was a result of a widely shared desire to provide aid to the elderly, and it was this political reality which led to the premature extension of the old age insurance system. By the time the law of 13 September 1946 was implemented, a wide-ranging anti-reformist coalition had emerged in opposition to social security, and the scope of the ensuing protests compelled the government to reconsider its policies. The Ministry of Labour was forced to acquiesce to the demands of its critics, resulting in the appointment of the Surleau commission and the passing of the law of 17 January 1948. The latter created a fragmented old age insurance system which catered to distinct socio-economic categories, including the artisans, merchants and industrialists, the liberal professions, and agricultural workers. The concept of occupational solidarity thus replaced the notion of social solidarity, an approach which rejected the redistributionist logic of universalization.

The main political parties, namely the MRP, PCF, and SFIO, claimed to support the principle of social security, but this consensus was an altogether shallow one, given their lack of interest in the issue. While they all agreed that social security represented a necessary appendage of the reformist politics associated with the legacy of the Resistance, it was never considered a priority by their respective leaders. The MRP had opposed the *caisse unique*, while neither the PCF nor the SFIO represented a reliable basis of support for the promotion of a universal social security system. The Left was preoccupied by other issues, as had been illustrated by the focus on the 'battle of production' and its support for the nationalization of industry. Both the Communists and Socialists had failed to articulate a coherent and comprehensive rationale for social security, a glaring omission in the light of the rise of public opposition to the universalization of old age insurance. The PCF and the SFIO eventually acquiesced to the fragmentation of the latter, but they could not do otherwise given the failure to implement the law of 13 September 1946.

It was in this context, moreover, that the MRP found its true voice, as it became the partisan instrument of middle class outrage, contributing to the legislative *dènouement* of the political crisis.

The introduction of the *caisse unique* remained consistent with the logic of administrative decentralization, and its structure was intended to promote the participation of the insured in the management of the social security system. The *conseils d'administration* of the relevant *caisses* provided for the inclusion of the representatives of various professional organizations, and a significant share of their seats was set aside for the representatives of the CGT. While this mechanism was meant to foster the participation of the working class, it was not altogether clear how this would result in the creation of institutions which were to transform social relations in post-war France. There was little indication that the new social security system would be able to achieve such an ambitious goal, given the fact that its development was met by a public indifference which easily gave way to the resolute hostility of an important cross section of French public opinion.

Pierre Laroque had long been concerned with the alienation of the working class, and he developed various proposals that sought to address this problem, be it through the corporatist management of industrial relations or the creation of a new social security system. Laroque's perception of social reality was anything but objective, and he undoubtedly glorified the working class while exhibiting little sympathy for the middle classes, not to mention the representatives of business and management. In *Réflexions sur le problème social*, a study published in 1953, he argued that the working classes easily accepted interventionism and regulation; unlike the middle classes, they viewed liberty in collective and not individual terms.[1] These views were simplistic at best, but they did illustrate the fact that he assumed that French workers exhibited a solidaristic outlook which contrasted with the perceived egotism of the middle classes. It should be noted, however, that this analysis was consistent with his understanding of the history of industrial relations, and it explained his response to the failure of the universalization of old age insurance.

Laroque had stated in *Les Rapports entre patrons et ouvriers* that social progress was a product of working class pressure, but the history of social insurance and social security did not necessarily support this line of analysis. While these policies enjoyed the support of an important segment of the labour movement, the initiative for these reforms came from civil servants like Georges Cahen-Salvador and Pierre Laroque. Both

---

[1] P. Laroque, *Réflexions sur le problème social*, 149–50.

Cahen-Salvador and Laroque developed innovative policies that were subjected to the criticism of concerned interest groups, a pattern which defined the political debates of the twenties and forties. There was little indication that public pressure had driven the policy process, and this track record pointed to Laroque's idealization of the working classes and his espousal of a teleological conception of history.

The development of the Laroque Plan invites a comparison with the publication of the Beveridge Report in wartime Britain. Much like the Beveridge Report, the Laroque Plan was an expression of an international trend which favoured the expansion of existing systems of social benefits.[2] Both Sir William Beveridge and Pierre Laroque sought to consolidate existing policies and structures within the framework of an expansive state, building upon past achievements and promoting greater state intervention in social and economic affairs. Though they shared a common set of concerns, they were divided as to the means by which they intended to achieve their objectives, a logical outcome of the respective histories of French and British social policy. Each country had developed its own specific responses to the social problems it faced, and both Laroque and Beveridge elaborated policies which took into account the administrative legacies associated with these different social policy traditions.

These institutional factors were matched by important social, cultural, and ideological differences. British political and intellectual life had long been characterized by a persistent interest in social policy questions, and the emergence of the Fabian Society and New Liberalism had best illustrated this phenomenon at the turn of the century. In France, however, the public discourse had largely been uninterested by these issues, despite the rise of the syndicalist, socialist, and solidarist movements. French social policy was propelled by the initiatives of reform-minded bureaucrats who had to contend with the general indifference of public opinion and the periodic manifestations of interest group pressure. The peculiarities of the French experience can be ascribed to a variety of factors. The tardy industrialization of the French economy did not give the social question the same political saliency, but it is also true that the revolutionary tradition contributed to the marginalization of social insurance and social security. Both the PCF and SFIO preferred to focus on policies like the nationalization of industry, an objective that was consistent with the revolutionary rhetoric of the political Left. Those Communists and Socialists who contributed to the relevant policy debates, like Étienne Antonelli and Alfred Costes for example, exerted little influence on their

---

[2] F. Netter, *La Sécurité sociale et ses principes.*

respective parties. After the Liberation, the Left supported the principle of social security without devoting much thought to the question, an attitude which was shared by their counterparts of the political Centre and Right.

Beveridge and Laroque were the products of different cultural and ideological environments, and their thought evoked a different set of formative influences. Nevertheless, their views exhibited similar concerns. In Beveridge's case, his thought invoked both scientific and 'republican' themes, wedding a pseudo-scientific approach to social problems with an ideal of active citizenship.[3] For Laroque, a belief in the rational organization of services was coupled with a preoccupation with the participation of those who would benefit from given social policies. Both men operated in political and ideological contexts which had been shaped by liberal and democratic values, not to mention the rise of the socialist and labour movements. They stressed that the expansion of social programmes served to promote positive freedom, but this was to be achieved in a manner which sought to preserve individual initiative.

The Beveridge Report and the Laroque Plan served different policy objectives. The former would be described as a blueprint for what would come to be known as the welfare state, presenting the guidelines of a comprehensive system of social benefits destined for the entire population. The latter, on the other hand, sought to rationalize a rather limited social insurance system in anticipation of the subsequent expansion of benefit programmes. Both initiatives were designed in the light of macroeconomic considerations, but these concerns were fundamental to the design of the Beveridge Report. Sir William Beveridge had outlined a comprehensive approach towards economic policy,[4] an approach which proved consistent with the long-standing preoccupations of British policymakers. The development of unemployment insurance had been central to the development of the British welfare state, a focus which could be understood given Britain's status as the world's first industrial power. French social security, however, did not even include an unemployment insurance scheme. Laroque would later explain that French social policy had preferred to focus upon the provision of support to the family and the elderly, a reflection of its focus on the demographic plight of early twentieth-century France.[5]

These conceptions of social policy were marked by their contrasting attitudes towards the administration of services. Laroque and his critics

---

[3] J. Harris, *William Beveridge: a biography*, 2nd edn., 488.

[4] See W. Beveridge, *Full Employment in a Free Society*.

[5] MAS, LP, box 71, lecture given by Laroque to the House of Commons, 31 March 1947.

were in agreement about the virtues of administrative decentralization, but they differed over its practical implications. While the mutual aid societies believed that decentralization entailed mutualist control of the social insurance system, the Laroque Plan promoted a rationalized administrative system defined by the expansion of a state-run administrative infrastructure. This concern with decentralization was foreign to the content of the Beveridge Report, and its author advocated a more centralized approach towards the delivery of social services and benefits.[6] The concept of administrative decentralization had long been central to the evolution of the social policies of early twentieth-century France. The rise of solidarism explained this bias, since its interventionism was matched by its support of intermediary social structures which somewhat limited the impact of the expansion of the power of the state. Political realities supported this trend because the mutual aid societies were intent on preserving the pre-eminent administrative role conferred on them by the *Retraites Ouvrières et Paysannes* of 1910 and the social insurance legislation of 1928–1930. Their influence was to be felt throughout the history of the Third Republic, and this remained the case during the short existence of the Vichy regime. The provisional government finally confronted the power of the mutual aid societies, and the ordinance of 4 October 1945 effectively divested them of their role in the distribution of social benefits.

The public response to the Beveridge Report and the Laroque Plan reflected the contrasting experiences of wartime Britain and France. In Great Britain, the shared sacrifices of wartime had produced a communitarian spirit which came to permeate British society. Professor José Harris has argued that the success of the Report was due to the fact that its substance addressed the aspirations of a people united by a new sense of common purpose, a result of the shared sacrifices of wartime.[7] This reformist consensus would eventually lead to the election of a government that espoused many of the objectives of the Beveridge Report. The same could not be said of France, despite the lofty rhetoric of the Resistance and the Free French movement, not to mention the reformist spirit of the Liberation. The Occupation had fostered new social and political tensions, as illustrated by the rise of the Vichy regime, the Resistance, and the Free French movement. While all agreed on the necessity of reform, reflecting a common rejection of the status quo antebellum, they were divided as to its nature and purpose. The question of social security did become the object of a political consensus and was included in the common programme of the CNR, but few understood what this actually entailed

---

[6] W. Beveridge, *Social Insurance and Allied Services*, 22–3.
[7] Harris, *William Beveridge*, 415–16.

and fewer seemed concerned by its prospective implementation by the provisional government.

The Laroque Plan was successfully implemented, but this outcome was the product of an exceptional political environment. The emergence of a revived legislative branch signalled the return of a truly democratic politics, and public opinion could now influence the legislative process. By the autumn of 1946, the *Assemblée Nationale Constituante* would exert its influence over social policy, and its initiatives contributed to the undoing of the universalist objectives of social security. Political considerations had led to the acceleration of the timetable of universalization, and the ensuing fiasco exposed the vulnerability of a plan which had never caught the public imagination nor sustained the interest of the political establishment. French social security had been conceived in a political vacuum of sorts, and this contributed to the reformist momentum of 1944–1945.

Pierre Laroque's background as a public lawyer and social policy expert explained his belief in a state interventionism which promoted social solidarity by encouraging public participation in the administration of decentralized services. By streamlining the bureaucracy and consolidating benefit programmes, the Laroque Plan set the stage for the subsequent expansion of the social security system. The *caisse unique* and universalization were the instruments of a renewed republican covenant: public participation in an expanded system of social services was meant to address working class alienation while transforming social relations in the post-war era. Laroque employed reformist means to achieve revolutionary objectives, but it was by no means clear how social security could actually fulfil these goals, and the same could be said of his proposals for the corporatist management of industrial relations. French social security reflected the contradictions of its architect, reflecting both the pragmatic and utopian aspects of his thinking. While Laroque put a premium on public participation and social solidarity, his plan was introduced by an authoritarian government and imposed upon a passive population. The attempt to extend old age insurance did not foster social solidarity but confirmed the social fragmentation and ideological polarization of the post-war years. Laroque might have failed to attain his ultimate policy objectives, but his work resulted in the rationalization of a complex network of services and benefits, deceptively modest goals that had escaped the grasp of his predecessors.

Bibliography

PRIMARY SOURCES

1) Archives

Archives Nationales
Cabinet du Maréchal Pétain
2 AG 499
Commissariat National à l'Intérieur (CFLN)
F1a 3726
F1a 3733
F1a 3840
Commission d'assurance (Chambre des Députés)
C 14646
C 14768
C 14878
Commission des finances (ACP, ANC, AN)
C 15311
Commission du travail (ACP, ANC, AN)
C 15166
C 15293
C 15313
C 15409
Conseil National Économique
CE 1
CE 43
CE 60
CE 65 (Cahen–Salvador papers)
Ministère du Travail
F 22
Présidence du Conseil
F 60

Assemblée Nationale (materials transferred to the Archives Nationales)
p–v de la commission du travail (ANC)
p–v de la commission des finances (ANC)

Centre des Archives Contemporaines
CAC 760145
CAC 760228
CAC 860269

CAC 920247

Other Archives

Centre des Archives Économiques et Financières

Pleven papers

Centre des Archives du Monde du Travail (CNPF archives)

72 AS 835

Chambre de Commerce de Paris

C.C.P III, 5.50 (7)
C.C.P III, 5.50 (13)
C.C.P III, 5.70 (1)

Confédération Française Démocratique du Travail (CFTC papers)

4h 112
4h 113

Fondation Nationale des Sciences Politiques

MRP papers
MRPS papers
Parodi papers

Institut d'Histoire Sociale

Belin papers
Tessier papers

Ministère des Affaires Sociales

Laroque papers

Mutualité Française (FNMF papers)

p–v des conseils d'administration
p–v des assemblées générales

Office Universitaire de Recherche Socialiste (SFIO papers)

Gazier papers
SFIO, *p–v du comité directeur*

Parti Communiste Français

décisions du Secrétariat
p–v du bureau politique
p–v du comité central

Peter Baldwin Papers
Notes taken by Prof. Peter Baldwin (UCLA) for the purposes of his doctoral research. The notes used relate to the proceedings of the commission which negotiated a new retirement scheme with the *Confédération Générale des Cadres*: *p–v de la commission paritaire d'étude des régimes complémentaires de sécurité sociale* (1946–1947)

Sénat
P–v de la commission d'hygiène

2) Interviews/oral histories
Histoire orale de la sécurité sociale (Centre des Archives Contemporaines):
Témoignage Pierre Laroque.
Témoignage Francis Netter.
Témoignage Alexandre Parodi.
Personal interviews:
Prof. Philippe–Jean Hesse, 9 December 1998.
Mme Colette Laroque (widow of Pierre Laroque), 5 November 1998.

3) Periodicals
L'Artisan d'Aunis et Saintonge
L'Artisan Comtois
L'Aube
Cadres de France
Combat
Droit Social
Le Figaro
Franc–Tireur
Front–National
L'Homme Nouveau
L'Humanité
Informations Sociales de L'INASAS
Journal Officiel
Le Monde
La Nouvelle Revue
Les Nouveaux Cahiers
Le Peuple
Le Populaire
Revue Française de Science Politique
La Santé de L'Homme
La Tribune des Nations
La Vie Socialiste
La Voix Artisanale

4) BOOKS AND ARTICLES

Albert, C., *L'État moderne, ses principes et ses institutions* (Paris: Valois, 1929).

Andreu, P., *Le Rouge et le blanc 1928–1944* (Paris: La Table Ronde, 1977).

——*Révoltes de l'esprit: les revues des années 30* (Paris: Éditions Kimé, 1991).

Antonelli, É., *La Démocratie sociale devant les idées présentes* (Paris: Marcel Rivière, 1911).

——*Conférence du mecredi 11 janvier 1933. Comment furent votées les lois sur les assurances sociales* (Paris: Édition de la Fédération National des Syndicats d'Employés, 1933).

Archambault, P., (ed.) *Aux sources du droit. Le Pouvoir, l'ordre et la liberté* (Paris: Librairie Blond & Gay, 1933).

Aron, R., *Le Spectateur engagé* (Paris: Julliard, 1981).

Belin, R., *Du secrétariat de la CGT au gouvernement de Vichy* (Paris: L'Albatros, 1978).

Berstein, S., (ed.) *Le 6 février 1934* (Paris: Julliard, 1975).

——*Leon Blum* (Paris: Fayard, 2006).

Beveridge, W., *Social Insurance and Allied Services* (London: HM Stationery Office, 1942).

——*Full Employment in a Free Society* (London: G. Allen & Unwin, 1944).

Bloch-Lainé, F. and C. Gruson, *Haut fonctionnaires sous l'occupation* (Paris: Odile Jacob, 1996).

Bonnard, R., *Syndicalisme, corporatisme et état corporatif* (Paris: Librairie générale de droit et de jurisprudence, 1937).

——et al., *À la mémoire de Léon Duguit, 1859–1928, doyen de la Faculté de droit de l'Université de Bordeaux (1919—1928)* (Bordeaux: Imprimerie de Cadoret, 1929).

Bouglé, C., *Le solidarisme* (Paris: Giard, 1907).

——*Proudhon et notre temps* (Paris: Chiron, 1920).

——(ed.) *Proudhon* (Paris: Félix Alcan, 1930).

——*Oeuvres complètes de Pierre-Joseph Proudhon*, 14 vols (Paris: Marcel Rivière, 1923–1959).

Bourgeois, L., *Solidarité*, 2nd edn (Paris: Armand Colin, 1897).

Bouthillier, Y. *Le Drame de Vichy*, 2 vols (Paris: Plon, 1951).

Bouvier-Ajam, M., *Du coopératisme au corporatisme* (Paris: Cercle d'Éditions Corporatives et Sociales, 1938).

Broderick, A, (ed.) *The French Institutionalists* (Cambridge, MA: Harvard University Press, 1970).

Buisson, G., C.G.T. *Pour connaître les assurances sociales, par Georges Buisson, entretiens sur la loi du 5 avril 1928, modifiée par les lois du 5 août et 30 avril 1930* (Paris: Éditions de la Confédération Générale du Travail, 1930).

Cahen-Salvador, G., *Les Assurances sociales. Le Nouveau Projet de loi. Rapport de M. Georges Cahen-Salvador* (Paris: Félix Alcan, 1921).

——'L'Économie disciplinée, ses methodes et son programme', *Revue Politique et Parlementaire* (Paris, 1934).

Cahen-Salvador, J., *La représentation des intérêts et les services publics* (Paris: Librairie du Recueil Sirey, 1935).

Centre Polytechnicien des Études Économiques, *X-crise: de la récurrence des Crises économiques* (Paris: Economica, 1982).

Comité du Plan, *Le Plan Français*, préface de Marcel Déat (Paris: Fasquelle, 1935).

de Gaulle, C., *Discours et messages 1940–1946* (Paris: Plon, 1970).

——Mémoires de Guerre: l'unite 1942–1944 (Paris: Presses pocket, 1980).

——Mémoires de Guerre: l'appel 1940–1942 (Paris: Presses pocket, 1980).

De Gaulle, P., *Mémoires accessoires* (Paris: Plon, 1997).

de Man, H., *Au delà du marxisme*, 2nd edn (Paris: Librairie Félix Alcan, 1929).

——*L'Idée socialiste* (Paris: Bernard Grasset, 1933).

——*Cavalier seul. 45 années de socialisme européen* (Geneva: Éditions du Cheval Ailé, 1948).

Déat, M., *Perspectives socialistes* (Paris: Valois, 1930).

——*Mémoires politiques* (Paris: Denoël, 1989).

Debré, M., *L'artisanat classe sociale. La Notion d'artisan. La Législation artisane* (Paris: Librairie Dalloz, 1934).

Detoeuf, A., *La Construction du syndicalisme* (Paris: Gallimard, 1938).

Dubreuil, H., *Employeurs et salariés en France* (Paris: Librairie Félix Alcan, 1934).

Duguit, L., *Le Droit constitutionnel et la sociologie* (Paris: Armand Colin, 1889).

——*L'État, le droit objectif et la loi positive* (Paris: Librairie générale de droit et de jurisprudence, 1901).

——*Le Droit social, le droit individuel* (Paris: Alcan, 1908).

——*Les Transformations du droit public* (Paris: Armand Colin, 1913).

——*Souveraineté et liberté* (Paris: Librairie Félix Alcan, 1922).

——*Traité de droit constitutionnel*, 2nd edn, 4 vols (Paris: Boccard, 1923).

du Moulin de Labarthète, H., *Le Temps des illusions* (Geneva: Éditions du Cheval Ailé, 1946).

Durkheim, É, *De la division du travail social: thèse présentée à la Faculté des lettres de Paris* (Paris: Alcan, 1893).

——*Leçons de sociologie. Physique des mœurs et du droit* (Paris: Presses Universitaires de France, 1950).

Frachon, B., *La Bataille de la production. Nouvelle étape du combat contre les trusts: rapports, articles et discours* (Paris: Éditions Sociales, 1946)

——*Au rythme des jours*, 2 vols. (Paris: Éditions Sociales, 1967).

Groupe du 9 Juillet, *Plan du 9 Juillet* (Paris: Gallimard, 1934).

Hauriou, M., *Les Facultés de droit et la sociologie* (Paris: Thorin et fils, 1893).

——*La Science sociale traditionelle* (Paris: Édition Larose, 1896).

——*Le Point de vue de l'ordre et de l'équilibre* (Toulouse: E. Private, 1909).

——*Études constitutionelles. La Souveraineté nationale* (Paris: L. Larose et L. Tenin, 1912).

——*Principes de droit public*, 2nd edn (Paris: Larose, 1916).

——*Précis de droit administratif et de droit public à l'usage des étudiants en licence (2e et 3e années) et en doctorat sciences politiques*, 10th edn (Paris: Sirey, 1921).

——*Precis elémentaire de droit constitutionnel* (Paris: Édition Sirey, 1925).

Ionescu, G., (ed.) *The Political Thought of Saint-Simon* (Oxford: OUP, 1976).

Lajugie, J., (ed.) *Pierre-Joseph Proudhon: textes choisis et présentés par J. Lajugie* (Paris: Dalloz, 1953).

Landry, A. *La Révolution démographique. Études et essais sur les problèmes de la population* (Paris: Librairie du Recueil Sirey, 1934).

Laroque, P., *Les Usagers des services publics industriels* (Paris: Librairie du Recueil Sirey, 1933).

——*Les Rapports entre patrons et ouvriers* (Paris: Aubier, 1938).

——'L'Avenir des asurances sociales française', —, *La Sante de L'Homme*, 28 (1945).

——*Réflexions sur le problème social* (Paris: Éditions Sociales Françaises, 1953).

——'La sécurité sociale de 1944 à 1951', *Revue Française des Affaires Sociales*, 25 (1971), 11–26.

——*Au service de l'homme et du droit: souvenirs et réflexions* (Paris: Comité d'histoire de la sécurité sociale, 1993).

——, P. Tissier et al, *Traité des assurances sociales. Supplément de mise au courant 31 octobre 1932* (Paris: Librairie des Juris-Classeurs, 1932).

Leriche, E., *Les Assurances sociales et notre apostolat ouvrier* (Paris: Librairie de Jeunesse Catholique, 1927).

Leroy, M., *Les Techniques nouvelles du syndicalisme* (Paris: Garnier, 1921).

——*Les Tendances du pouvoir et de la liberté* (Paris: Librairie du Recueil Sirey, 1937).

Lyttelton, A., (ed.) *Italian Fascisms from Pareto to Gentile* (London: Jonathan Cape, 1973).

Malterre, A., *La Confédération générale des cadres, la révolte des mal aimés* (Paris: Épi, 1972).

Manoislesco, M., *Le Siècle du corporatisme. Doctrine du corporatisme intégral et pur* (Paris: Félix Alcan, 1934).

Maspétiol, R. and P. Laroque, *La tutelle administrative* (Paris: Librairie du Recueil Sirey, 1930).

Maxence, J.-P., *Histoire de dix ans : chronique des années 30* (Paris: Éditions du Rocher, 2005).

Mer, G., *La Réforme de l'état* (Paris: Librairie du Recueil Sirey, 1934).

Montagon, B., et al. *Ordre-Autorité-Nation* (Paris: Grasset, 1934).

Les Motifs de la loi sur les assurances sociales (Strasbourg: Éditeur La Vie Sociale en Alsace et Lorraine, 1921).

Mounier, E., *Mounier et sa génération: lettres, carnets et inédits* (Saint-Maur: Parole et Silence, 2000).

Mussolini, B., *Four Speeches on the Corporate State* (Rome: Laboremus, 1935).

Netter, F., *La Sécurité sociale et ses principes* (Paris: Librairie du Recueil Sirey, 1959).

——'Les Retraites en France au cours de la période 1895–1945', *Droit Social*, 7/8 (1965), 448–55.

——'Les Retraites en France au cours de la période 1895–1945', *Droit Social*, 9/10 (1965), 514–26.

——'L'Histoire des retraites: les non-salariés', *Droit Social*, 1 (1967), 45–51.

Noufflard-Guy-Loé, H., P. Laroque, O. Raffalovich, J. Cahen-Salvador, et al., *Alexandre Parodi* (Paris: Association des membres et anciens membres du Conseil d'État, 1980).

Parlato, G., (ed.) *Il convegno italo-francese di studi corporativi (1935) con il testo integrale degli Atti* (Rome: Fondazione Ugo Spirito, 1990).

Paul-Boncour, J., *Le Fédéralisme économique*, 2nd edn (Paris: Alcan, 1901).

——*Entre deux guerres*, 2 vols. (Paris: Plon, 1945).

Pétain, P., *Actes et écrits* (Paris: Flammarion, 1974).

——*Discours aux Français: 17 juin 1940–20 août 1944* (Paris: Albin Michel, 1989).

Perroux, F., *Capitalisme et communauté de travail* (Paris: Éditions Librairie du Recueil Sirey, 1937).

Pic, P., *Traité Elémentaire de Législation Industrielle*, 6th edn (Paris: A. Rousseau, 1930).

Pirou, G., *Le corporatisme* (Paris: Éditions Librairie du Recueil Sirey, 1934).

Prélot, M., *L'Empire fasciste. Les origines, les tendances et les institutions de la dictature et du corporatisme italiens* (Paris: Libraire du: Recueil Sirey, 1936).

Qu'est-ce que l'artisanat? préface d'André Siegfried (Paris: Horizons de France, 1941).

Rappoport, C., *Jean Jaurès: l'homme, le penseur, le socialiste* (Paris: Rivière, 1925).

Raynaud, H., *La défense de la sécurité sociale* (Paris: Éditions de la Confédération Générale du Travail, 1947).

Rey, A., *La Question des assurances sociales* (Paris, 1925).

Rosenstock-Franck, L., *L'économie corporative fasciste en doctrine et en fait* (Paris: J. Gamber, 1934).

Rossoni, E., *Dans l'Italie fasciste. Aspects politiques et moraux de la nouvelle économie corporative, conférence de Edmondo Rossoni à Berlin, le 29 avril 1936* (Rome: Società Editrice di Novissima, 1937).

Sacerdoti, P., *Le Corporatisme et le régime de la production et du travail en Italie* (Paris: Librairie du Recueil Sirey, 1938).

Sauvy, A., 'Adolphe Landry', *Population*, 11 (1954), 609–20.

Scelle, G., *Le Droit ouvrier. Tableau de la législation française actuelle* (Paris: Armand Colin, 1922).

Sorel, G., *Réflexions sur la violence*, 13th edn (Paris: M. Rivière et Cie, 1912).

——*Les illusions du progrès*, 5th edn (Paris: M. Rivière et Cie, 1947).

——*Matériaux d'une théorie du prolétariat*, 2nd edn (Paris: M. Rivière et Cie, 1921).

Stern, E., (ed.) *Les Assurances sociales en Tchécoslovaquie* (Prague: Librairie Orbis, 1931).

Tissier, P., P. O. de Sardan, and P. Closset. *Traiteé des assurances sociales. Supplément de mise au courant au 31 octobre 1932, par Pierre Laroque*. Préface de M. Adolphe Landry (Paris: Librairie des Juris-Classeurs, 1933).

Villiers, G., *Les Leçons du passé. Réponse de M. Georges Villiers à des déclarations de M. Guy Mollet* (Paris: J. Petit/Conseil national du patronat français, 1957).

——*Témoignages* (Paris: France-Empire, 1978).

SECONDARY SOURCES

Adam, G., *La CFTC* (Paris: Armand Colin, 1964).

Addison, P., *The Road to 1945* (London: Jonathan Cape, 1975).

Ambler, J., (ed.) *The French Welfare State: surviving social and ideological change* (New York: NYU Press, 1991).

Amoyal, J., 'Les Origines socialistes et syndicalistes de la planification en France', *Le Mouvement social*, 87 (1974), 137–69.

Anderson, R. D., *France 1870–1914: politics and society* (London: Routledge, Kegan & Paul, 1977).

Andrieu, C., *Le Programme commun de la Résistance* (Paris: Les Éditions de l'Érudit, 1984).

——, et al. *Les Nationalisations de la libération. De l'utopie au compromis* (Paris: Presses de Sciences Po., 1987).

Aron, R., *Histoire de Vichy* (Paris: Fayard, 1954).

Ashford, D., *The Emergence of the Welfare States* (Oxford: Blackwell, 1986).

——*Policy and Politics in France: Living with Uncertainty* (Philadelphia: Temple University Press, 1982).

Azèma, J. P., *1940: L'Année terrible* (Paris: Éditions du Seuil, 1990).

Baldwin, P., *The Politics of Social Solidarity: Class Bases of the European Welfare States 1875–1975* (Cambridge: CUP, 1990).

Bancal, J., *Proudhon: pluralisme et autogestion*, 2 vols (Paris: Aubier-Montaigne, 1970).

Barjot, A. *La Sécurité sociale: son histoire à travers les textes, Tome III, 1945–1981* (Paris: Comité d'histoire de la sécurité sociale, 1988).

Baruch, M. O., *Servir l'état français* (Paris: Fayard, 1997).

Belhoste, B., A. Dahan-Dalmedico, and A. Picon, (eds.) *La Formation polytechnicienne: 1794–1994* (Paris: Dunod, 1994).

Bernard, G. and D. Tintant, *Léon Jouhaux: cinquante ans de syndicalisme*, 2 vols. (Paris: Presses universitaires de France, 1962–1979).

Berstein, S., *La France des années 30* (Paris: Armand Colin, 1988).

——and O. Rudelle (eds.) *Le Modèle républicain* (Paris: Presses universitaires de France, 1992).

Béthouart, B., *Des syndicalistes chrétiens en politique: de la Libération à la Vième Republique* (Paris: Presses universitaires du Septentrion, 1999).

Biard, J.-F., *Le socialisme devant ses choix. La naissance de l'idée de plan* (Paris: Publications de la Sorbonne, 1985).

Black, A., *Guilds and Civil Society in European Thought From the Twelfth Century to the Present* (London: Methuen, 1984).

Bloch-Lainé, F. and J. Bouvier, *La France restaurée 1944–1954* (Paris: Fayard, 1986).

Boltanski, L., *Les cadres, formation d'un groupe social* (Paris: Les Éditions de Minuit, 1982).

Bougeard, C., *René Pleven: un français libre en politique* (Rennes: Presses universitaires de Rennes, 1994).

Brun, G., *Technocrates et Technocratie en France (1918–1945)* (Paris: Albatros, 1985).

Burrin, P., *La Dérive fasciste: Doriot, Déat et Bergery 1933–1945* (Paris: Éditions du Seuil, 1986).

Callot, E., *Le Mouvement Républicain Populaire* (Paris: Rivière, 1978).

Castel, R., *Les Métamorphoses de la question sociale: une chronique du salariat* (Paris: Éditions du Seuil, 1995).

Chase, M., *Élie Halévy: an intellectual biography* (New York: Columbia University Press, 1980).

Chatriot, A., *La Démocratie sociale à la française: l'expérience du Conseil national économique 1924–1940* (Paris: Éditions La Découverte, 2002).

Chavardes, M. *Le 6 février 1934: La république en danger* (Paris: Calmann-Lévy, 1966).

——*Une Campagne de presse, la droite française et le 6 février 1934* (Paris: Flammarion, 1970).

Chevallier, J., (ed.) *Variations autour de l'idéologie de l'intérêt général*, 2 vols. (Paris: Presses universitaires de France, 1978).

Choisnel, E., *L'Assemblée Consultative Provisoire (1943–1945): le sursaut républicain* (Paris: L'Harmattan, 2007).

Cointet, J.-P., *Histoire de Vichy* (Paris: Perrin, 2003).

Cointet, M., *De Gaulle et Giraud: l'affrontement* (Paris: Perrin, 2005).

Comité d'Histoire de la Deuxième Guerre Mondiale, *La Libération de la France.* (Paris: Éditions du CNRS, 1976).

Comité d'Histoire de la Sécurité Sociale, *Actes du 105ième Congrès National des Sociétés Savantes* (Lyons: Éditions du CTHS, 1980).

——*Actes du 112ième Congrès National des Sociétés Savantes* (Lyons: Éditions du CTHS, 1987).

Courtois, S., *Le PCF dans la guerre* (Paris: Ramsay, 1980).

Crémieux-Brilhac, J.-L., *La France libre: de l'appel du 18 juin à la Liberation* (Paris: Gallimard, 1996).

Dard, O., *Le Rendez-vous manqué des relèves des années 30* (Paris: Presses universitaires de France, 2002).

de Bellescize, D., *Les Neufs sages de la résistance: le Comité Général d'Études dans la clandestinité* (Paris: Plon, 1979).

Demier, F., *Histoire des politiques sociales* (Paris: Éditions du Seuil, 1995).

Dodge, P., *Beyond Marxism: The Faith and Works of Hendrik de Man* (The Hague: Martinus Nijhoff, 1966).

Donzelot, J., *L'invention du social. Essai sur le déclin des passions politiques* (Paris: Fayard, 1994).

Douglas, A., *From Fascism to Libertarian Communism: Georges Valois against the Third Republic* (Oxford: University of California Press, 1992).

Dreyfus, F.-G., *Histoire de la Résistance* (Paris: Éditions de Fallois, 1996).

Dreyfus, M. et al., *Se protéger, être protégé: une histoire des assurances sociales en France* (Rennes: Presses universitaires de Rennes, 2006).

Dumons, B. and G. Pollet, *L'État et les retraites* (Paris: Belin, 1994).

Dupeyroux, J.-J. and X. Prétot, *Sécurité sociale*, 8th edn., (Paris: Dalloz, 1994).

Durand, P., *La Politique contemporaine de sécurité sociale* (Paris: Dalloz, 1953).

Dutton, P. V., *Origins of the French Welfare State: the struggle for social reform in France 1914–1947* (Cambridge: CUP, 2002).

Ehrmann, H., *Organised Business in France* (Princeton: Princeton University Press, 1957).

Elbow, M. H., *French Corporative Theory 1789–1948: A chapter on the history of ideas* (New York: Columbia University Press, 1953).

Elwitt, S., *The Third Republic Defended: bourgeois reform in France 1880–1914* (Baton Rouge, LA: Louisiana State University Press, 1986).

Esping-Andersen, G., *The Three Worlds of Welfare Capitalism* (Princeton: Princeton University Press, 1990).

Ewald, F., *L'État providence* (Paris: Grasset, 1986).

Faure, B., 'Généralisation de l'assurance vieillesse à l'ensemble de la population', *Droit Social,* 12 (1949), 25–8.

Fine, M., 'Albert Thomas: a reformer's vision of modernisation 1914–32', *Journal of Contemporary History,* 12 (1977), 545–64.

——'Hyacinthe Dubreuil: le témoignage d'un ouvrier sur le syndicalisme, les relations industrielles et l'évolution technologique de 1921 à 1940', *Le Mouvement Social,* 106 (1979), 45–63.

Fondation Charles de Gaulle, *Le Rétablissement de la legalité républicaine* (Brussels: Éditions Complexe, 1996).

Fournié, F., *Recherches sur la décentralisation dans l'œuvre de Maurice Hauriou* (Paris: LGDJ, 2005).

Freedeman, C. E., *The Conseil d'État in Modern France* (New York: Columbia University Press, 1961).

Galant, H. C., *Histoire politique de la sécurité sociale française 1945–1952* (Paris: Armand Colin, 1955).

Gautier, C., 'Corporation, Société et Démocratie chez Durkheim', *Revue Française de Science Politique,* 44 (1994), 836–55.

Gibaud, B., *De la mutualité à la sécurité sociale: conflits et convergences* (Paris: Éditions Ouvrières, 1986).

——'Mutualité/Sécurité sociale: un couple sous tension', *Vingtième Siecle,* 48 (1995), 119–30.

Giddens, A., *Durkheim* (Glasgow: William Collins, 1978).

Girard, A., 'Adolphe Landry et la démographie', *Revue Française de Sociologie,* 23 (1982), 111–26.

Graham, B. D. *The French Socialists and Tripartisme, 1944–1947* (Toronto: University of Toronto Press, 1965).

Gueslin, A., *L'État, l'économie et la société française XIXe—Xxe siècle* (Paris: Hachette, 1992).

——(ed.) *De la charité médiévale à la sécurité sociale* (Paris: Éditions Ouvrières, 1992).

Guillaume, S., *Confédération Générale des Petites et Moyennes Entreprises* (Bordeaux: Presses universitaire de Bordeaux, 1987).

Guillemard, A.-M., *Le Déclin du social* (Paris: Presses universitaires de France, 1986).

Guy-Grand, G., *Pour connaître la pensée de Proudhon* (Paris: Bordas, 1947).

Harris, J, *William Beveridge: a biography*, 2nd edn (Oxford: Clarendon Press, 1997).

Hatzfeld, H., *Du paupérisme à la sécurité sociale* (Paris: Armand Colin, 1971).

Hawkins, M. J., 'Durkheim on Occupational Corporations: an exegesis and interpretation', *Journal of the History of Ideas*, 55 (1994), 461–81.

Hayward, J. E. S., 'Solidarity: the social history of an idea in nineteenth century France', *International Review of Social History*, 4 (1959), 261–84.

—— 'Solidarist syndicalism: Durkheim and Duguit', *The Sociological Review*, 8, 1 (1960), 17–33.

—— 'Solidarist syndicalism: Durkheim and Duguit', *The Sociological Review*, 8, 2 (1960), 185–202.

—— 'The Official Social Philosophy of the French Third Republic: Léon Bourgeois and Solidarism', *International Review of Social History*, 6 (1961), 19–48.

——*After the French Revolution: six critics of democracy and nationalism* (New York: Harvester Wheatsheaf, 1991).

Hesse, P.-J. and J.-P. Le Crom, 'Travail, salaire, protection sociale: le tournant des années quarante', *Revue Française des Affaires Sociales*, 3–4 (2000), 17–27.

——(eds.) *La Protection sociale sous Vichy* (Rennes: Presses universitaire de Rennes 2010).

Hoffmann, S., *Decline or Renewal? France since the 1930s* (New York: Viking Press, 1974).

Hostache, R., *Le Conseil National de la Résistance. Les institutions de la clandestinité* (Paris: Presses universitaires de France, 1958).

Irving, R. E. M., *Christian Democracy in France* (London: Allen & Unwin, 1973).

Jabbari, E., 'Law and Politics in Interwar France: Pierre Laroque's search for a democratic corporatism', *French Politics Culture and Society*, 24 (2006), 93–113.

Jackson, J., *The Politics of Depression in France 1932–1936* (Cambridge: CUP, 1985).

——*The Popular Front in France: defending democracy, 1934–1938* (Cambridge: CUP, 1988).

Jambu-Merlin, R., 'Le Problème de la sécurité sociale des travailleurs non-salariés au lendemain de la libération', *Droit Social*, 3 (1970), 11–16.

Jankowski, P., *Cette vilaine affaire Stavisky: histoire d'un scandale politique* (Paris: Fayard, 2000).

Jennings, J., *Syndicalism in France: a study of ideas* (New York: Macmillan, 1991).

Jones, H. S., *The French State in Question* (Cambridge: CUP, 1993).

Judt, T., *Marxism and the French Left: studies on labour and politics in France, 1830–1981* (Oxford: OUP, 1986).

Julliard, J. and S. Sand, (eds.) *Georges Sorel en son temps* (Paris: Éditions du Seuil, 1985).

Karady, V., 'Stratégies de réussite et mode de faire valoir de la sociologie chez les Durkheimiens', *Revue Française de Sociologie*, 20 (1979), 49–82.

Kaspi, A. et al., *La Libération de la France, juin 1944–janvier 1946* (Paris: Perrin, 1995).

Kaufman-Osborn, T. V., 'Émile Durkheim and the Science of Corporatism', *Political Theory*, 13/4 (1986), 638–59.

Kedward, H. R., *Resistance in Vichy France: a study of ideas and motivation in the Southern Zone 1940–1942* (Oxford: OUP, 1978).

——and A. Roger, (eds.) *Vichy France and the Resistance: culture and ideology* (Beckenham: Croom Helm, 1985).

Kessler, M.-C., *Le Conseil d'État* (Paris: Armand Colin, 1968).

Kriegel, A., *Le pain et les roses, jalons pours une histoire des socialismes* (Paris: Presses universitaires de France, 1968).

Kuisel, R., 'Auguste Detoeuf, Conscience of French Industry: 1926–1947', *International Review of Social History*, 20 (1975), 149–76.

——*Capitalism and the State in Modern France: renovation and economic management in the twentieth century* (Cambridge: CUP, 1981).

——*Le Capitalisme et l'État en France: modernisation et dirigisme au XXe siècle*, trans. A. Charpentier (Paris: Gallimard, 1984).

Laborde, C., *Pluralist Thought and the State in Britain and France, 1900–1925* (Basingstoke: Palgrave Macmillan, 2000).

Lacouture, J., *De Gaulle*, 3 vols. (Paris: Éditions du Seuil, 1986).

Lacroix-Riz, A., *La CGT de la Libération à la scission, de 1944 à 1947* (Paris: Éditions Sociales, 1983).

Landauer, C., *Corporate State Ideologies* (Berkeley: University of California Press, 1983).

Latour, B., *La Fabrique du droit: une ethnographie du Conseil d'État* (Paris: Découverte, 2004).

Launay, J.-P., *Francis Netter: une vie pour le développement du progrès social* (Paris: Comité d'histoire de la sécurité sociale, 1989).

Lavau, G., (ed.) *L'Univers politique des classes moyennes* (Paris: Presses de Sciences Po., 1983).

Leclerc, P., *La Sécurité sociale: son histoire à travers les textes, Tome II (1870–1945)* (Paris: Comité d'histoire de la sécurité sociale, 1996).

Le Crom, J.-P., *Syndicats nous voila! Vichy et le corporatisme* (Paris: Éditions de l'Atelier, 1990).

Lefranc, G., *Les Expériences syndicales en France de 1939 à 1950* (Paris: Montaigne, 1950).

——*Le Mouvement socialiste sous la Troisième République, 1875–1940* (Paris: Payot, 1963).

——*Le Mouvement syndical sous la Troisième Republique* (Paris: Payot, 1967).

——'La Diffusion des idées planistes en France', *Revue Européenne des Sciences Sociales: cahiers Vilfreto Pareto*, 12 (1974), 151–67.

——*Les Organisations patronales en France* (Paris: Payot, 1976).

Ligou, D., *Histoire du socialisme en France, 1871–1961* (Paris: Presses universitaires de France, 1961).

Lion, H., 'La Convention du 14 mars 1947 et son évolution', *Droit Social*, 7–8 (1962), 396–402.

Logue, W., 'Sociologie et politique: le libéralisme de Célestin Bouglé', *Revue Française de Sociologie*, 20 (1979), 141–52.

——*From Philosophy to Sociology: the evolution of French liberalism, 1870–1924* (DeKalb: Illinois University Press, 1983).

Loubet del Bayle, J.-L., *Les Non-conformistes des années 30: uue tentative de renouvellement de la penseé française* (Paris: Éditions du Seuil, 1969).

Lukes, S., *Émile Durkheim* (London: Penguin, 1973).

Lynch, F., *France and the International Economy from Vichy to the Treaty of Rome* (London: Routledge, 1997).

Lynes, T., *French Pensions* (London: Bell and Sons, 1967).

Machefer, P., *Ligues et fascisme en France, 1919–1939* (Paris: Presses universitaires de France, 1974).

Magraw, R., *France 1815–1914: the bourgeois century* (Oxford: OUP, 1986).

Maier, C. S., 'Between Taylorism and Technocracy: European ideologies and the vision of industrial productivity in the 1920s', *Journal of Contemporary History*, 5 (1970), 27–61.

——*Recasting Bourgeois Europe* (Princeton: Princeton University Press, 1975).

Margairaz, M., *L'État, les finances et l'économie. Histoire d'une conversion*, 2 vols. (Paris: Comité pour l'Histoire Économique et Financière de la France, 1991).

Marquand, D. and A. Seldon, (eds.) *The Ideas That Shaped Post-War Britain* (London: Fontana Press, 1996).

Marshall, T. H and T. Bottomore, *Citizenship and Social Class* (London: Pluto Press, 1992).

Marwick, A., *War and Social Change in the Twentieth Century* (New York: Palgrave Macmillan, 1974).

Merrien, F.-X., *Étude comparative de l'édification et de l'évolution de l'état-protecteur en France et en Grande Bretagne* (Paris: Mission interministérielle de recherche-expérimentation, 1990).

——*L'État-Providence* (Paris: Presses universitaires de France, 1997).

Metton, N., *Brève histoire de l'artisanat en France 1925–1963* (Lyons: Artisan de la Metallurgie du Rhône, 1964).

Michel, H., *Les Courants de pensée de la Résistance* (Paris: Presses universitaires de France, 1962).

——*Histoire de la France Libre* (Paris: Presses universitaires de France, 1963).

——*François Darlan* (Paris: Hachette, 1993).

Milhau, J., 'L'Action politique d'Étienne Antonelli', *Revue d'Histoire Économique et Sociale*, 31, 4 (1951), 364–82.

Milward, A., *The Reconstruction of Western Europe 1945–1951* (Berkeley: University of California Press, 1984).

Milza, P., *Fascisme français passé et présent* (Paris: Flammarion, 1987).

Mioche, P., *Le Plan Monnet: genèse et élaboration 1941—1947* (Paris: Publications de la Sorbonne, 1987).

Miquel, P., *Les Polytechniciens* (Paris: Plon, 1994).

Mitchell, D., *The Divided Path: the German influence on social reform in France 1871–1914* (Chapel Hill: University of North Carolina Press, 1991).

Montaye, J. and P. Bony, 'Le Refus par les commerçants et industriels de la loi du 22 mai 1946', Congrés National des Sociétés Savantes, Actes du 112éme Congrés National des Sociétés Savantes, Lyon, 1987 (Paris: Éditions du CTHS, 1987).

Morgan, K. O., *Labour in Power, 1945–1951* (Oxford: OUP, 1984).

Mortimer, E., *The Rise of the French Communist Party, 1920–1947* (London: Faber & Faber, 1984).

Mouriaux, R., *La CGT* (Paris: Éditions du Seuil, 1982).

Muracciole, J.-F., *Histoire de la Résistance en France*, 3rd edn (Paris: Presses universitaires de France, 1993).

Nicolet, C., *L'Idée républicaine en France. Essai d'histoire critique* (Paris: Gallimard, 1982).

Noguères, H. et al., *Histoire de la Résistance en France*, 5 vols (Paris: Robert Laffont, 1967–1981).

Palier, B., (ed.) *Comparer les systèmes de protection sociale en Europe*, 3 vols (Nantes: Maisons des sciences de l'homme Ange-Guépin, 1995).

——*Gouverner la sécurité sociale: les réformes du système de protection sociale depuis 1945* (Paris: Presses universitaires de France, 2005).

Paxton, R., *La France de Vichy, 1940–1944*, 2nd edn (Paris: Éditions du Seuil, 1997).

Pedersen, S., *Family, Dependence and the Origins of the Welfare State: Britain and France, 1914–1945* (Cambridge: CUP, 1994).

Peterson, W. C., *The Welfare State in France* (Lincoln: University of Nebraska Press, 1964).

Pisier-Kouchner, E. *Le Service public dans la théorie de l'État de Léon Duguit* (Paris: Librairie générale de droit de jurisprudence, 1972).

Prost, A., 'Jalons pour une histoire des pensions et des retraites (1914–1939)', *Revue d'Histoire Moderne et Contemporaine*, 11 (1964), 263–89.

Quilliot, R., *La SFIO et l'exercice du pouvoir, 1944–1958* (Paris: Fayard, 1972).

Rémond, R. and J. Bourdin, (eds.) *Le Gouvernement de Vichy, 1940–1944* (Paris: Fondation nationale des sciences politiques, 1972).

Renouvin, P. et al., *Léon Blum, chef de gouvernement 1936–1937* (Paris: Fondation nationale des sciences politiques, 1965).

Ritter, A., *The Political Thought of Pierre-Joseph Proudhon* (Princeton: Princeton University Press, 1969).

Ritter, G., *Der Sozialstaat: Entstehung und Entwicklung im Internationalen Vergleich* (Munich: Oldenbourg Verlag, 1991).

Rioux, J.-P., *The Fourth Republic* (Cambridge: CUP, 1987).

Robineau, Y. and D. Truchet, *Le Conseil d'État* (Paris: Presses universitaires de France, 1994).

Rony, O., *Jules Romains ou l'appel au monde* (Paris: Robert Laffont, 1992).

Rosanvallon, P., *L'État en France de 1789 à nos jours* (Paris: Éditions du Seuil, 1990).

Sadoun, M., *Les Socialistes sous l'Occupation: résistance et collaboration* (Paris: Presses de Sciences Po, 1982).

Sarti, R., *Fascism and the Industrial Leadership in Italy 1919–1940* (Berkeley: University of California Press, 1971).

Schmitter, P. C., 'Still the Century of Corporatism?' *The Review of Politics*, 36 (1974), 85–126.

Sfez, L., *Essai sur la contribution du doyen Hauriou au droit administratif français* (Paris: Librairie générale de droit et de jurisprudence, 1966).

Shennan, A., *Rethinking France* (Oxford: OUP, 1989).

Simon, D., 'Le Patronat face aux assurances sociales: 1920–1930', *Le Mouvement Social*, 137 (1986), 7–28.

——'Les Assurances sociales et les mutualistes 1920–1932', *Revue d'Histoire Moderne et Contemporaine*, 34 (1987), 587–615.

Smith, T. B., *Creating the Welfare State in France, 1880–1940* (Montreal: McGill-Queens University Press, 2003).

Sternhell, Z., *Neither Right Nor Left*, trans. by D. Maisel (Berkeley: University of California Press, 1986).

Sternhell. Z. *Ni droite ni gauche: l'idéologie fasciste en France.* Nouvelle edition revue et augmentée (Paris: Éditions Complexe, 1987).

——*The Birth of Fascist Ideology*, trans. by D. Maisel, (Princeton: Princeton University Press, 1994).

Stone, J. F., *The Search for Social Peace: Reform Legislation in France 1890–1914* (Albany: State University of New York Press, 1985).

Suleiman, E. N., *Politics, Power and Bureaucracy in France* (Princeton: Princeton University Press, 1974).

Touchard, J., *Le Gaullisme, 1940–1969* (Paris: Éditions du Seuil, 1969).

Tournerie, J. A., *Le Ministère du Travail. Origines et premiers développements* (Paris: Éditions Cujas, 1971).

Valat, B., 'Résistance et sécurité sociale 1941–1944', *Revue Historique*, 292, 2 (1995), 315–46.

——*Histoire de la sécurité sociale*, (1945–1967) (Paris: Économica, 2001).

Vincent, K. S., *Pierre-Joseph Proudhon and the Rise of French Republican Socialism* (Oxford: OUP, 1984).

Vinen, R., *The Politics of French Business 1936–1945* (Cambridge: CUP, 1991).

——*Bourgeois Politics in France 1945–1951* (Cambridge: CUP, 1995).

Vogt, P., 'Un Durkheimien ambivalent: Célestin Bouglé 1870–1940', *Revue Française de Sociologie*, 20 (1979), 123–38.

Weber, E., *The Hollow Years: France in the 1930s* (London: Sinclair Stevenson, 1995).

Weber, H., *Le Parti des patrons. Le CNPF 1946–1990* (Paris: Éditions du Seuil, 1991).

Weisz, G., 'L'Idéologie républicaine et les sciences sociales', *Revue Française de Sociologie*, 20 (1979), 83–112.

Williams, P. M., *Politics in Post-War France* (London: Longmans, 1954).

Wright, G., *The Reshaping of French Democracy* (New York: Reynald & Hitchcock, 1948).

Zeldin, T., *France 1848–1945*, 2 vols (Oxford: OUP, 1979).

THESES

Brun, G., 'Techniciens et technocratie en France (1918–1945)', PhD thesis, University of Paris II, Paris, 1977.

Dard, O., 'Les novations intellectuelles des années trente: l'exemple de Jean Coutrot', PhD thesis, Institut d'Études Politiques, Paris, 1993.

Laborde, C., 'State, Groups and Individuals: pluralist thinking in Britain and France (1900–1925)', DPhil thesis, University of Oxford, 1996.

Rossiter, A., 'Corporatist Experiments in Interwar France', DPhil thesis, University of Oxford, 1986.

Simon, D., 'Les Origines des assurances sociales au début des années 30', PhD thesis, University of Paris I, 1983.

Youlden, C. A., 'The Political Evolution of Marcel Déat', DPhil thesis, University of Oxford, 1979.